INDIGENOUS RESURGENCE IN AN AGE OF RECONCILIATION

Edited by Heidi Kiiwetinepinesiik Stark, Aimée Craft, and Hōkūlani K. Aikau

What would Indigenous resurgence look like if the parameters were not set with a focus on the state, settlers, or an achievement of reconciliation? *Indigenous Resurgence in an Age of Reconciliation* explores the central concerns and challenges facing Indigenous nations in their resurgence efforts, while also mapping the gaps and limitations of both reconciliation and resurgence frameworks.

The essays in this collection centre the work of Indigenous communities, knowledge, and strategies for resurgence and, where appropriate, reconciliation. The book challenges narrow interpretations of indigeneity and resurgence, asking readers to take up a critical analysis of how settler colonial and heteronormative framings have infiltrated our own ways of relating to our selves, one another, and to place. The authors seek to (re)claim Indigenous relationships to the political and offer critical self-reflection to ensure Indigenous resurgence efforts do not reproduce the very conditions and contexts from which liberation is sought.

Illuminating the interconnectivity between and across life in all its forms, this important collection calls on readers to think expansively and critically about Indigenous resurgence in an age of reconciliation.

HEIDI KIIWETINEPINESIIK STARK is an associate professor of Indigenous governance at the University of Victoria.

AIMÉE CRAFT is an associate professor in the faculty of law at the University of Ottawa.

HŌKŪLANI K. AIKAU is a professor of Indigenous governance at the University of Victoria.

Indigenous Resurgence in an Age of Reconciliation

EDITED BY HEIDI KIIWETINEPINESIIK STARK, AIMÉE CRAFT, AND HŌKŪLANI K. AIKAU

UNIVERSITY OF TORONTO PRESS
Toronto Buffalo London

ISBN 978-1-4875-4459-1 (cloth)   ISBN 978-1-4875-4461-4 (EPUB)
ISBN 978-1-4875-4460-7 (paper)   ISBN 978-1-4875-4462-1 (PDF)

Library and Archives Canada Cataloguing in Publication

Title: Indigenous resurgence in an age of reconciliation / edited by Heidi
    Kiiwetinepinesiik Stark, Aimée Craft, and Hōkūlani K. Aikau.
Names: Stark, Heidi Kiiwetinepinesiik, editor. | Craft, Aimée, 1980– editor. |
Aikau, Hokulani K., 1970– editor.
Description: Includes bibliographical references and index.
Identifiers: Canadiana (print) 20220496439 | Canadiana (ebook) 20220496498 |
    ISBN 9781487544607 (softcover) | ISBN 9781487544591 (hardcover) |
    ISBN 9781487544614 (EPUB) | ISBN 9781487544621 (PDF)
Subjects: LCSH: Indigenous peoples – North America – Social conditions. |
    LCSH: Reconciliation. | LCSH: North America – Race relations. |
    LCSH: North America – Ethnic relations.
Classification: LCC E98.S67 I53 2023 | DDC 305.897–dc23

We wish to acknowledge the land on which the University of Toronto Press
operates. This land is the traditional territory of the Wendat, the Anishnaabeg,
the Haudenosaunee, the Métis, and the Mississaugas of the Credit First Nation.

This book has been published with the help of a grant from the Federation
for the Humanities and Social Sciences, through the Awards to Scholarly
Publications Program, using funds provided by the Social Sciences and
Humanities Research Council of Canada.

University of Toronto Press acknowledges the financial support of the
Government of Canada, the Canada Council for the Arts, and the Ontario Arts
Council, an agency of the Government of Ontario, for its publishing activities.

Canada Council   Conseil des Arts
for the Arts   du Canada

ONTARIO ARTS COUNCIL
CONSEIL DES ARTS DE L'ONTARIO
an Ontario government agency
un organisme du gouvernement de l'Ontario

Funded by the   Financé par le
Government   gouvernement
of Canada   du Canada

Canada

Contents

Acknowledgments

We would like to express our appreciation and acknowledge the funding supports that made this book possible. The National Centre for Truth and Reconciliation provided initial funding that covered the costs of the symposium, "Indigenous Resurgence in an Age of Reconciliation" held 16–18 March 2017. The success of the symposium was also made possible with support from The Centre for Indigenous Research and Community-Led Engagement, the Director of Indigenous Academic and Community Engagement, the President's Office, the Faculty of Social Sciences, the School of Indigenous Governance, the Department of Political Science, and the Faculty of Law at the University of Victoria. The University of Victoria also provided a subvention supporting publication of this book. In addition, the editors would like to thank the presenters at the symposium and the contributors to this book for their commitment to Indigenous resurgence. Their work is generative and inspiring.

Ìyénłan | My Relative

We emerge out of the bush a bit different than before.
Renewed by the rain.
We look more familiar to our ancestors,
Who see us as we once were and how we are meant to be:
Indistinguishable from the earth.

Lianne Marie Leda Charlie

INDIGENOUS RESURGENCE IN AN AGE OF RECONCILIATION

Generating a Critical Resurgence Together[1]

HEIDI KIIWETINEPINESIIK STARK

The vision for this collection grew out of conversations many of us had been having around Indigenous resurgence – conversations that both focused on how Indigenous communities are trying to revitalize their language, culture, and political practices as well as concerns about the pitfalls and traps we can sometimes fall into in our efforts to conduct this grounded work. We were also intrigued and maybe even a bit troubled by the increased uptake of the term within the academy, as it has too often involved a narrow characterization of resurgence with critiques focused largely on feasibility or fundamentalism. These invocations that resurgence literature is either utopic or essentializing seemed to be largely tethered to or placed in dialogue with discourses of reconciliation. We were also intrigued in thinking through how our framing and calls for Indigenous resurgence were being shaped and affected by nation-state interest in the project of reconciliation.

In the wake of the proliferation of scholarship focusing on reconciliation (and sometimes resurgence), which often centres the voices of non-Indigenous scholars, there is an assumption that space must be shared equally between Indigenous and non-Indigenous scholars, and attention is given to the relationship between Indigenous and non-Indigenous people. With this edited collection, we seek to create a space primarily, though not exclusively, for Indigenous scholars to come together to discuss the central concerns and challenges facing Indigenous nations in their resurgence while also mapping the gaps and limits of both reconciliation *and* resurgence. We ask what discussions of resurgence look like if we didn't focus on the state, settlers, or an achievement of reconciliation? We knew that a focus on all three would be present throughout. That was not surprising when reconciliation was in the title of the symposium. Indigenous resurgence efforts often entail engagement with the state or involve settler alliances. These important conversations are included in this collection. But we also wanted to ensure we were making space for other critiques and visions of Indigenous resurgence.

While resurgence is a concept often associated with a few key intellectuals, initially Mohawk scholar Taiaiake Alfred, Cherokee scholar Jeff Ganohalidoh Corntassel, and later Dene scholar Glen Coulthard and Anishinaabe scholar Leanne Simpson, this framing of resurgence ignores both the work of Indigenous communities and the broader Indigenous studies literature these intellectuals are drawing from and engaging with.[2] Indeed, they often note that they are not the originators of this concept but instead are seeking to theorize the efforts they are engaged in with Indigenous communities. In fact, the initial use of the term *resurgence* did not arise from the aforementioned scholars' work but instead was found titling Anishinaabe scholar John Borrows's acclaimed *Recovering Canada: The Resurgence of Indigenous Law*, which calls for the recognition and invigoration of Indigenous legal traditions across and in engagement with Canada. And if we think beyond the word *resurgence* to what this concept invokes, there is a vast literature in Indigenous studies that predates and informs the literature explicitly taking up resurgence.

Reconfiguring Resurgence and Reconciliation

In reflecting on the widespread use, continuous contestation, and ongoing reconfiguration of the terms *resurgence* and *reconciliation*, John Borrows and James Tully recognize there is a plurality of meanings affixed to them. In tracing these out, they find the field has been polarizing, framing one camp as the *rejectionist-resurgence* perspective, which rejects reconciliation because it is understood as assimilative or colonizing. They argue that the other position, the *resurgence-reconciliation* perspective, "strives to live more holistically," pursues "more constructively provocative approaches," and rejects "isolationism," which they assert "can lead to self-absorption and become marginalizing and disempowering."[3] Despite their statements that polarization in the field has arisen largely from misunderstandings and misuse of these terms, this reproduction of a binary reading of the literature fails to account for the full breadth and range of both the resurgence literature and the grounded efforts and actions it arises from. Consequently, it valorizes the *resurgence-reconciliation* perspective while foreclosing the transformative potential of the work within the *rejectionist-resurgence* perspective.

Borrows and Tully reproduce a predominant characterization and critique of the Indigenous resurgence literature – that it is insular and calls for a turn away from the state. This reading of resurgence collapses varied concepts and arguments put forward by Indigenous scholars. Too often this characterization of the field comes out of a reading of Glen Coulthard's *Red Skins, White Masks: Rejecting the Colonial Politics of Recognition* that tethers his rich discussion of grounded normativity (read: resurgence of Indigenous normative lifeways) with his call to turn away from the state, effectively either dismissing both as improbable or problematic or embracing the "turn away" with a critique that failure to do so makes grounded normativity impossible or inauthentic. These readings miss the point that grounded normativity, while perhaps strengthened or benefitting from it, isn't contingent on a "turn away."

Coulthard calls for this turn in his seminal work, but it is a strategic shift, not necessarily requiring it to be a permanent position. The "turn away" crucially enables Indigenous investment in shoring up the grounded normative lifeways that can guide critical engagement with the state – lifeways that have largely been under attack and affected by colonialism. His critique of state engagement is not a decontextualized attack on state apparatuses but instead is deeply contextualized, situated in the wake of four decades of state engagement that too often contorted and constrained Indigenous visions of nationhood and liberation. And more concerning, it was four decades in which many of our people deeply invested in state engagement, to the expense of grounded normativity and the resurgence of Indigenous lifeways, despite initial motivations that extended beyond recognition by the state. Indeed, many Indigenous nations were seeking to augment paralyzing relationships with the state that left them little agency and control over themselves and perpetuated conditions for their people such as poverty, unemployment, and poor health. Many Indigenous nations found themselves in the courts, for example, solely as the result of carrying out their grounded lifeways and, in the process, running up against provincial and federal laws that curtailed these practices. But, as nations turned their energies to securing recognized title to their lands and liberating their citizens from incarceration or steep fines for carrying out their legal, political, and cultural traditions, these interests diverted focus from the cultivation of grounded Indigenous philosophies and lifeways.

It is no surprise that many Indigenous youth have been encouraged to become lawyers. Two of my own siblings were lawyers and I was set to follow this path as well until backing out a week before law school started. We came of age in an era where our nations were fighting for recognition of our Aboriginal title and treaty rights. And while we saw Indigenous nations equally committed to the resurgence of our lifeways, and were even participating in these resurgence efforts, many of us thought the legal avenue would best serve our nations. Indeed, many lawyers have done and continue to do important work for Indigenous nations. But it's no surprise that the generation that followed mine often turned not to law (or social work, as both fields had prominence) but instead towards language revitalization or to the arts when they found the politics of recognition was failing to produce the security and space for Indigenous nations to flourish. They instead directed their energies at drawing on grounded Indigenous lifeways and a decolonial praxis that confronted and challenged the heteronormative patriarchy that has too often entangled our communities to try to imagine a new future for our nations. And those who continued to pursue law rarely thought section 35 of the Canadian Constitution (alone) would liberate our nations, so they too largely turned inward to focus on Indigenous legal traditions while critiquing the limits of Canadian law.

Though the critiques of the colonial politics of recognition teased out in the resurgence literature may produce anxieties about the paths we have chosen, many of these scholars are also sympathetic to these choices, understanding the complex terrains we were and are navigating as we came to make these decisions. It is important that we don't let our own discomfort produced by these critiques result in a misreading, distortion, or disregard for the argument being made. We must open our ears and our hearts. It is equally important that we don't also let the affirmation and empowerment that resurgence literature may produce cause us to distill calls to action into essentialized and too-often exclusionary hashtags. We must be careful not to reproduce harmful relationships in our efforts towards a resurgent politic that seeks to liberate us from these injuries.

The resurgence literature is vast and extends beyond the work of Coulthard. Although he is often taken up as a pinnacle thinker in the field, it is important to trace the nuance in his work that recognizes the complex terrain that Indigenous nations must traverse. He asks whether in our struggles for land and freedom, "it requires that we vacate the field of state negotiations and participation entirely," to which he answers, "Of course not. Settler colonialism has rendered us a radical minority in our own homelands and this necessitates that we continue to engage with the state's legal and political system."[4] Coulthard's turn away from the state then is a call to decolonize on our own terms and recognize the profound power disparity between Indigenous nations and the state. Instead of completely discounting the work of many who direct their energies towards engagement with the state, he asserts that present conditions demand that engagement with the state be conducted with caution, scepticism, and self-reflection. Furthermore, "it also demands that we begin to shift our attention away from the largely rights-based/recognition orientation that has emerged as hegemonic over the last four decades to a resurgent politics of recognition that seeks to practise decolonial, gender-emancipatory, and economic nonexploitative alternatives of law and sovereign authority grounded on a critical refashioning of the best of Indigenous legal and political traditions."[5] He closes by noting, "It is only by privileging and grounding ourselves in these normative lifeways and resurgent practices that we have a hope of surviving our strategic engagements with the colonial state with integrity and as Indigenous peoples."[6]

Certainly Coulthard is concerned that the transformative potential of state engagement is limited without a radical reconfiguration of the state. But he is also seeking to remind Indigenous nations that to strategically engage with the state requires we are firmly grounded in our Indigenous lifeways that should be shaping and determining this engagement. And we may find that our critical engagements with the state, rooted in our grounded normativity, may not be enough. In fact, we often think of our nineteenth-century ancestors as being deeply grounded in Indigenous lifeways, yet their critical engagement with the state (for treaty nations) or strategic refusal (for those nations that didn't sign historic or modern treaties) did not leave these nations unscathed by colonialism or prevent contortion of their relationship with the Crown. Indeed, treaty nations are still calling on the Crown to honour the treaties, and those nations outside of these historic agreements continue to challenge Canada's assertion of title and rights over their territories. And yet achieving Indigenous visions for a new world, or what the Anishinaabe refer to as lighting the eighth fire, requires settler engagement. As Leanne Simpson notes, "In order for the Eighth fire to be lit, settler society must also choose to change their ways, to decolonize their relationships with the land and Indigenous nations and to join with us in building a sustainable future based on mutual recognition, justice and respect."[7]

Furthermore, the resurgence literature is equally informed by and cognizant of the trappings that befell Indigenous sovereignty and self-determination movements, which problematically excluded the voices and concerns of Indigenous women and sought recognition of Indigenous political authority to the expense of addressing how heteronormative patriarchy is shaping and harming our communities. Coulthard draws on Leanne Simpson's calls to queer resurgence, demanding "that we remain cognizant of the pitfalls associated with retreating into an uncritical essentialism in our practices of cultural revitalization."[8] And when we expand our reading of Indigenous resurgence, we find both a variant and vibrant multiplicity of visions for Indigenous nations that similarly aim for critical self-reflection to ensure our resurgence efforts don't reproduce the very conditions and contexts from which we seek liberation. Throughout this collection, our contributors call on us to think expansively and critically about Indigenous resurgence in an age of reconciliation. Rather than detail each chapter that follows, in this introduction I seek to engage the central themes that shape this collection, referencing the contributors and their contributions as well as drawing from the larger body of scholarship that contributes to how we may think about resurgence inside and outside an age of reconciliation.

This collection is structured through four central actions: realizing, claiming, narrating, and reconciling. We open with a focus on what it may look like to *realize resurgence together.* Here we see this framing operating through two registers. The first is process-oriented. What processes arise from and for Indigenous ways of knowing? Ways of generating new knowledge? Ways of interpreting and applying knowledge? The second register pushes back against essentialist and fundamental constructions of indigeneity and resurgence. The contributions that comprise this first section challenge narrow interpretations of indigenity and resurgence, calling on us to take up a critical analysis of how settler colonial and heteronormative framings have infiltrated our own ways of relating to our self, one another, and place.

The second section brings together contributions that seek to *(re)claim our relationships to the political.* These scholars expose and challenge state interpretations of treaty and law, rejecting fixed notions of relationship. They orient us towards a relational resurgence that captures the myriad ways we come together with one another and the world around us. The third section builds on these themes through attention to dialogue, story, and truth-telling. These contributions draw on narrative while also *narrating possibilities for reconciliation and resurgence.* They call for us to envision enriching and enduring ways of relating. The fourth section, *reconciling lands, bodies, and gender,* centres our attention on the particular experiences and connections that are too often muted and severed by settler colonialism. Illuminating the interconnectivity between and across creation (life in all their forms), these chapters call for visions of resurgence that remain accountable to all our relations (women, two-spirit, queer, and the various life-forms and forces that comprise creation). Cree scholar Billy-Ray Belcourt concludes this conversation by calling on us to envision new futures, ones that are not wholly encumbered by settler colonialism and instead are centred in Indigenous joy.

Accounting for Location: Accountability, Land, and Mobility

Seneca scholar Mishuana Goeman opens this collection with an important discussion about the first step necessary for decolonization: accountability. She does so through a focus on self-location and land

acknowledgments. She reminds us that failure to engage Indigenous studies and Indigenous knowledge eclipses more fulsome understandings of
relationships to land and place. She notes, "In settler colonial studies,
focused as it is on structures without the flesh of Indigenous thought,
land is already property accumulating into settler state territory." To stop
short of engaging Indigenous knowledge leaves concepts of *terra nullius*
intact, as these ideas are insidiously embedded logics organizing the state
rhetoric and structures that disavow the concept in name.

Land acknowledgments have become commonplace in Canada. One
reporter in 2017 noted, "But you know a phenomenon has really arrived in Canada when it involves hockey. Both the Winnipeg Jets and
the Edmonton Oilers began acknowledging traditional lands in their
announcements before all home games last season."[9] Land acknowledgments can be important reminders of our position as visitors on these
lands or treaty partners whose rights to live here are contingent on embodying the relationships with the Indigenous nations outlined in these
agreements. Land acknowledgment, while a long-standing tradition
across Indigenous nations who have detailed their relationships to the
lands they traverse and make their home upon since time immemorial,
began to be expressed by non-Indigenous leaders in British Columbia in
the early 1970s in order to highlight the outstanding Indigenous land
question that was plaguing BC government and industry. Land acknowledgments were powerful reminders of the unresolved question of how
BC came to have the "right" to be there, who had the authority to govern
the land, etc. Unfortunately, the courts and state reconciliation efforts
have largely been stalled by questions of authority.

Indigenous stories of how we engage with place unearth possibilities
that imagine other ways of relating to one another. As Inupiat/Inuvialuit
scholar Gordon Christie notes, "Questions about how people might interact with one another and the land and sea around did not trace back to
first-order questions about which body had the rightful authority to make
decisions in this context. First-order questions would be about *how* one
might act – they were about the appropriateness of the action in questions,
not who might be appropriately positioned to decide how to act."[10] Unfortunately our invocation of land acknowledgments today rarely questions
who has the rightful authority to make decisions or, more importantly,
how we might act. Instead they are now largely symbolic demonstrations
of cultural inclusion at best and, at worst, close down further examination.
Anishinaabe scholar Hayden King cautions that a danger of land acknowledgment is that it "offers them [settlers] an alibi for doing the hard work
of learning about their neighbours and learning about the treaties of the
territory and learning about those nations that should have jurisdiction."[11]

King states, "For me, personally, I think I started to see how the territorial acknowledgement could become very superficial and also how it sort of fetishizes these actual tangible, concrete treaties. They're not metaphors — they're real institutions, and for us to write and recite a territorial acknowledgement that sort of obscures that fact, I think we do a disservice to that treaty and to those nations."[12] The dangers that King warns us about are potentially present in any efforts towards reconciliation, whether that be land acknowledgements or efforts towards Indigenizing the academy. And our relationships with place also risk becoming eclipsed in resurgence efforts that reproduce Native-settler binaries in ways that excuse Indigenous peoples from being attentive to questions of our own responsibilities and obligations as we move through our own and others' territories.

The field of critical Indigenous resurgence reminds us that our position on these lands requires that we daily consider our responsibilities to these nations and their territories. We are all encumbered by these obligations, Indigenous and non-indigenous peoples alike. As such, it is crucial for us to find ways to explore what these obligations are and find pathways to enact our relationships with these nations and the lands and water. It is our mobility, our movement across the lands and waters that activates our relationships and responsibilities. The flattening of Indigenous space to territorial delineations of bounded spaces marking "ours" and "theirs" not only reifies settler claims to unceded lands and settler modes of possession but also presumes Indigenous spaces are unregulated, failing to account for the ordering of relationships that produce the balanced interactions with creation.

A broad examination of resurgence literature encourages us to combat colonial framings of land that reify Western containments or elide a broader understanding of the range of relationships we have to place. These works remind us that in our efforts to assert our political authority in the face of state assertions of title over our territories, we must be careful not to foreclose alternative forms of resistance and resurgence by centring our attentions on articulations of land that are wedded to Western notions of bounded space. In our aim to revitalize our grounded lifeways, we must remain vigilant in our considerations of how our attempts to assert that our political authority has become wedded to territorial boundaries and fixed political formations that foreclose rich understandings of relating to one another. We don't want to enable the fulfilment of colonial efforts to restrict Indigenous mobility by tethering Indigeneity to land.

Within the broader resurgence literature, Pohnpeian and Filipino scholar Vicente Diaz reminds us to be attentive to this trap, noting the need to be "cognizant of how we as Native peoples sometimes unwittingly perpetuate colonial definitions of land (and self) through ways that we invoke primordial connectedness to landedness, particularly in political programs of reclaiming stolen land bases."[13] This romanticizing of pre-contact Indigenous life poses at least two significant risks for Indigenous nations: (1) it obscures the hard work that produces Indigenous knowledge and enables flourishing relationships with humans and non-humans,[14] and (2) in the absence of this attention to the work involved in living out our relationality, makes space for settler replacement narratives that posit Indigenous relationships and knowledge as *natural* and *innate*. Consequently, these narratives position Indigenous realities as *inauthentic* and *contaminated* by colonialism and frame the rise of settler-states as *inevitable* and thus *inculpable*.[15] As Mishuana Goeman also highlights in her scholarship, "A consequence of colonialism has meant a translation or too easy collapsing of *land* to *property*, a move that perpetuates the logics of containment."[16] This valuation of land to jurisdictional legal value fails to account for the relationality of land as a "storied site of human interactions."[17] In the process of this power-knowledge dynamic, land becomes devoid of its agency and meaning-making potential and instead becomes objectified as a quantifiable good we live *on* rather than a living entity we live *with* and generate knowledge *through*.[18]

We need to work against colonial narratives that seek to divorce us from these relationships by configuring land as bounded territories in which only our primordial practices can permeate so long as they are understood as temporally and spatially fixed and discursively remade as "cultural rights" to ensure minimal material impacts for the state. We can resist this move, however, by ensuring we are creating space for relationships that are generative, that cultivate not just the continued *transmission* of Indigenous knowledge but also ensure the *production* of Indigenous knowledge.

In detailing land as pedagogy, Leanne Simpson relays the story of Kwezens, a young girl who learns both *from* the land and in interaction *with* the land, bringing the knowledge of how to make maple syrup to her people. It is not just her ability to learn with and from the land that generates this knowledge. It is further cultivated through her loving relationships with her family, her mother, and her aunties who trust in her knowledge and support her in working through her understanding of the land and, in this context, the maple trees, when she is unable to reproduce the running sap at first attempt. Simpson asserts, in this way, "The land, aki, is both context and process."[19] It is through the activation of our relationships with the living entities that constitute this expansive space – the land, animals, spirits, and humans – that knowledge is produced and transmitted. The generative quality of our movement across Creation necessitates attention to and accountability for our positionality. This requires we be attentive to and ground our analysis of relationships in the place we are, and where we are is always changing.[20] Containment of Indigenous lands to reserves or even the more expansive Indigenous/Aboriginal territory can risk our assuming that our movements through our own territories are not also always regulated and conditioned by relationships and responsibilities. In fact, it is our engagement with place and others in these places that gives rise to our political practices, exchanges, and development of new relationships. Greater understanding of how our mobility is generative can also enable us to see how discourses that fix us spatially (and temporally) are reductive.

For example, the story of Kwezens nicely demonstrates the danger of failing to see *land as pedagogy*. If we fail to account for how our movement across and engagement with place give rise to our knowledge production and practices then we see the practice of making maple sugar as a primordial practice of Anishinaabeness instead of seeing the practice of engaging creation and nurturing new knowledge production as essential. Certainly this story is about how the Anishinaabe came to receive the gift of maple syrup. But more importantly, it serves as a guide for how we can bring forward new gifts to aid us in this ever-changing world. The greatest tool available to Indigenous peoples is not revitalization of our traditional practices but instead is the processes that gave rise to these ever-growing and flourishing traditions.

Towards the Resurgence of Indigenous Knowledge

The resurgence literature reminds us that we must contend with how we are engaging with and producing knowledge. We have to ask ourselves what knowledge counts and in what ways. I believe we must move beyond merely a considerate citational politic. Beyond *which* sources of knowledge we take up, we are also intently focused on *how* we take up them up. For example, why do we classify some works as theory and others as stories? What is lost when we fail to understand *theory* as a set of *stories?* Or when we fail to consider theories produced and contained within stories. And story is not just theory. It is also a practice. As Leanne Simpson reminds us, within Anishinaabe thought, "'Theory' is generated and regenerated continually through embodied practice and within each family, community, and generation of people."[21] It is rooted in relationality – in our relationships with one another and with creation.

Taking Indigenous knowledge seriously means not just taking up different answers but instead (or at least in addition) requires raising a different set of questions. Indigenous knowledge is too often treated as an additive to Western knowledge, eclipsing its transformative powers. The Indigenous resurgence literature calls on us to be attentive to how power structures and determines which narratives, modes of understanding our world and the web of relationships in operation, are given primacy. Furthermore, we must untangle how these narratives have ordered *how* we relate to one another and to creation. Too often, conventional Western knowledge is willing to turn to the relational only insofar as this attention to relationships doesn't threaten the stability of the state. For example, Cree scholar Gina Starblanket's chapter shows how foreclosing more expansive conceptions of treaty relationships eclipses the concomitant questions these understandings produce in relation to state claims to sovereignty, land title, and political authority over Indigenous lives. We need to be attentive to how asymmetrical power relationships have enabled conventional Western knowledge to produce hierarchies of knowledge that too often mute modes of understanding the world as deeply relational and interconnected.

We can see similar forms of containment operating in educational contexts, such as with efforts to indigenize the academy. This rarely involves the expansion of Indigenous programming that takes Indigenous knowledge production as its base or is directed and driven by the questions and concerns of Indigenous communities (both the grounded concerns of Indigenous nations and their citizens or the related intellectual inquiries coming from Indigenous studies). Instead, widespread attention and resources are dedicated to the expansion of Indigenous responses to and critiques of the central tenets and concerns within the Western disciplines. Indigenous knowledge becomes contained within these disciplinary traditions that drive both the questions deemed important to their respective field and determines the metrics for successful engagement and mobilization of knowledge.

In fact, even within Indigenous studies, much of the celebrated and well-funded scholarship is focused on works that make critical interventions in long-standing Western disciplines, dismantling the theories central to a particular field. These works often brilliantly theorize both Indigenous resurgence and Indigenous experiences with and responses to settler colonialism and warrant considerable engagement. Indeed, Indigenous studies scholarship recognizes we are not outside of colonialism, but are engaging with and affected by the structures and logics that enable its continued flourishing. This is important work. But the question remains why Western academic fields will often *only* engage Indigenous knowledge when it's translated through the language of their discipline. Why does the onus continue to reside with Indigenous knowledge holders to translate Indigenous knowledge into cognizable frames? And even when Indigenous and non-Indigenous scholars do this work, Indigenous knowledge is most often given consideration or taken up by Western thinkers when there is either a *vacancy* or *bankruptcy* in Western thought, replicating a power binary between Western and Indigenous knowledge.

For example, when Western scientific knowledge fails to provide insights for how to live in a precarious world affected by devastating natural events such as earthquakes and tsunamis, attention will be given to Indigenous knowledge systems, recognizing that Indigenous peoples have had to contend with these concerns since time immemorial. Yet, even when Western thinkers are willing to consider the stories that detail these historic events that are absent from the Western historical record, they often fail to give consideration to how Indigenous knowledge posits we are a part of the web of relationships that give rise to these moments. Instead, Western divisions between humans and nature are reified even while considering the Indigenous stories that work against this categorization and binary by detailing the interconnectedness of Creation.[22] These tendencies minimize or contain the transformative potential of Indigenous knowledge, rendering it easier to incorporate and assimilate into the Western categories of knowledge. It is not enough to make space for Indigenous knowledge. We must allow for this space to be reconfigured by Indigenous knowledge.

In this collection, Anishinaabe-Métis scholar Aimée Craft unpacks resurgence and reconciliation within Canadian law to consider how language is constraining Indigenous aspirations and expressions. She highlights the troubling tradition within Canadian law in which Crown sovereignty is assumed and thus requires the reconciliation of Aboriginal occupancy with this presumed sovereignty. Reordering our relationships to our lands, the courts configure the parameters of the questions presented to ensure the answers found will enable the state to remain intact. This is despite the Truth and Reconciliation Commission's calls to action asserting that primacy should be given to Indigenous legal traditions. Craft demonstrates how the appropriation of language can reorient our own efforts towards resurgence and asks us to be considerate in the language we draw on. Cree scholar Darcy Lindberg cautions us of the risks in teaching Indigenous laws within Canadian university frameworks and pedagogies, which tend to separate and isolate law and legal principles from the lifeworlds they are embedded in. Yet Lindberg also reminds us that Indigenous resurgence efforts today are always running up against the multi-juridical landscape of Canada and continued colonization pressures that necessitate our engagements with the state.

The Process of a Relational Resurgence

Glen Coulthard, in his public presentation for the Indigenous resurgence symposium that is reflected in Hunt and Simpson's contribution to this collection, encouraged us to consider the containment of our intellectual traditions. He reminded us that Indigenous intellectuals are not some new phenomenon of the Western academy but instead have always been a bedrock of our communities, communities that have always privileged and encouraged the expansion of our knowledge and thinking. Critical engagement with others has always been an Indigenous tradition. Tracing the myriad ways Indigenous intellectuals such as George and Art Manuel engaged with Fanon's work in the 1970s, Coulthard challenges and pushes back against newer trends within our fields that either naively posit this form of engagement as new, or worse, as somehow "un-Indigenous." In the process, he reminds us that we can better understand our contemporary realities that have been so thoroughly conditioned by colonization by looking to the important works that have long spoken of settler colonialism but by another name, such as internal colonization. He asserts that doing so can get us out of the binds of settler colonial framings that too often ignore process and relationship by focusing on subjects. Instead, he encourages us to question not *who we are* in our relationships (the settler or the Native) as this positional orientation is too often vacant of accountability, but to instead consider *how we are* in our relationship (the colonizer and the colonized), as this framing highlights our relational practices, not our subjectivities.[23]

Similarly Kanaka scholar Noelani Goodyear-Kaʻōpua frames the term *Indigenous* "as an always already historically situated category of alliance rather than a static, ahistorical category of identity."[24] For Goodyear-Kaʻōpua, "To use the term Indigenous is not only to speak from that grounding [as a Kanaka Maoli] but also to emphasize our relationality to other Native peoples who similarly maintain their connection to their lands and aboriginal ancestors, often against forces seeking to sever those ties."[25] Kanaka scholar Hōkūlani Aikau's chapter reminds us that we must be careful not to reproduce racial and colonial logics of purity in our efforts towards the revitalization of Indigenous practices. In looking to the metaphor of the non-Native as an invasive species, Aikau cautions us of the harms of (re)producing binary thinking, noting how racial logics of purity and authenticity undergird the invasive species metaphor and work against our efforts towards resurgence. She reminds us of the importance of diversity to ensure the flourishing of our nations.

Tanana Athabascan scholar Dian Million, in the chapter the precedes Aikau's, asks us to consider what it would mean to take seriously that everything is spirit. She reminds us that spirit refuses enclosure. Million refuses the damage-centred narratives of Indigenous peoples in urban centres, of disconnection, trauma, and harm at the hands of colonialism. Resisting fundamental and essentializing conceptions of Indigeneity and resurgence, she recognizes our pots are never empty but instead bubbling over with spirit. Following Million and Aikau, Cree scholar Dallas Hunt complicates how we understand masculinity, highlighting how it helps set the terms of what is intelligible and legible in Indigenous studies. Hunt is concerned with how masculinity becomes tethered to wisdom, constructing and orienting Indigenous politics to put forward imaginaries that direct us away from relational obligations and forecloses possibilities of liberatory futures premised on an ethic of care for all our relations. Hunt utilizes the work of Cree scholar and poet Billy Ray Belcourt to interrogate Taiaiake Alfred's conceptions of masculinity. Hunt challenges fundamental and essentialist notions of resurgence that have too long characterized a narrow reading of the field of resurgence.

Many of our contributors explore Indigenous visions for what it means to be flourishing nations and communities as well as how these narrations have been reconfigured by others, curtailing their abilities to breathe new life into how we understand the world and our relationships. Gina Starblanket focuses on the resurgence of treaty relationships. She asks what this looks like when their current form is not of our choosing and instead have been configured from the top down by violence and dispossession. Her examination of treaty reminds us that resurgence cannot be just an invocation of the past into the present without understanding how our ancestors' visions for us outlined in treaty relationships have been largely reconfigured. Critiquing colonial mythologies of treaty, she calls on us to resist this singular story that eclipses the transformative potential of relational understandings of treaty.

Jeff Ganohalidoh Corntassel examines reconciliation discourses to ask when and how Indigenous knowledge and living histories have agency in order to understand how Indigenous self-determination is practised amidst reconciliation. He demonstrates how witnessing and storytelling offer different but overlapping directions for sustainable self-determination and ways to enable the transmission and production of Indigenous knowledge for future generations. Corey Snelgrove and Cree scholar Matthew Wildcat also take up reconciliation discourse to ask what opportunities exist in this special conjuncture. Focusing on the Maskwacis Cree and their efforts to create a new education authority, Snelgrove and Wildcat demonstrate that we can understand reconciliation as a response to Indigenous action that has produced a colonial reconfiguring of Canada. And though this may be a colonial reconfiguring, they argue the outcomes are not predetermined or fixed. Instead reconciliation offers and signals an opening for strategic action. In doing so, they remind us of the efficacy of Indigenous political action, as well as the ruptures and openings it produces.

Biniza (Zapotec) scholar Isabel Altamirano-Jiménez takes up an Indigenous feminist analysis of resurgence to trace out the intersections of capitalism and Indigenous place-based practices of resurgence. Mapping a body-land analytic, Altamirano-Jiménez historicizes gendered dispossession and grounds resurgence in the colonial capitalist conditions within which it occurs to demonstrate how collective Indigenous struggles to protect lifeways must centre protecting Indigenous trans, two-spirit, and women, whose lives are too often rendered violable by the modern settler state.

The contributors in this collection call for us to think collectively. Kwagu'ł scholar Sarah Hunt and Leanne Simpson ask us to think through together by engaging in dialogue with one another. In doing so they make a critical intervention. Instead of telling us what Indigenous resurgence should look like, they model it, reminding us all that resurgence is process-oriented. It requires careful and considerate work. We must open our ears and our hearts. We must listen to one another and have enough respect and love for one another to ask the difficult questions, not just of others but also of ourselves. They model healthy engagement that is rooted in respect and care for one another and the unique views and perspectives brought forward by their own experiences and knowledges. Their modelling of process also highlights tensions we must attend to in our considerations of Indigenous resurgence, asking us to consider the exclusionary tactics we are reproducing in our relationships.

Leanne Simpson reminds us that we must be attentive to the ways in which our relationships have been reordered by colonization, highlighting how restrictive notions of gender and sexuality have been effectively taken up by our own communities for over three centuries. She asks us to consider why we see some work as political and not other work. Why, when families are so central to the facilitation and embodiment of healthy relationships, do we consider this work as somehow outside the political? Indeed, she reminds us that nothing is more political than raising new generations that are equipped with our practices and the knowledges embedded within them and thoroughly inculcated in our processes for relating with creation that they can dream into existence new traditions for how to make our way through this ever-changing world. In learning with Black Lives Matters, she also reminds us that resurgence isn't the language used in all communities and that we shouldn't be overly committed to a word. It's actions that matter. She encourages us to look broadly in defining and determining pathways for resurgence.

Sarah Hunt similarly asks us to consider whose voices contour resurgence, reminding us that engagement in resurgence is a luxury and privilege that is not afforded to all. In fact, much of the immediate and urgent work needed in our communities is not about the resurgence of Indigenous lifeways but instead is focused on reducing the harms of colonialism that continue to wreak havoc on our people. She highlights the need to be attentive to the violences that too often order our relationships and play out disproportionately on the bodies of Indigenous women and two-spirited people. She reminds us that intimate practices of care are resurgence, countering violence, transphobia, and homophobia while expanding and opening space for all our people. Hunt calls on us to consider what it means if we are missing vast numbers of our people from the spaces in which we are carrying out resurgence and theorizing these practices.

Turning to a discussion of the Olympics, Abenaki scholar Christine O'Bonsawin importantly reminds us of the dangers of reconciliation frameworks that appropriate Indigenous peoples in name and image while failing to consider the long history of exploitation that Indigenous nations have faced through the structures of these international sporting events. Through a meticulous study of Indigenous peoples and the Olympics, O'Bonsawin reminds us that this tradition is not only steeped in nationalism and Western notions of hetero-patriarchy that put forward very particular notions of masculinity, but also have significant material implications for Indigenous peoples in our relationships with the land, water, and animals that are severely and often irreparably harmed by the infrastructures of these events. Métis scholar Daniel Voth reimagines Métis nationalism through the connections between women and the land in order to produce a framework of Métis governance that can be operationalized outside of the patriarchal logics that have too often shaped Indigenous-Métis political interactions.

We close this collection with Belcourt's "Red Utopia," as it's a fitting reminder of the power of Indigenous joy. He shows how a "culture of radical hope puts pressure on the vulgarities of settlement." Through the resurgent act of breathing together, resisting being out of breath, Belcourt reminds us that sometimes we have to tilt our heads a bit to see the world to come. Forcing us to confront the limits of language and linearity, Belcourt reminds us that the political violences of colonialism cannot "wholly negate that which it despises." He encourages us to look around and see hints of a world to come – a Red utopia.

NOTES

1 Portions of this chapter are drawn from Gina Starblanket and Heidi Kiiwetinepinesiik Stark, "Toward a Relational Paradigm – Four Points for
   Consideration: Knowledge, Gender, Land and Modernity," in *Resurgence
   and Reconciliation: Indigenous-Settler Relations and Earth Teachings*, edited
   by Michael Asch, John Borrows, and James Tully (Toronto: University of
   Toronto Press, 2018), 179–208.
2 Sheryl R. Lightfoot, "The Pessimism Traps of Indigenous Resurgence,"
   in *Pessimism in International Relations: Provocations, Possibilities, Politics*, ed. Tim
   Stevens and Nicholas Michelsen (Nature, Switzerland: Palgrave Macmillan,
   2020), 155–72; Michael Elliot, "Indigenous Resurgence: The Drive for
   Renewed Engagement and Reciprocity in the Turn Away from the State,"
   Canadian Journal of Political Science 51, no. 1 (March 2018): 61–81; John
   Borrows and James Tully, "Introduction," in *Resurgence and Reconciliation:
   Indigenous-Settler Relations and Earth Teachings*, ed. Michael Asch, John
   Borrows, and James Tully (Toronto: University of Toronto Press, 2018), 3–25.
3 Michael Asch, John Borrows, and James Tully, eds., *Resurgence and Reconciliation: Indigenous-Settler Relations and Earth Teachings* (Toronto: University of
   Toronto Press, 2018), 4.
4 Glen Sean Coulthard. *Red Skins, White Masks: Rejecting the Colonial Politics of
   Recognition* (Minneapolis: University of Minnesota Press, 2014), 179.
5 Coulthard, *Red Skins, White Masks*, 179.
6 Coulthard, *Red Skins, White Masks*, 179.
7 Leanne Betasamosake Simpson, *Lighting the Eighth Fire: The Liberation, Resurgence,
   and Protection of Indigenous Nations* (Winnipeg: Arbeiter Ring, 2008), 14.
8 Simpson, *Lighting the Eighth Fire*, 156.
9 Stephen Marche, "Canada's Impossible Acknowledgment," *New Yorker*,
   7 September, https://www.newyorker.com/culture/culture-desk/canadas
   -impossible-acknowledgment.
10 Marche, "Canada's Impossible Acknowledgment," 341.
11 "'I Regret It': Hayden King on Writing Ryerson University's Territorial
   Acknowledgement," CBC Radio, 18 January 2019. https://www.cbc.ca
   /radio/unreserved/redrawing-the-lines-1.4973363/i-regret-it-hayden-king
   -on-writing-ryerson-university-s-territorial-acknowledgement-1.4973371.
12 "'I Regret It.'"
13 Vicente M Diaz, "No Island Is an Island," in *Native Studies Keywords*, ed. S.N.
   Teves, A.S. Smith, and M. Raheja (Tucson: University of Arizona Press, 2015), 19.
14 Hokulani K. Aikau, Maile Arvin, Mishuana Goeman, and Scott Morgensen,
   "Indigenous Feminisms Roundtable," *Frontiers* 36, no. 3 (2015): 94.
15 Jean M. O'Brien, *Firsting and Lasting: Writing Indians Out of Existence in New
   England, Indigenous Americas* (Minneapolis: University of Minnesota Press,

2010). For discussion of American innocence, see Boyd Cothran, *Remembering the Modoc War: Redemptive Violence and the Making of American Innocence* (Chapel Hill: University of North Carolina Press, 2014).

16 Mishuana Goeman, "Land as Life: Unsettling the Logics of Containment," in *Native Studies Keywords*, ed. Teves, Smith, and Raheja (Tucson: University of Arizona Press, 2015), 72.

17 Goeman, "Land as Life," 72.

18 Goeman notes, "Land is foundation to people's cultural practices and if we define *culture* as meaning making rather than as differentiation and isolation in a multicultural neoliberal model, then by thinking through *land* as a meaning-making process rather than a claimed object the aspirations of Native people are apparent and clear." "Land as Life," 73.

19 Leanne Betasamosake Simpson, "Land as Pedagogy: Nishnaabeg Intelligence and Rebellious Transformation," *Decolonization: Indigeneity, Education, and Society* 3, no. 3 (2014): 7.

20 Aikau et al., "Indigenous Feminisms Roundtable."

21 Simpson, "Land as Pedagogy," 7.

22 See, for example, Ann Finkbeiner, "The Great Quake and the Great Drowning," *Hakai Magazine*, 14 September 2015, https://www.hakaimagazine.com /article-long/great-quake-and-great-drowning.

23 For additional information about the symposium and recorded panels, see "Symposium: Indigenous Resurgence in an Age of Reconciliation," University of Victoria, 16–18 March 2017, https://www.uvic.ca/socialsciences/intd /indigenousnationhood/workshops/irar/index.php

24 Noelani Goodyear-Kaʻōpua, *The Seeds We Planted: Portraits of a Native Hawaiian Charter School.* First Peoples: New Directions in Indigenous Studies (Minneapolis: University of Minnesota Press, 2013), 11.

25 Goodyear-Kaʻōpua, *The Seeds We Planted*, 11.

PART ONE

Realizing Resurgence Together

1 Beyond the Grammar of Settler Apologies

MISHUANA GOEMAN

Nya:wëh sgë:nö. Mishuana Goeman gya:söh, Onöndowa'ga:'Ni'ah Ta:növödé:onö'. Here I am following Indigenous protocols to introduce myself. It briefly translates to Hello (or I hope this finds you in good health)! My name is Mishuana Goeman, and I am Tonawanda Band of Seneca from the Great Hill People. Before I begin, Nya:weh to the Gabrielino Tongva,[1] on whose lands, Tovaangnar, I teach, research, raise my children, and live. I am grateful to work in this place. This chapter is about what it means to be in place as a guest in Tovaangnar. How do you, how should the university, introduce oneself?

Let us begin where we began with my introduction. My introduction is a common practice, one we learn at an early age as Native children. When we ask, as Native people, where you are from, it does much more than relay a fact that I am from or live in Los Angeles. Rather, this common protocol is to place yourself. That is, it is a gesture not only to place yourself in a physical geographic location, although it does just that, but also to place oneself in a trajectory of cultural, intellectual, and political lineages. It is to put yourself in relation to a nation, and as such that also comes with particular and reasonable expectations. Yet it should not be understood as a move towards essentialism or authentication, though all too often it is taken this way. Policies of disconnecting families and individuals from each other have long been part of settler practices.[2] Rather, the question of where one is from and introduction are key to resisting this disconnection and defining oneself not as a racialized American Indian but in relation to others, a place, and a community. It is an anti-colonial tool to root Indigenous meaning, and it recognizes alterNative knowledges. The introduction is a route to find connection between each other.

The simple introduction of placing oneself in relation to their people can generate abundant possibilities – possibilities across time and geographies. In many cases, and this depends on the community as I will talk about shortly, the response of each party will be followed up by locating oneself by families or other markers. If you are a Parker, a Hill – or in my own very odd case a Lone or Goeman – the introduction creates a particular and at times unarticulated understanding. Native communities are small and our inclinations towards expansive relationalities large.[3] In Haudenosaunee communities, we have a phrase for extending our knowledge systems, called extending the rafters.[4] It reflects the longhouse and its expansion – whether that be into new lands, incorporating new nations as we did with Tuscarora, or making new concepts and ideas our own. These are expansive relationalities that do not rest on exclusionary binaries relying on differences of us/them, foreigner/ citizen, colonized/colonizer, but rather considers our relationship as humans and non-humans to each other on this ground we live. These relationalities and the ability to remember and connect are the key to surviving attempts to the settling and taking of lands through policies, lands given to what would become white citizens at the exclusion and expense of Black and Native people. In the words of the town destroyer Theodore Roosevelt, the breaking up of Indigenous land was meant to be "a mighty pulverizing engine to break up the Tribal mass."[5] This belies the often stagnant, essentialized, and uncomplicated ways that Indians are produced in literature, the media, academia, and the everyday of settler society.

Now I say "simple introductions," but it is not that simple to have survived years of brutal colonization meant to eradicate a tribal sense of place, a tribal people's and Indigenous nation's futurity. Deborah Miranda, of the Coastan Esselen people in California, eloquently speaks to the difficulty and demand by settler society that somehow Indigenous people remain "whole" through brutal violence. She begins by quoting Chickasaw author Linda Hogan who profoundly acknowledges, "I am the result of the love of thousands." Miranda, however, continues, "And sometimes we are the result of the bitter survival of thousands, as well. Sometimes we get here any way we can. Sometimes our bodies are the bridges over which our descendants cross, spanning unimaginable landscapes of loss."[6] So while introductions and acknowledgments place us, they place us in relationships with specific families and nations and become a way to remain accountable; yet there is also the recognition of how loss can displace those connections. In the introduction there is an acknowledgment of how words can bring them, weave them, back together again. Still, it is the placing that will help forge the path back. It is the smallest of breadcrumb paths that have brought people home through unimaginable circumstances of boarding schools, the child welfare system, adoption sweeps, federal policy aimed at dispossessing, and systems of surveillance that create highways, not just pipelines, to prison. Oh, yes, and pipelines that destroy water supplies, leaving entire swathes of Native communities and Nations as expendable peoples. This is exacerbated by pipelines that bring destruction as women and children become targets for sexual violence in oilfields.[7] At Standing Rock, people used the introduction to forge relationships to each other, to remind ourselves that ancestors had gathered here before. They used the introduction to extend their rafters and invite others in. The pole in the middle of the camp was "an infrastructure" that directed people to camps based on their introductions.[8] The introduction is an anti-colonial tool in this instance. It is not an apology for the past or a single thread to a past, it weaves a future forward. The introduction is a mechanism for the beginning of not only acknowledging your place in the world but also of creating Indigenous and allied networks. It reframes landscapes and our relationships to them. The introduction is a first step in organizing Indigenous belonging and place-making.

So you might be asking by now, why is she unpacking this commonplace practice? I do so because it has been readily apparent in my work that many are willing to take up the examination of the United States as a settler power and Indians as unfortunate bystanders in need of saving and thus an object of research, Indians as somehow something we begin with in our discussions and then let drop out in a settler temporal reiteration of power, Indians as, well, Indians without a specificity to place or community and without particular colonial histories and particular histories of resistance. Simply, the Indigenous disappear or are evacuated in empty containers. American Indians and Indigenous people are all too often solely associated with loss – whether it be our lands or our lives. At times decolonization is not even about us, and often neither is settler colonialism. That is, decolonization is not often about returning land to the Tongva, for instance. Often moves towards decolonization do not address Native epistemology or ontology about land; settler colonialism too often does not recognize the vast literature written by Native scholars over the preceding decades. Yet both terms are still about a transfer of land as property just on a wider scale. We recognize settler structures but do not acknowledge possibilities of impermanence or other ways of organizing our societies. That is, settler colonialism becomes the analytic, and Indigenous futurities are not part of the practice. You can study settler colonial structures without ever talking to Indigenous communities or peoples. I do not recommend it, but I state this because I consistently see settler colonialism being taken up across many fields in the social sciences or humanities without a discussion of Indigenous scholarship that has not only discussed these issues for decades, but worked on materializing alterNative ways of addressing mass capitalism and property regimes by working with tribal communities. The window dressing of settler colonialism or decolonization that does not recognize even the land or peoples troubles me. We do not "move beyond the blessing."[9] In examining the land introduction, it is my hope to begin this process of seriously reframing settler landscapes by rethinking the role of the university in disposessing the original caretakers of the land, emboldening relationships to tribal communities in unpacking accountability not as a neoliberal diversity project but one of accountability and learning, and moving forward with a future of working with tribal communities in our places of learning.

As I relate at the start of my first book, *Mark My Words: Native Women Mapping Our Nations*, my interest and understanding of embodied geographies and racialized settler landscapes began at a very young age as I moved back and forth from reservation to urban to rural spaces. My dad was an ironworker, like many men from Haudenosaunee communities. My mom was white and, in our communities, land is caretaken by the women. This is not a new formation of land and property rights, but a practice of care Tonawanda has maintained since time immemorial. Thus we moved with my father and his jobs, from one community to the next. It was the unspoken racialized and gendered knowledge of what these movements meant, our understandings of Native mobilities and settler grammar of places that ensured our tribal, community, and family survival, albeit with losses en route. When we met people along our routes, we introduced ourselves. To this day, I run across people who remember my family of ironworkers, crazy kids, and constantly changing array of visiting relatives and friends. It was Indian chaos at its finest. The life of a professor has been similar in some ways. You take the job you get, you meet people along the way and know you may someday meet up again, you are always on the go, and academia has its own moments of high-steel manoeuvring with fatalities along the way – and there is always academic chaos. Finding a place can be difficult and challenging as an American Indian and Indigenous scholar.

When I finally received tenure at UCLA, I had to wrestle with the idea of permanence, of staying and not moving on, of not knowing for instance that Los Angeles is not a dry desert but is full of microclimates forever changed by ongoing mass development and the theft of water. I had to reconcile myself to the fact that I am a long-term guest on Tongva land. To what am I accountable? How should UCLA and I as an Haudenosaunee woman and member of the faculty, be accountable as a land-grant institution? After all, our cultural practices, though often land-based, should not be tossed away as we move across colonial borders in all their scales. In my work I aim towards the first steps of decolonization – which is knowing your positionality and holding yourself accountable.

It is common practice in New Zealand and then later Canada to have an acknowledgment of whose lands you are on as part of an institutional practice. As chair of the American Indian Studies (AIS) Interdepartmental Program, I drew up a model of an acknowledgment to run past the faculty. After input, which also involved paying careful attention to the legal concerns at the top of so many of our universities' minds as neoliberal institutions worried about giving land back, I contacted Tongva cultural educators I have been working with as part of the Mapping Indigenous LA project.[10] They tweaked the meaningful place-based element of this acknowledgment, enmeshing it in a place-based language and community caring. Pam Munro, professor emeritus in linguistics at UCLA, also aided with the language element.[11] Here the work would take an unexpected turn, as working with community so often does if you are listening and learning. Through a series of emails back and forth, we came up with an acknowledgment together that was far more meaningful than the original attempt. While we place the words in our signatures and invite others to do so as well, it also reminds us daily of our actions. Dissemination of digital work is often hard, but dissemination of email has become not only commonplace but overwhelming. By placing the acknowledgment here, the community takes the first step of recognizing Tongva as the original landowners. AIS faculty, staff, and students can use it and have used it as a reminder to our colleagues of their responsibility for being in this place. By repeating it in front of our talks and in our teaching practice, we can also disseminate this knowledge. The more it circulates, the more it becomes part of the fibre of our land-grant institutions.

AIS and AISC at UCLA acknowledge the Tongva peoples as the traditional land caretakers of Tovaangar (Los Angeles basin, So. Channel Islands) and are grateful to have the opportunity to work for the taraax-atom (Indigenous peoples) in this place. As a land grant institution, we pay our respects to honuukvetam (ancestors), 'ahiihirom (elders), and 'eyoohiinkem (our relatives/relations) past, present, and emerging.[12]

Now there has been some worry that this will result in lip service and no real material tangibility and it actually has taken that turn in some cases. (Re)writing Native people – in Cutcha Risling Baldy's words to describe a method of an Indigenous-driven agenda of research, teaching, and learning, especially in California – will be a long process. There are material gains to not acknowledge or to do so on the surface level.

Just as Cutcha Risling Baldy encourages "Indigenous scholars to reclaim the historical, anthropological, and ethnographic record with a more discerning analysis in order to (re)write, (re)right, and (re)rite gender epistemologies and Native feminisms from a perspective that values oral narratives accounts as 'archive' and 'documentary' evidence,"[13] the universities who fomented those fields too must practise an appropriate self-reflection. Institutionalizing acknowledgment cannot repair the past 150 years of exploitation, theft, genocide, and erasure of California Indians that make possible the UC system and the fifth-largest economy in the world, but an introduction followed by furthering that ongoing relationship is ripe with possibility for all.

A land introduction is situated in place, with a place-based assessment of the needs and desires of the local first peoples. To incorporate community feedback moves it from a nod to a past and more towards a land introduction that only begins the (re)writing and (re)righting that Risling Baldy refers to in her push for community revitalization. The local situation at UCLA is that, to the Tongva community whose lands and deaths were the soil and fertilizer for the metropolis of Los Angeles, there is much meaning in these first steps of introduction as they have been ignored by the non-Native and Native diaspora for many years.[14] To not acknowledge their existence is to continue to pave mass capitalist pathways devouring their lands, ancestors, and waterways. So, while the acknowledgment is not perfect, so is ignoring the account of the histories of dispossession. Anishinabeg scholar Hayden King is often quoted on his misgivings in implementing an acknowledgment at Ryerson, yet rarely is the line that advocates for action and the particularity of place part of the dismissive conversation: "I'd like to move towards a territorial acknowledgment where you provide people with a sort of framework and then let them write it themselves. The really important aspect of a territorial acknowledgment for me, anyway, is this sort of obligation that comes on the back end of it."[15]

As UCLA consulted with the Tongva from the beginning through our previous working relationships, we incorporated language. In doing so, it became a land introduction that disputes many damaging misconceptions. As settler colonial studies makes headway, there is often a misconception that Native peoples did not have a concept of territory. This statement is a result of stopping at settler colonial studies and not reading the richness of Indigenous studies, which have a much fuller idea of land and relationality. In settler colonial studies, focused on structures without the flesh of Indigenous thought, land is already property accumulating into settler state territory.[16] It does not break from *terra nullius,* no-man's-land, the language embedded in propertied relationships, resurrected from the papal bull of 1049 and reformulated into a doctrine discovery and the Marshall trilogy, the very foundation of settler law or what is known as federal Indian law. Tovaangar comprises many villages across Southern California, as noted by academics and Tongva themselves, who have held ideas of place, some of whom have become academics themselves in order to assert control over place without recognition for a foreign government, such as Spain, then Mexico, and most recently the United States as of 1850.[17] Each village had its own resources and trading practices. Each had its own relationship to the land and non-humans that constituted a complex system of trade and relationships. Many members of the Tongva know today these places that continue to exist under the pavement. This in large part was part of our work in the Mapping Indigenous LA project. For instance, from our website you can see how we worked with digital tools to undo colonial concepts of mapping.

Maps are not always about exact locations. Craig Torres, Cindi Alvitre, and others have helped create this map on the basis of years of research on Tongva place-making, landscapes, and cultural history and what that knowledge has meant for them. Maps are about relationships. For the Tongva, mapping occurs in many forms depicting relationships between villages in the LA basin. These relationships include environmental factors, such as wetlands, ceremonial relationships, and kinship systems that reflect intermarriage. Many of the mainstream maps that have been used to depict Indigenous peoples spatially were largely based on linguistic genealogies, yet this leaves out so much of the story. Rather than the maps we present here being based on restrictive boundaries or territories, we look to how storied maps show connection, alliance, and mobility within the Tongva landscape.[18]

In thinking through the Tongva world, it is our attempt not to start with loss of landscapes but rather to point out what is retained and passed down. This is at the heart of an anti-colonial land introduction and Indigenous forms of mapping; it starts with acknowledgment of the continuity and futurity of the Tongva, which comes through the use of Tovaangar that translates as "the world." It is not an acknowledgment of past occupancy or past wrongdoings in an apology – these grammars of settler apologies can never suffice.

That said, let's turn to the root, or theft, for a moment so we can (re)write and unpack just how important using Tovaangar is as an anti-colonial tool. While I want to describe the process of this collaborative moment, it is absolutely necessary to address the history of land grants, theft, and colonial unknowing, especially as UCLA's adoption came at the 150th anniversary and a moment in the larger UC system when there was a push to complete complying with the thirty-year-old Native American Graves and Protection Act (NAGPRA) passed in 1990. The push to return ancestors begins, however, well before the passing of NAGPRA with the first legal case waged against the UC system, particularly Berkeley's anthropology department, by Yokayo Pomo Rancheria in 1906.[19] This time of turmoil was also marked by an ever-changing exchange of land title garnered through the capitalist exchange of paper title in service to establishing a settler governance. UCLA itself started as a Spanish land grant, which then with the Mexican revolution became Rancho San Jose de Buenos Ayres (see figure 1.1).

While the figure resembles a childlike drawing and has no to-scale formations of the particular cartography that Western science and land surveying uses to position itself in power, it nonetheless was used to deny Tongva their right to land and, thus, life.

After California was passed through title to the United States, a claim was filed through the nefarious 1851 Public Land Commission Act, which sought to settle uncontested land and have pure property title in 1852. Through a series of passing titles, it eventually landed in the hands of English citizen Arthur Letts, who moved to Canada pursuing entrepreneurial endeavours. Eventually, after fighting Indians and quelling the Louis Rebellion in 1869, he obtained wealth in the form of a Canadian land grant. Too often our ideas of territory overlook these important co-constitutive recognitions of title to land. Letts eventually moved from Canada to new burgeoning frontiers and a landscape ripe for his voracious entrepreneurial appetites. He sensed that the push for a new citizenship would lend itself to the development of the west side of Los Angeles, what was then mostly farmland. He died in 1923, however, before he had the chance to see his bid for the downtown UCLA campus come to fruition. Los Angeles was the promised land, a settler paradise built on racial inequalities[20] that enabled Letts to build a fortune that he would pass on to his sons-in-law, the Janss brothers of the famed UCLA steps. While a majority of students, until recently with the introduction of land acknowledgment, had no idea who or what the Tongva were, they knew well of these developers that created the city of Westwood and founded UCLA through "donated" plots. This pass of title and grifting were not unique to UCLA, but in fact indicative of larger national processes of making land into property.

It is not coincidental that the first iterations of land-grant colleges took place at the same time as what historians term "the reservation era" and what Californians experienced as a period of mass genocide, that is, a time when the US government herded Native peoples onto contained reservations and away from populations it chose to protect. The early

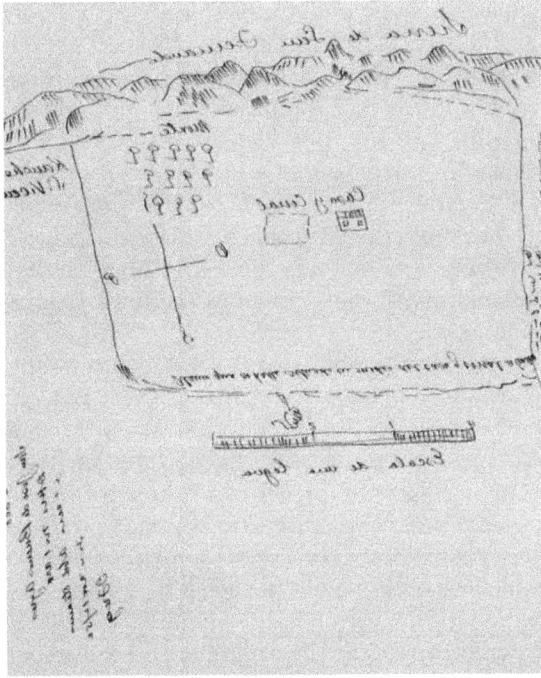

Figure 1.1. *Diseños*: Maps and plans of ranchos of Southern California, mostly within Los Angeles and Orange counties, Bound Manuscripts Collection (collection 170, item 368), Library Special Collections, Charles E. Young Research Library, UCLA.

transfer of land into property came not only through mass violence, but at the start of American legal practices. The "conquest by law"[21] that came after mass physical violence of domesticating land, a violence now relegated to individual liberal models, is largely concerned with protecting *and making* property.[22] Abraham Lincoln signed the first Morrill Act (7 U.S.C § 301) in 1862, only after conciliatory amendments to the bill demanded that the colleges supplement training in agriculture, mechanics, and engineering with military training. Notwithstanding the *Chronicle of Higher Education* assertion about increased weaponry and militarization,[23] the US campus is not a modern implementation of governmental force but rather a constitutive fact of its existence. Among the features to be found at the University of California at Berkeley, established in 1868 on Ohlone land, was a campus armoury. UC students underwent two hours of mandatory training per week in "tactics, dismounted drill, marksmanship, camp duty, military engineering, and fortifications."[24] The building of military forces and its use in the westward movement of settlement was entwined with education at the start, as the absorption of land was coupled with the subjugation of American Indian children into mandatory boarding schools. Berkeley was also the site of the second founded anthropology department – producers of knowledge, conveyers of colonial ideology – supported through conquest of thought. At the time of its founding, the UC collected mass amounts of Indigenous knowledge, artefacts, and our very ancestors. Many ancestors still find themselves detained under the cement of the Berkeley pool, waiting to be returned home.

Five months after signing the Morrill Act, Lincoln would approve the largest mass execution in the United States, which further opened the floodgates for Native land to become white property. The Dakota 38 were executed.[25] They fought against the US program of starvation and slow death to their communities as well as the encroachment of white settlers.[26] The 1862 Morrill Act gave to each state – which was not experiencing a state of Native insurrection or not currently in revolt against the Union – 300,000 acres of land. In cases where there was not enough federally held land within a given state, the state could option for well-resourced land elsewhere to line their coffers. To be clear, Native land by this time was held in trust by the US government, and rich resource land was often leased to private companies well under the market value. In a recent exposé titled "Land-Grab Universities," researchers collected data on the afterlife of the Act. They "located more than 99% of all Morrill Act acres, identified their original Indigenous inhabitants and caretakers, and researched the principal raised from their sale in the late 19th and early 20th centuries. [They] reconstructed approximately 10.7 million acres taken from nearly 250 tribes, bands, and communities through over 160 violence-backed land cessions, a legal term for the giving up of territory."[27] In preparation for the 150th anniversary and acknowledgment, I too attempted to trace land title in all its iterations as California passed from one colonial entity to another. Tongva scholar Teresa Ambo-Stewart examines what this means to higher education recruitment and activism and how the promise of public institutions will not be upheld until more California Indians find a place on these campuses. Data collected by the Land-Grab Universities' researchers were then mapped by Margaret Pearce to create a stunning visual of how education in the United States was funded.[28]

Cornell University, for instance, was built on the land of Cayuga people, a nation in the Haudenosaunee Confederacy. Cornell used its land-grant scrip to invest in 500,000 acres of valuable timberland in Wisconsin.

Two land-grant universities and their **Morrill Act parcels.**

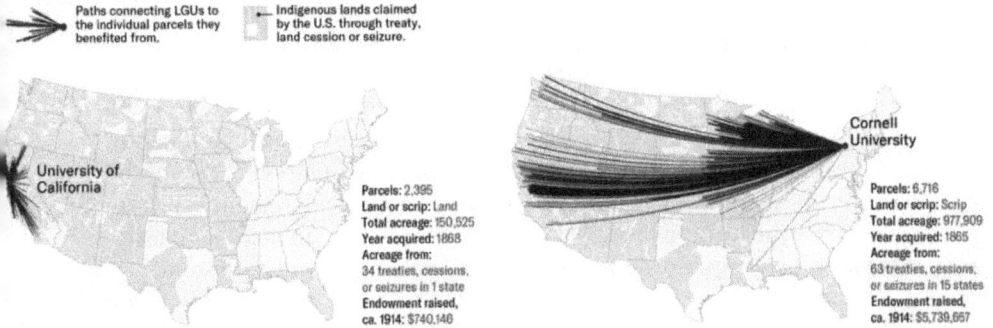

Paths connecting LGUs to the individual parcels they benefited from.

Indigenous lands claimed by the U.S. through treaty, land cession or seizure.

University of California

Parcels: 2,395
Land or scrip: Land
Total acreage: 150,525
Year acquired: 1868
Acreage from:
34 treaties, cessions,
or seizures in 1 state
Endowment raised,
ca. 1914: $740,148

Cornell University

Parcels: 6,716
Land or scrip: Scrip
Total acreage: 977,909
Year acquired: 1865
Acreage from:
63 treaties, cessions,
or seizures in 15 states
Endowment raised,
ca. 1914: $5,739,667

SOURCES: Andrews 1918; GLO, BLM; Royce 1896-1897; USFS; USGS; Natural Earth.

Figure 1.2. From Cornell to the UC financial funds

Anticipating the appreciation of the land's value – and thereby investing in the expansion of the settler state's conversion of land into property – Cornell waited decades while the land, and the timber to which it was home, appreciated in value, ultimately adding $5 million (or $59 million in contemporary dollars) to its endowment after selling the land in the 1920s. Ultimately, over 17,400,000 acres of Indigenous land transferred to these land-grant colleges meant to prepare a new class of labourers to build the nation.

These schools were built in the redemption period during reconstruction as whites worked to solidify racial hierarchies and established Black codes simultaneously. While I do not have time to do the full work justice here, it must be noted that anti-blackness and land theft are woven together through educational histories as they were used to assimilate, exclude, and create racialized economic and political hierarchies. Craig Wilder, while primarily speaking to Ivy League schools on the East Coast at an earlier colonial period of education, examines the underbelly of dispossession and slavery as well as the aftermath, as the nation's white elite strove to keep hold of power through containing land. In bringing together the push for "racial clearances in the South" and the violence of Indian removal in the southeast, Wilder poignantly remarks, "It was through Indian removal that the desire to eliminate non-white, non-Christian presences came to dominate the popular culture."[29] Weaving these relational threads is necessary. It strengthens the braid in a fight for holding the university systems across the United States accountable for colonization as well as the institution of slavery. In California the development that led to the violence of theft of California Indians was done through what Manu Karuka names as railroad colonialism. Rather than exemplifying rugged individualism characterizing American exceptionalism – two components too often undergirding resistance to opening up the public university to marginalized groups – the privatized railroad companies subsidized by the government were lining their coffers through the racialized and gendered dispossession of land, labour, and belonging.[30] This loss of land – or Indigenous lifeblood – was not the end of the story, however. Land continues to be demarcated as private property instead of a living relation. Our acknowledgment, our introductions, and our knowledge systems reframe these landscapes.

Although Indian land had already begun to be allotted – that is, made into private parcels of property – as early as 1798, Congress formalized this strategy of completely eliminating Native access to their land after the end of the treaty-making era (1871) by passing the Dawes Act of 1887. In this act, which was implemented over the course of several years, settler surveyors divided the communally held land into property parcels that could more easily be piecemealed away from tribal nations. Each parcel was to be handed out to a Western-defined head of household, which was most commonly the husband or male or, more rarely, a widow, whose name was fortuitously signed onto base rolls of their nation. While there is variation in the way this was handled regionally, the policy's overall purpose was to domesticate land under US regimes.

This was done without regard to varying epistemologies of gender systems, clan systems, and relationships to land and water. "Surplus" land, a concept foreign to Indigenous peoples, was demarcated and folded into the settler state. Of course, a multitude of shenanigans that took place, leading to listing people not on these rolls and whites who were close to Indian agent managers as Indian recipients. These rolls, even with known fraudulent practices, gender impositions causing large inequities for women and two-spirits, and large absences used to expunge "holdouts" from the records, remain an important basis for tribal citizenship today and a continued tool of deracination and elimination. The afterlife of this period was mired in an imperfect coercive tactic for survival that continues today.

Property development and dispossession with bio-political laws and systems intended to eradicate Native peoples were and are still implemented in order to open up more bodies – bodies of Native lands, waters, and beings – to transition to private property. Once in private property, land was passed through economic tyranny in which delinquent taxes, illegally applied to Indian land, caused such a huge amount of debt that the land transferred to the settler state. Often the US government did not hold up its end of the bargain by providing promised rations and food while restricting movement outside territorial bounds so that people could live off traditional food sources. Trading stores became a major source of food, yet most traders jacked up the prices of necessities so high that debt accumulated quickly, and more land passed into the hands of developers and white landowners as Native peoples struggled to provide for their families. The lost property title and rights of occupancy became the place where we live, learn, and teach at our public universities. The land, however, is still often in relationship to the living Indigenous communities.

At UCLA the role of title-shifting combines with religion, access to citizenship, and the shifting of property title between colonial entities. The settler government at the time was also fully aware that the lands and those Americans who would now be set in place to occupy Native places would need education in the form of agricultural, mining, and resource programs to do so. Thus, they continued to bolster the land grants and implemented the Hatch Act in 1887 – the exact same year as the Dawes Act – that extended federal grant money for establishing and developing land-grant colleges. This land itself was left over from corporate accumulation and from that given to the transcontinental railroad. Native people and the massive breaking of treaty rights continue to not be mentioned in these charters. This history has long been forcibly erased.

Though land grants derived from theft of Native land and lives, it was not until 1994 that tribal colleges became part of land-grant institutions' access to resources – and they are limited resources at that. At a time when restorative justice, particularly through moves to decolonize, are being taken up by feminists, educators, and social movements, it is important to particularly engage these specifics of dispossession. Anti-colonial tools such as a land introduction will hold us accountable for the willful disposal and knowledge of such violence to certain populations that enabled others to live and prosper.

Even in our current situation, we continue to see the ongoing dispossession of Tongva people and Indians in general. A reply from one of the Tongva elders I was in conversation with regarding feedback on my original attempt sums up the lack of accountability in the UC system:

Dear Mishuana,
No one asked us, and no one ever wanted to know about us. Thank you for this incredible gift of acknowledgment.
   In Spirit, Barbara

I relate this story not to pat myself on the back, but because it was a profound moment in the process of the acknowledgment that was a gift. Working with the Tongva – the difficulties, my mistakes at times, and the good – have all taught me an immense amount about tackling a colonial unknowing. Vimalassery, Hu Pegues, and Goldstein's words aptly define colonial unknowing as what "establishes what can count as evidence and proof – aiming to secure the terms of reason and reasonableness as much as to disassociate," in order to observe how it materially acts in practice: "Produced and practiced in concert with material violences and differential devaluations, colonial unknowing strives to preclude relational modes of analysis and ways of knowing otherwise."[31] What if we listened to tribal voices that have always held a relational position to the land the university occupies and responsibility to welcome Native students and others? How do we begin to act in meaningful ways? Despite the current land title being held by the University of California system, there was still a way of understanding the elderberry, oak, and sage across the university landscapes.

It is in this sense that we contend that colonial unknowing is always itself a response, an epistemological counter-formation, that takes shape in reaction to the lived relations and incommensurable knowledges it seeks to render impossible and inconceivable.[32]

What if we considered our relationality to the vast expanse of history and geographies that are surely connected? The way I was taught to introduce myself, to conduct myself as a guest on others' land, to extend my personal rafters, were the anti-colonial tools at my disposal for fighting a colonial unknowing – an unknowing we see here in the UC's testimony in 2012 at the anniversary of the land grants:

> The impact [of the land grants] rippled far beyond the campus borders, providing opportunity to the children of immigrants and settlers just as it did for the offspring of landowners and industrial barons. A well-educated populace helped the state's economy thrive. The nascent university also led to the creation of agricultural extension offices and other programs that took innovations out of the labs and put them into practice in fields and farms around the state. That historic partnership remains just as important today, helping to sustain a $37.5 billion farm economy in the state.[33]

Rather than return to erasure and disavowal, we must return to the ongoing dispossession – not merely of property but of life itself. This is not only a temporal return but a return that demands we encounter, engage, and assess the foundations of settler nation states, empire-building, and the ethos of violence and disposability.

As Jodi Byrd makes clear at the outset of her book *Transit of Empire*, we need to "think through the syllogistic traps of participatory democracy born out of violent occupation of lands."[34] At a time when there is a great dismantling of hopes that constitute the American Dream – a dream that itself depends on dispossession and forgetting, a colonial unknowing – may also be the moment to address the structure itself, to interrogate the philosophies of democracy, multiculturalism, diversity, or any of the liberal catchwords and conservative fodder for debate that circulate to render the ongoing structures of colonialism and empire invisible but in full working order. We need to interrogate the ways the making of land and lives into property and its normalization of property into relation to whiteness still functions, even in a moment when those previously disenfranchised are given access to structures of accumulating property as full, individual citizens.[35]

This use of Indian as a transit of colonialism and empire, again here I refer to Byrd who sees transit as "exist[ing] liminally in the ungrievable spaces of suspicion and unintelligibility,"[36] is consistent within university politics, the nodding of heads that express sympathy but nothing more, or the hard core who say the numbers aren't there, administration claiming the quality of Native students is so bad, or any other numerous remarks made to avoid accountability to colonialism that would engender new structures and thinking of race, land, and our politics. Lisa Lowe reminds us that "the affirmation of the desire for freedom is so inhabited by the forgetting of its conditions of possibility, that every narrative articulation of freedom is haunted by its burial, by the violence of forgetting."[37] "Race" and "gender" in Lowe become the traces of such humanist forgetting – a modern humanism whose conditions, she explains, were created by "New World" people for whom the production of "freedom" was first predicated on the creation of the racialized category of the "unfree" and the "enslaved," next to whom it was then possible to racialize otherwise those liminal or *transitional* subjects in-between, as well as those thought to be on their way towards "freedom." Yet as Byrd states, in this configuration Indigenous land and dispossession often become folded into slavery, and again the Indian becomes a transit whose agency and historical presence are unacknowledged. The urge and indeed coercion at times to belong in the space of the university or even a fight to rearrange the structures of the university, often results in an obfuscation of the roots of injustice at the core. That first move in dispossessing Native people of land and life is obscured in the lauding of the public university.

Let's return to the acknowledgment, the important collaboration that took place, one that I hope does not fall into the trap of a politics of recognition[38] but rather moves us forward into a relationship of accountability and gain. Once language was brought into the acknowledgment by the Tongva educators, I became a bit nervous, as language is not my strong suit. Yet once I read the new version, I could not help but think of how it reconfigures Tongva as well as those making the statement as active participants. I have had to work very hard on my pronunciations and am still not getting it right! Pam Munro, curator of the Tongva Word of the Day on Facebook, created sound waves downloadable on the AISC web page. In working with tribal groups towards the acknowledgment, a discussion arose regarding elders or 'ahiihirom. There was a discussion of the word – also used for "carpenter" – and its application. Now there was another word for "old people," but that just meant aged and one for wise people who were not elders. Here is the discussion that followed:

> So on 'ahiihirom: "I thought about the word for Elder and it looks as if we really didn't have a word that translates as 'Elder,' but there is a word that signifies a 'wise' person. One who carries wisdom or knowledge (of one's culture) is 'ahyoorot (plural = 'ahiihirom) from the word hynooax = to know or know. Tataarawtam seems to refer more to old, as in old person." So maybe carpenters – who would carry wisdom and knowledge – could be translated to Elders if the meaning was coming from song?[39]

Now for those who have not had the pleasure of meeting Tongva people, canoes are profoundly important to the community, which makes sense because they live on the Pacific. Waterways were abundant, and Pimu, or Catalina, was a very special place in the chain of coastal communities.[40] To make canoes takes years of knowledge and understanding. As Moomat Ahiiko is recovered, traditional language, aesthetics, and relationships are forged. The acknowledgment and its process resemble the new forging of place-based relationships to UCLA. The Ti'at society is an important part of Tongva resurgence and 'ahiihirom makes our acknowledgment richly place-based yet connective. It is an anti-colonial tool as it doesn't differentiate on the basis of race but is deeply connected to place-based needs. It is not an apology to an "other" attached to a whereas statement that leaves one free of all wrongdoing. It is a lived relation requiring responsibility. This land introduction undoes a grammar of settler apologies, it remakes a landscape of dispossession, and it holds us accountable to the history related above. It pushes us forward in our relationship to the original caretakers and this land. All of us who participate in the university system are the past, the present, and the emerging relationships.

Since this essay was first published in the Western Humanities Review,[41] *several initiatives at UCLA have continued to build relationships with the Gabrielino Tongva, local Indigenous communities, and create a better environment for learning better relationships. Tuition waivers, a hiring initiative, a living and learning community, implementing a plan for sustainability that accounts for local knowledge of planting practices, and an agreement on access to harvesting, gathering, and caretaking rights, as well as efforts to ensure Southern California tribes are served by UCLA. While it is not decolonized, anti-colonial efforts are ongoing. Building relationships is an everyday task that requires vigilance.*

NOTES

1 Gabrielino Tongva is the preferred name by the original peoples who were taken from village sites around Los Angeles and enslaved in the mission. The consensus of the endonym arose in modern times as a means of asserting self-determination by moving away from being solely associated with the mission and as a commitment to being a people and nation.

2 See Margaret D. Jacobs, *White Mother to a Dark Race: Settler Colonialism, Maternalism, and the Removal of Indigenous Children in the American West and Australia, 1880–1940* (Lincoln: University of Nebraska Press, 2009); Margaret D. Jacobs, *A Generation Removed: The Fostering and Adoption of Indigenous Children in the Postwar World* (Lincoln: University of Nebraska Press, 2014); K.T. Lomawaima and T.L. McCarty, *To Remain an Indian: Lessons in Democracy from a Century of Native American Education* (New York: Teachers College Press, 2006); Matthew L. Fletcher, Wenona T. Singel, and Kathryn E. Fort, *Facing the Future: The Indian Child Welfare Act at 30* (East Lansing: Michigan State University Press, 2009).

3 Note that I am not saying all tribal nations are small. Some are in fact quite large. But even in the nations with large territory, the introduction of place where one comes from acts similarly to those who have retained smaller land mass.

4 See John Mohawk and José Barreiro, *Thinking in Indian: A John Mohawk Reader* (Golden, CO: Fulcrum, 2010); and Stephanie J. Waterman and Lorinda Lindley, "Cultural Strengths to Persevere: American Indian Women in Higher Education," *NASPA Journal about Women in Higher Education* 6, no. 1 (2013), 139–65.

5 Francis Paul Prucha, *The Great Father: The United States Government and the American Indians* (Lincoln: University of Nebraska Press, 1984), 671.

6 Deborah A. Miranda, *Bad Indians: A Tribal Memoir* (Berkeley: Heyday, 2012), 74.

7 Sarah Pytalski, Cindy Burns, and Malia Villegas, "Human Trafficking: Trends and Responses across Indian Country" (Washington, DC: National Congress of American Indians, 2016).

8 Dana E. Powell, *Indian Cities: Histories of Indigenous Urbanization*, ed. K. Blansett, C.D. Cahill, and A. Needham (Norman: University of Oklahoma Press, 2022).

9　I tribute this to Cindi Alvitre, Tongva T'iat Society for naming what so many of us have felt as a perfunctory component of pulling an elder on stage with no real engagement for what this knowledge might or could do to productively change the structure of an event.

10　For an important critique of land acknowledgments, see Chelsea Vowel, "Beyond Territorial Acknowledgments," âpihtawikosisân, 25 January 2017, https://apihtawikosisan.com/2016/09/beyond-territorial-acknowledgments.

11　For a look at Professor Munroe's important language-based work with the Tongva, which followed the instituting of the acknowledgment at UCLA, see "Behind the Story: Step into This Tongva Classroom and Witness Love in an Act of Redemption," *Los Angeles Times*, 9 May 2019, https://www.latimes.com/local/california/la-me-col1-tongva-first-person-20190509-story.html.

12　Since this publication of the original land introduction, community members also point out that the San Gabriel Mountains should also be considered.

13　Cutcha Risling Baldy, *We Are Dancing for You: Native Feminisms and the Revitalization of Women's Coming-of-Age Ceremonies* (Seattle: University of Washington Press, 2018), 34.

14　Los Angeles County lands are also the lands of the Fernandeño Tataviam Band of Mission Indians in the north, the Chumash, and the Juaneño Band of Mission Indians, Acjachemen Nation to the south. As UCLA is squarely located in Tongva territory with the closest-known village site being Kuruvungna, we acknowledge them as the original caretakers, but also have relationships to the other nations as well.

15　Hayden King, "'I Regret It': Hayden King on Writing Ryerson University's Territorial Acknowledgement," CBC/Radio Canada, 18 January 2019, https://www.cbc.ca/amp/1.4973371.

16　See my "Notes towards a Native Feminism's Spatial Practice," *Wicazo Sa* 24, no. 2 (2009): 169–87.

17　See, for example, the work of Cindi Alvitre in arts and culture, Teresa Ambo-Stewart in education, Desiree Martinez in archaeology, and Charles Sepulveda in ethnohistory.

18　Alvitre C.Torres, A. Fischer-Olson, M. Goeman, and W.Teeter, "Perspectives on a Selection of Gabrieleño/Tongva Places," Mapping Indigenous LA, http://www.arcgis.com/apps/MapJournal/index.html?appid=4942348fa8bd427fae02f7e020e98764.

19　This was waged against Kroeber in particular, as they demanded the return of remains that had been dug up by a student he recruited, anthropologist and collector Samuel Barrett. He provided the locations of remains, having lived in the area. See Tony Platt, "The Yokayo vs. the University of California: An Untold Story of Repatriation," *News from Native California* 26, no. 2 (Winter

2012–13): 9–14. For the later engagement with NAGPRA, see "Timeline," http://coah-repat.com/.

20 For an excellent history of the convergence of racialization and settler-colonialism, refer to Kelly L. Hernandez, *City of Inmates: Conquest, Rebellion, and the Rise of Human Caging in Los Angeles, 1771–1965* (Chapel Hill: University of North Carolina Press, 2017).

21 Lindsay Gordon Robertson, *Conquest by Law: How the Discovery of America Dispossessed Indigenous Peoples of Their Lands* (Oxford: Oxford University Press, 2007).

22 Robertson, *Conquest by Law*.

23 Dan Bauman, "On Campus, Grenade Launchers, M-16, and Armored Vehicles," Chronicle of Higher Education, 11 September 2014, http://chronicle.com/article/On-Campus-Grenade-Launchers/148749/.

24 Bonnie Azab Powell, "The Histories of Berkeley and the U.S. Military Have Long Been Allied," Berkeley Campus News, 11 October 2002, http://berkeley.edu/news/media/releases/2002/10/11_rotc_history.html.

25 Nick Estes, *Our History Is the Future: Standing Rock versus the Dakota Access Pipeline, and the Long Tradition of Indigenous Resistance* (New York: Verso, 2019).

26 See Waziyatawin. *What Does Justice Look Like?: The Struggle for Liberation in Dakota Homeland* (St. Paul, MN: Living Justice Press, 2008), for work on this period for the Dakota and its ongoing injustice.

27 The article continues to extrapolate the meaning of these institutions, which are required to keep the money from these "land sales [which] must be used in perpetuity, meaning those funds still remain on the ledgers." These funds were "endowment principal for 52 institutions" and 12 of them still maintain mineral-rich lands used for profit. Robert Lee, "Morrill Act of 1862 Indigenous Land Parcels Database," High Country News, March 2020, https://www.hcn.org/issues/52.4/Indigenous-affairseducation-land-grab-universities.

28 Margaret Pearce, "Land-Grab Universities." High Country News, 30 March 2020. https://www.hcn.org/issues/52.4/Indigenous-affairs-education-land-grab-universities. Journalists Tristan Ahtone and Robert Lee have gone on to investigate further the afterlife of the Morrill Grant in establishing higher education in the United States.

29 Craig S. Wilder, *Ebony & Ivy: Race, Slavery, and the Troubled History of America's Universities* (New York: Bloomsbury, 2013), 250.

30 Manu Karuka, *Empire's Tracks: Indigenous Nations, Chinese Workers and the Transcontinental Railroad* (Oakland: University of California Press, 2019).

31 Manu Vimalassery, Juliana Hu Pegues, and Alyosha Goldstein, "Colonial Unknowing and Relations Study," *Theory & Event* 20, no. 4 (October 2017): 1042, https://muse.jhu.edu/article/675631/pdf.

32 Manu Vimalassery, Juliana Hu Pegues, and Alyosha Goldstein, "Colonial Unknowing and Relations Study," *Theory & Event*, 20, no. 4 (October 2017): 1042, https://muse.jhu.edu/article/675631/pd.

33 Nicole Freeling, "Morrill Act: Honoring Our Land Grant History," UC Office of the President, 6 July 2012, https://www.universityofcalifornia.edu /news/morrill-act-honoring-our-land-grant-history.

34 Jodi Byrd, *The Transit of Empire: Indigenous Critiques of Colonialism* (Minneapolis: University of Minnesota Press, 2011), xii.

35 Cheryl Harris, "Whiteness as Property," in *Critical Race Theory: The Key Writings That Formed the Movement*, ed. Kimberlé Crenshaw, Neil Gotanda, Gary Peller, and Kendall Thomas (New York: New Press, 1995), 276–91.

36 Byrd, *Transit of Empire*, xv.

37 Lisa Lowe, "The Intimacies of Four Continents," in *Haunted by Empire: Geographies of Intimacy in North American History*, ed. Ann Laura Stoler (Durham, NC: Duke University Press, 2006), 206.

38 Elizabeth A. Povinelli, *The Cunning of Recognition: Indigenous Alterities and the Making of Australian Multiculturalism* (Durham, NC: Duke University Press, 2002).

39 Tongva Word of the Day, Facebook, 14 October 2017.

40 For more information see Mishuana Goeman, "Eastern Oceania: Los Angeles Region Canoe Societies," Mapping Indigenous LA, 15 December 2015, https:// mila.ss.ucla.edu/2015/12/15/eastern-oceania/.

41 Mishuana Goeman, "The Land Introduction: Beyond the Grammar of Settler Landscapes and Apologies," *Western Humanities Review* 74, no. 3 (Fall 2020): 35–65.

2 Spirit as Matter: Resurgence as Rising and (Re)Creation as Ethos

DIAN MILLION

What if we took it seriously what our elders told us, everything is spirit? What would it mean for our Indigenous spirits to rise, as ethos? To make our relations, or presence and spirit permeate and move what is now only thought of as ineffable inert matter?

Dian Million

Spirit
Salmon leaps into fine mist and the old scaffolds
shiver, the structures protrude from the rocky shore.
My sore hands grasp the braided metal,
and I watch fishermen dip their long poles, the bone
colored nets skim the water. The drifting aroma
of fish permeates the cable car as we sway in the wind...
I don't consider them dead, even though I clubbed
their heads with a sawed-off bat. And I don't feel
as though I am killing them. They are food.
I watch as their shiny bodies wriggle, arch and dance
on the earth. I feel their spirit. I pray, I sing
and dance for them. We understand each other.

Earle Thompson[1]

Earle Thompson was an amazing poet in a burgeoning Native writing community forming in the Pacific Northwest in the 1980s. Later, after years living on the streets of Seattle, he died in Yakama, at Wapato with his family. In the twenty-six intervening years, much of it spent in the city, far from the river and the salmon spirits that were his kin, you might picture disconnection and dissolution. Many of us pictured it that way when we later wrote about these streets as part of our experience. We might imagine this transition from the fishing scaffolds of his youth to the streets *as* his downfall. But, these *places*, the streets that he later enshrined in writing, were not places where he experienced an *absence* of communion with the spirits that once nourished him. Earle Thompson was a man of large spirit, a spiritual man whose death after many years of alcoholism produced a great sadness in many of us. We might read this street life, often lived so far away from the life that produced a poem like "Spirit," as a failure of his relations. He seemingly chose relations with the spirit alcohol, a relationship that stole his life. At the same time, alcohol can never be the full truth of this life and his spirit. His spirit, in those places we knew him, is now forever entangled with the spirit of other Yakama, of other Columbia River peoples in that time and in those streets.

Their spirit infused Indigenous life far beyond their place and time. Their example of the fusing of "land" and "urban lives" in spirit remains exemplary. The Columbia River peoples along with many other Northwest and Northern peoples present in Portland and in Seattle during the trial of Washat religious leader David Sohappy Sr. and his co-defendants, his son David Sohappy Jr., Wilbur Slockish Jr., Leroy Yocash, and Matt McConville physically and spiritually fed many of us, far from our own Native homes. David Sohappy Sr. and his co-defendants were criminalized for defending their participation in a web of traditional economies that then and now unite the entire Pacific Northwest. For the Sohappy family, the salmon they continued to take from the Columbia River were an important practice of spiritual connection to place. This particular Columbia River struggle is now often read as a federal fiasco. An intervention aimed at the peoples at the heart of the 1855 treaties upheld in Judge George Boldt's famous decision on the allocation of the Northwest salmon runs. In this chapter I am going to emphasize a different reading. The Columbia River people's fight to protect their livelihood and way of life was/is a spiritually informed struggle.

We, as "urban" peoples displaced into the cities by many colonial acts of spiritual war, travesty, law, and policies, also fought for these river ways of life just as surely as if we had been in our own homelands. The River Peoples fed our bodies, in struggle, in heart, and in spirit. Earle Thompson fed our spirits with his poetry. He wrote, "I don't consider them dead, even though I clubbed / their heads with a sawed-off bat. And I don't feel / as though I am killing them. They are food. / I watch as their shiny bodies wriggle, arch and dance / on the earth. I feel their spirit. I pray, I sing / and dance for them. We understand each other." Joined as we were in struggle, "urban" and "river," we ate this Columbia River food offering as a communion.

In this chapter I argue for the transforming spirit of an Indigenous ethos that we must claim, because to claim this spirit *is* to claim these Indigenous spaces again, not as a bound space, or a space necessary to recognition, but one where we must declare, as Eve Tuck has asked, to articulate "our relations of place" acknowledging their dynamics and living contingency in larger webs of lived experience.[2] I believe that this question of *where we are* and what we can declare from these places is one that is critical to any discussion of Indigenous resurgence.

First, I want to tell you a story.

Where Are We?

Let us speak of cartographies of struggle (Mohanty, Russo, and Torres) then, if solidarity is too compromised a word. More, let us speak of cartographies of dispossession – the kind that rips away, distances, alienates – but also the kind that is waged upon us like war. The kind that is manufactured for my destruction."[3]

Angie Morrill and Eve Tuck

So I go back to Portland in the 1980s to talk about relations – dynamic, contingent relations – that changed and reverberated through all who were involved in that moment. I go back to those intense few years when David Sohappy Sr. (Tucknashut) was imprisoned for what was at the time known as the salmon scam. The federal agents who arrested him knew him well. David Sohappy had been arrested and tried in an earlier fishing rights case, one that preceded the case of Billy Frank Jr., one perhaps not as well known as Frank's. David Sohappy's trial in 1969 resulted in upholding Indian treaty rights all over the Pacific Northwest. Like Billy Frank, David Sohappy Sr. had defied the authority of Washington State to tell him where he could or couldn't live and fish over many years. David Sohappy's 1969 case established the right to take fish "in common," while Billy Frank Jr.'s case established the allocation of these salmon – the amount that federally recognized tribes could potentially harvest. David Sohappy Sr. fished on Cook's Landing because he was a direct descendent of the Washat prophet Smohalla, and his traditional Columbia River fishing site had been appropriated in the land grab for the Hanford Nuclear Reservation.[4] His arrest and second trial in 1983 for fishing resulted in an imprisonment many believe was the United States settling a score.

The Columbia River peoples were numerous. They fought fiercely for their homelands, for their lives, before some signed treaties in 1855, forcing their consolidation into the four larger federally recognized tribes of the Warm Springs, Umatilla, Yakama, and Nez Perce. Others became federally recognized through executive order and became the upper River peoples of the Spokane and Confederated Tribes of the Colville Indian reservations. The Colville are fourteen upper Columbia River tribes, many from what is for now the Canadian side of a border placed between them. For 12,000 years the Columbia River peoples and those peoples who came to be known as the Plateau tribes fished at Celilo (on the lower Columbia) and Kettle Falls (on the upper Columbia). Both Celilo and Kettle Falls disappeared within a generation, swallowed by dams to feed the insatiable US need for energy, the same need that had brought atomic bomb makers to the Columbia. The loss of these two fishing sites is a loss beyond description to the Native peoples of the Pacific Northwest. The Columbia River people's loss cannot be measured. Their loss was a spiritual blow to lives of Native peoples in the Pacific Northwest and to all of us who contemplated the silencing of these places.

Both Portland and Seattle had large Indigenous populations, in spite of Seattle's ban on the Duwamish, whose homelands the city denied and built over. The c'inúk or Chinook, and máłnumax or Multnomah peoples were the ancient inhabitants of both sides of the Columbia where Portland is now. Like many of the peoples in what became Oregon Territory, the Chinook were forced off their land. Many of these people suffered dispersion south with their descendants now enrolled among the Grande Ronde and Warm Springs peoples. Yet Portland and Seattle are Indigenous despite the strong settler desire to disappear us. The Native population in Portland had grown exponentially after the Second World War and the surge of programs to move Indians off the remaining lands. By the 1980s, tense currents of resistance generated an energy that tied the Northwest coastal cities, including Vancouver, BC, in a large web of relations, vibrant and caring and loudly resurgent. Both Portland and Seattle were sites of numerous movements and movement support groups whose care encompassed Cook's Landing where volunteers sought to winterize the small house where Myra, David Sohappy's wife, and their family still lived and fished. It was there where some in this winterization crew witnessed the feathers and spiritual items that belonged to the family thrown to the floor and broken by federal agents who raided the Sohappy home. The desire to help each other was very strong. I worked along other urban peoples that nourished and struggled for the lives of fellow Native men, women, and children, for families in the city and outside of it. In the community that was the Urban Indian Council and later the one that formed around Red Spirit Creations in Portland in the 1980s, relocation, termination, and the violence we knew as colonialism had placed many of us far from places and relations that would have once been our comfort. I participated in feeding older people in meal programs and I washed their bodies at their deaths as we searched for relatives who might still be in Pine Ridge, or Rocky Boy, or some other landed community to receive them "at home."

The irony of Cook's landing and David Sohappy Sr. in this conversation about *where we are*, is that this particular struggle for the "land" and a Washat way of life occurred where Columbia River peoples fished, not on any federally recognized lands. Cook's Landing, like other such sites, was "in-lieu." It existed in limbo in the 1980s because of disagreements between the state and tribes and families over hereditarily owned fishing camps and jurisdiction. The Columbia River peoples had once been many, many bands living all along the Nch'iWana (Big River). These were people who didn't always claim their federally recognized identities (enrolment) over their actual practices in the places where these practices made sense.[5] Just as they inhabited "land," outside of reservations, they were also mobile in their relation to cities that became marketing places for their salmon and for us who received gifts from them for our support of their Indigenous informal economy. That was the real issue for the states of Oregon and Washington and the feds. David Sohappy Sr., like Billy Frank Jr. belonged to families that still believed in hereditary and spiritual responsibility to places. Cook's Landing, at the mouth of Little White Salmon River, was one of these places. The Sohappys were criminalized by the states and the feds for their spiritual audacity to be "off the rez" and making a living in a mixed economy that made them less reliant on governments. They sought to live like many of their people had, before the dams and the tightening regulation on their ways of life. The current poet laureate of Oregon, Elizabeth Woody, was with us in Portland then. She wrote about this policing in her poem "Black Fear": "Explanations of renegades are hinted, / never known fully, until / you are blackened in the act, in night, / libeled as illegal fishermen." She ends with "the fear is to see the police trespass / on other people's land to break / the Indian renegade's fingers, / leaving him darkly bruised."[6]

This way of life where urban communities were informed by spiritual sites of sustenance recedes often in the memory of what was or not won by the Boldt decision. There was law involved. The law that integrated us in common with the Columbia River Indians was Indian law, perhaps as Tamánwit. In Thomas Morning Owl's words, Tamánwit teaches "all things of the earth were placed by the Creator for a purpose" and that "until times end, these laws are to be kept."[7] In this law there is respect for all and every place and entity. As Phil Cash Cash says in his explanation of spirit and place, "There is a spirit or mind in all of nature."[8] The ceremonial respect for fish and life tied us into a relationship, acting in Portland, a place between the Willamette River (named for a tribe that Portland knew nothing about) and the Columbia River. The re-enactment of

ceremony and belief in this place desecrated by the removal and dispersion of its prior Indigenous peoples did not make it devoid of Indigenous spirit and intent. Its streets teemed with Indigenous lives from all
over the Pacific Northwest, Canada, and Alaska. Down river from Cook's
Landing, Portland was and is an Indigenous place, in the sense that Glen
Coulthard has articulated: "Place is a way of knowing, experiencing, and
relating with the world – and these ways of knowing often guide forms of
resistance to power relations that threaten to erase or destroy our senses
of place."[9] Our resistance took many forms, only one being the establishment of Indigenous informal economies in the undercommons with
off-rez fishing peoples. It was about maintaining an Indigenous identity
in community and in family even if we could not be at "home."

What is an informal economy? A network of subsistence is never just
a matter of food or the circulation of money. I claim here that it is a
spiritual act binding those who take part in the responsibilities of care
and continuance for ways of life. The salmon were sacred, as were the
berries and all the foods that the Washat taught us to respect. In settler law, the "in common" that the treaties established did not protect
circulations of food and trade among Native peoples except in settler
law. These "traditional economies" or "informal exchanges," as Winona
LaDuke once called them,[10] were the non-capitalist mainstay of Indigenous peoples on and off the rez, ones that established a set of relations
that recognized Tamánwit. A quote from the Declaration of Atitlan, an
early Indigenous food sovereignty conference, stated, "The denial of the
Right to Food for Indigenous Peoples not only denies us our physical
survival, but also denies us our social organization, our cultures, traditions, languages, spirituality, sovereignty, and total identity; it is a denial
of our collective indigenous existence."[11] The Columbia River fishing
peoples, like the Sohappys, fought for this larger spiritual meaning of
our practices and what they produced, not just for a treaty right that settlers sought to define through their own sense of what "common" meant.

An insult in Athabascan is to be an empty pot – someone who does
not feed others, who has nothing to share, or refuses to share. Earle
Thompson was a Yakama genius, full, not empty. The spirit, the ethos of
Indigenous struggle, life, water, and salmon had formed and informed
life in what was often an inhospitable place, the jails, federal courthouses
and streets of a city built over the bones of Indigenous peoples, which a
show like Portlandia can only be a mockery of. I attempt to tell a different story. I move to contrast a contingent and powerful ethos of presence
and resistance against a more prevalent narrative, a narrative where such
urban streets are the spirit and ethos of capital.[12] Inside this narrative, urban presence is characterized as Indigenous desperation and dissolution

in spaces of intense capitalization. These stories rely on an even more prevalent settler fantasy imagining our assimilation and final disappearance. I iterate another story here of Indigenous spirit, to counteract our propensity to believe that our own Indigenous presence in these *unrecognized* places is of no consequence, that this presence does not also represent Indigenous *place*, places of Indigenous memory, of ethos and spirit that have the power to transform.

Spirit as Affective Ethos

Unlike the maps that designate Indian land as existing only in certain places, wherever we went there were Natives and Native spaces, and if there weren't, we carved them out.[13]

Mishuana Goeman

Ethos: character, atmosphere, climate, mood, feeling, tenor, essence; disposition, rationale, morality, moral code, value system, principles, standards, ethics

What does a resurgence of our Indigenous presence mean in these "urban" centres of capitalism – or actually anywhere we are, "recognized" or not. What would it mean to act if our presence was always potential, that our living lives "otherwise" is witness and transformative, morphing, having effect on our own relations as well as on the relations of capital. I believe it is dangerous to imagine our presence in these "urban" places as solely corrupting, or corrupted, unable to acknowledge potentiality in what appears as concrete. We look to home, to land to be the places of our heart, our spirit. I claim that anywhere we are is *already* an Indigenous place first. An Indigenous ethos rises when we take responsibility for where we are, in the power and depth of our relations and responsibility to the Indigenous peoples of the places we are – to know and honour their ancient relations in *that place*. We have a responsibility to know the languages of these places and recognize them in the land, in their names for food and kinship. We need to honour and uphold these relations first, and to know that our Indigenous spirit reconnects any lands we are on, even – and especially when – these lands appear to be encased in concrete. As a reminder, we already (re)Indigenize these places by pointing out their considerable and continuing relations to spirits and Indigenous presence prior to any settler. Still, I think, concrete remains – in our hearts.

"Concrete" is a word that is both material and metaphorical – as a word it readily conveys the essential capitalist form in architecture, where it is meant to convey *permanence*, when nothing is permanent, where there is only and always change. The infrastructure of capitalism makes us believe in its dominance and enclosure through its seeming permanence. And more so even, through seemingly unbreakable patterns that appear to capture spirit, which is affective matter. To think otherwise is to have the knowledge that at some time the fourteen dams blocking the salmon on the Columbia will come down. As Aimée Craft told us in her presentation in our conference in Vancouver in the fall of 2017, "It is natural law ... that water must flow."

Stefano Harney and Fred Moten tell us something about the nature of enclosure, real and as part of our imaginaries: "The self-defense of revolution is confronted not only by the brutalities but also by the false image of enclosure. The hard materiality of the unreal convinces us that we are surrounded, that we must take possession of ourselves, correct ourselves, remain in the emergency, on a permanent footing, settled, determined, protecting nothing but an illusory right to what we do not have, which the settler takes for and as the commons."[14] In Moten and Harney's thought, we (fugitive life, the Indigenous life, the Black life, the queer, the outside) surround the enclosure. For the Indigenous, our relations with this living land make us who we are, and those relations, however they appear encased in concrete, are alive and change and recognize each other in our serious intent to free our places, our hearts, and our minds of concrete, wherever we are.[15]

One might say I am more interested in the life places we make when we enact vitality, different forms of taking something on, something valuable about the warmth of the food given, even when the pot looks irreparably damaged. I hear the truth in Peter Morin's (Tahltan) words: "We are the land and the land is in us," in his healing performance of ceremony that sought to move beyond the enclosure of Canada's reconciliation scripts.[16] Like Morin, I am interested that we as Indigenous peoples not remain in perpetual crisis, remaining only in emergency. If we live what we are as the vital spirit of these lands, our ancestors, their ancient knowledges we informed/transformed into present acts of governance and society by spirit and our kinships, into the way that we treat each other, everyone, in the way that we engage rather than disengage, when we change what wants to appear unchangeable. It is this spirit that needs to inform us, that we do not and will not stand for the violence that ravages our lives as women and children and men.

I think about flows, rivers, kinships, and knowledges that do not create enclosure, but that create relations, help, support, other ways of thinking and moving concrete. These are familiar words now – relations, reciprocity, resurgence – but it is also our responsibility to look closely at what we practise to bring these into living acts of sovereignty. What is the work that concepts do? Trauma appears as a fact in these ecocidal times that sends thousands fleeing across the globe, with their children dead in the tides and on the shores of sought refuge. Trauma might be a fact and an outcome of the different scales of settler violence that swirl through our lives, but it is also an enclosure where we often live in fear and frozen spirit. I look to my parents' and grandparents' generation, and like them, I seek to get up the next morning and ask our kinships for food for life to put in our pot. I seek to recognize abundance in what gets shared. I seek relations that feed us and make us strong and not those that seek to imprison our embodied spirits. Spirit and matter are not separate, and spirit, as Audra Simpson would say, "refuses" enclosure. It is the reclaiming of every moment as a chance to live differently, as Leanne Simpson urges. Spirit and affect transform will. Our Indigenous spirits are an ethos that can transform institutions, can transform capitalist ways of being by refusing to be enclosed by concrete in the form of disconnection. We transform by claiming our relations as responsibilities to act beyond disconnection to ask what it is that must be done in establishing the care that makes us more than individuals with racial identity.

I met Jeannette Armstrong when we were much younger, in Portland, and I was still in what I felt was a life lived in strife, but I became impressed by her spirit and movement. As a Syilx person, Jeannette believes strongly in our ability to connect to spirit, the life forces that are always part of us, and part of all our places. She states, "Indigeneity is a viable tool toward transformation of the people-to-be into being part of the social order as tmixʷ and to be a life-force in a life-force place rather than being part of the social order of depletion and destruction."[17]

We can be this force. It is our birthright through our generations to be this force, not enclosed and detached. Our bodies as spirit, affective will, are political orders if we refuse enclosure. We must manifest our difference into ways of life, into demands for responsibility, for respect rather than violence, for health rather than policing bodies. Indigenous epistemologies are practices and disciplines of place, the protocol for relations between people, all life forms, the spirits that move us in the face of hegemonic capitalist ways of life. The "stake" in all our relations is the living dynamic of Indigenous, is what resurgence means in a time of increasing capitalist-driven ecocide. This is spirit that exists as us and in all our Indigenous places, ones claimed and inhabited and transformational. We continue to stand for sovereignty. After Wounded Knee, at Oka, and in the collective *no* that is Idle No More, and now in Standing Rock, the force of Indigenous presence has sent Canada and the United States strong messages. In response Canada speaks a language of reconciliation. The United States relies on a conversation of self-determination as a US policy meant to entangle dreams of sovereignty with the neoliberal project of capitalist self-management. We need all of us to claim the places where we are as our part of our relations and part of our responsibility.

So maybe my term for loss or refusal to share is "empty pot." I honour that our pots are the ones that are always bubbling, always producing, even when they appear low. We are ones who honour the relations that make pots full enough to share. In the spirit of the land, our Indigenous spirit and ethos, if we are diametrically opposed to capitalism's bottom line, we must not separate what we are collectively.

Ana Baasi, I am done.

NOTES

1 Earle Thompson, "Spirit," in *Dancing on the Rim of the World: An Anthology of Contemporary Northwest Native American Writing*, ed. Andrea Lerner (Tucson: University of Arizona Press, 1990), 211–12.

2 Eve Tuck, Allison Guess, and Hannah Sultan, "Not Nowhere: Collaborating on Selfsame Land," *Decolonization: Indigeneity, Education & Society Journal*, 26 June (2014): 1–11.

3 Angie Morrill and Eve Tuck, "Before Dispossession, or Surviving It," *Liminalities: A Journal of Performance Studies* 12, no. 1 (2016): 4.

4 David Sohappy's relation to Smohalla, a Washat shaman, is discussed in the excellent film made during Sohappy's ordeal. It can be watched online: Michal Conford and Michele Zaccheo, *River People: Behind the Case of David Sohappy*, VAST – Academic Video Online. New York, NY: Filmakers Library, 1991, https://search.alexanderstreet.com/view/work/bibliographic_entity %7Cvideo_work%7C1784859.

5 A good account of these particular peoples' occupation of their "in-lieu" fishing sites is Andrew H. Fisher, *Shadow Tribe: The Making of the Columbia River Indian Identity* (Seattle: University of Washington Press, 2010). These fishing sites were bound up in Indigenous heritage rights through descent established prior to treaties and enrolments, that later put these fishing families at odds with their federally recognized tribes. One of Sohappy's co-defendants, Wilbur Slockish Jr., speaks to their way of life in Johnny Jackson and Wilbur Slockish Jr., "Oregon Voices: Johnny Jackson and Wilbur Slockish Jr.," *Oregon Historical Quarterly* 108, no. 4 (2007): 706–16.

6 Elizabeth Woody, *Hand into Stone* (New York: Contact II Publications, 1988). Excerpt from "Black Fear" from *Seven Hands, Seven Hearts: Prose and Poetry* by Elizabeth Woody, © 1994 by Elizabeth Woody, published by the Eighth Mountain Press, Portland, Oregon 1994. Reprinted by permission of the author and publisher.

7 Thomas Morning Owl, "Tamánwit," in *Wiyáx̱Ayx̱T/Wiyáakaáawn = as Days Go By: Our History, Our Land, and Our People – the Cayuse, Umatilla, and Walla Walla*, ed. Jennifer Karson (Pendleton: Tamástslikt Cultural Institute and Oregon Historical Society, 2006), 24.

8 Phillip E. Cash Cash, "Nuunim Titwatiitin? Weetes, Our Storied Earth," in *Čáw Pawá Láakni = They Are Not Forgotten: Sahaptian Place Names Atlas of the Cayuse, Umatilla, and Walla Walla*, ed. Eugene S. Hunn et al. (Pendleton, OR: Tamástslikt Cultural Institute, 2015).

9 Glen Coulthard, "Place against Empire: Understanding Indigenous Anti-Colonialism," *Affinities: A Journal of Radical Theory, Culture and Action* 4, no. 2 (2010), 79–80.

10 See *Mino-bimaadiziwin: The Good Life*, dir. Deborah Wallwork. https://www.folkstreams.net/films/the-good-life.

11 "The Declaration of Atitlán," Indigenous Peoples' Global Consultation on the Right to Food, Atitlán, Sololá, Guatemala, 17–19 April 2002.

12 I more fully articulate "cities" in their capitalist function in my chapter "'We Are the Land and the Land Is Us': Indigenous Land, Lives, and Embodied Ecologies in the Twenty-First Century," in *Racial Ecologies*, ed. LeiLani Nishime and Kim D. Hester Williams (Seattle: University of Washington Press, 2018), 21: "One increasingly antithetical split created in our minds is that there is an 'urban' and a 'rural.' What exactly do these terms mean? In the 2016 US presidential election, that split was imagined by one political party as a racial and class divide, between 'multicultural' and 'educated' white urban dwellers and poor rural uneducated 'whites.' We should be suspicious of this oversimplification."

13 Mishuana Goeman, *Mark My Words: Native Women Mapping Our Nations*, First Peoples: New Directions in Indigenous Studies (Minneapolis: University of Minnesota Press, 2013), 5.

14 Stefano Harney and Fred Moten, *The Undercommons: Fugitive Planning & Black Study* (Wivenhoe, UK: Minor Compositions), 18.

15 A beautiful example is the work that Megan Bang and her colleagues did in Chicago with Indigenous children and families, reconnecting language and place. See Megan Bang, Lawrence Curley, Adam Kessel, Ananda Marin, Eli S. Suzukovich, and George Strack. 2014. "Muskrat Theories, Tobacco in the Streets, and Living Chicago as Indigenous Land," *Environmental Education Research* 20, no. 1 (2014): 37–55. https://doi.org/10.1080/13504622.2013.865113.

16 Peter Morin, "This Is What Happens When We Perform the Memory of the Land," in *Arts of Engagement: Taking Aesthetic Action in and Beyond the Truth and Reconciliation Commission of Canada*, ed. Dylan Robinson and Keavy Martin, 67–91 (Waterloo, ON: Wilfrid Laurier University Press, 2016).

17 Jeannette Christine Armstrong, *Constructing Indigeneity* (Greifswald: University of Greifswald, 2009).

3 Removing Weeds so Natives Can Grow: A Metaphor Reconsidered

HŌKŪLANI K. AIKAU

Part 1: California Grass

It is 12 May 2012 at 8:00 on Saturday morning. There is still a chill in the air even though the days are getting warmer. The cloudless sky and the still, thick, humid air suggest it will be a hot day. The new intern begins the orientation of the project for volunteers who have gathered to help return the nearly 400 acres of wetland into productive wetland taro fields called loʻi. After this brief introduction Kalani, a staff member who has been with the project for at least two years, notes that they have planted about two acres of kalo (taro) so far. One challenge they face is that after the loʻi were filled in with topsoil and the families who lived in the surrounding areas were evicted by the landowners, the wetland was used for raising cattle. California grass (*Brachiaria mutica*) was introduced to feed the cows. The ranch was a temporary economic solution with lasting effects. Kalani explains that in the 1970s the landowners planned to dredge the wetland to create luxury condominiums with private boat docks along a lagoon, a country club, and a golf course. Community resistance blocked these development plans, and when they resurfaced in the 1990s the community mobilized opposition again. In 1992 the state stepped in and negotiated a land swap in which it traded a commercial property in Kakaʻako for the more than 300 acres of wetland in Heʻeia. Kākoʻo ʻŌiwi, a Native Hawaiian non-profit, is leading a project that will produce food and jobs. The project also allows Kanaka ʻŌiwi (Native Hawaiians) to practise their Hawaiian culture. This background is preparation for the work scheduled for that day – removing California grass from an area that will become a new loʻi.

After the orientation, the staff member walks the volunteers from the staging tent to the taro fields. Before she organizes the volunteers into work crews, Kalani tells them the story of kalo. According on one of our Kanaka

'Ōiwi ko'i honua (origin stories), kalo is the plant form of Hāloanākala-ukapalili, the first-born child of Wākea (Sky Father) and Ho'ohōkūkalani (the maker of stars and the daughter of Papahānaumoku – Earth Mother and Wākea). The child was stillborn and his lifeless body was buried beside their home. From that place grew the first kalo plant. Wākea and Ho'ohōkūkalani had a second child, he kāne, he kanaka (a boy, a human person). They named him Hāloa, who became an ali'i (leader, ruler) of Kanaka 'Ōiwi. One lesson that Kalani wants volunteers to remember is that through this story we know that Kanaka and kalo are kin, that kalo is our elder sibling and as such we have a responsibility to care for them and in turn they are responsible for caring for and feeding us. This story also tells us that Kanaka and kalo share a sacred lineage that connects us to the elemental persons who surround us – the sky, the stars, and the earth. This is the value of kalo and Kanaka according to our origin stories.

Staff members of Kāko'o 'Ōiwi – a Native Hawaiian non-profit organization working to restore wetland taro farming in the ahupua'a (watershed) of He'eia on the island of O'ahu– such as Kalani remove weeds so that native plants and animals can return and thrive. At most community work days, staff members tell some version of the story above. They characterize weeds such as California grass (*Brachiaria mutica*) and trees such as mangrove (*Rhizophora mangle*) as invasive species that choke out native plants and create an inhospitable environment for native animals. At Hoi, the removal of invasive species – weeds – is both material and metaphorical. The staff include California grass in the orientation because on any community work day volunteers will be expected to pull California grass from the filled-in lo'i so that staff and future volunteers can cultivate kalo.

The removal of invasive species of plants is also a powerful metaphor and rhetorical device for the decolonization and eradication of settler colonial structures in Hawai'i. This chapter takes up the potential and problems associated with the metaphor. I want to reconsider how non-native plants are framed as always already invasive and in need of eradication. I argue that undergirding this metaphor are racial logics of purity and authenticity that work against Indigenous resurgence. The chapter is organized around mo'olelo (ethnographic stories/moments) that reflect the stickiness and messiness of this work and how important it is to reconsider the relation between metaphor and materiality in order to move from critique to action. These mo'olelo indicate the spiritual transformation that can come from this work as well as the struggles that emerge when we try to put Indigenous resurgence into practice within contexts that are already laden with racist logics of elimination.

Indeed, it is difficult to not see settler state structures such as private property, conservation strategies, and recognition policy as invasive institutions that have inundated Indigenous communities, lands, and identities. These institutions have pushed out the Native structures that once thrived in these environments. While this metaphor has power and potential to mobilize people and inspire resurgence, there are at least two problematic ways it is deployed. First, it relies on the assumption that all non-native plants and animals are invasive by their nature and must be removed. This idea relies upon notions of purity and authenticity that serve white supremacy and the eliminatory logics of settler colonialism.[1] A second assumption that follows is that we can achieve decolonization only after these invasive species are removed and native species are replanted. This idea relies upon teleological, linear thinking about decolonization where all things not native must be removed before restoration can take place. Both assumptions rely upon binary racial and gendered discourses about natives and settlers, tradition and modernity that undermine Indigenous resurgence. They also create divisions within Indigenous communities about who are the real Hawaiians and who are not.[2]

This critique is not intended to take away from the value of the work of pulling up and digging out weeds so there is a space to replant kalo. Indeed, this work is rewarding at a very practical level. During my interview with a staff member who started working at the loʻi in 2014, he described his first two years as a seemingly never-ending process of removing California grass that was so overgrown it stood taller than he. While he described the magnitude of the process of getting the California grass under control, on a smaller scale there is something personally satisfying, gratifying even, in the physicality of pulling weeds and seeing a clear field. And at an ecological level, this work is also critical.

California grass (*Brachiaria mutica*) is a pesky kind of plant.

Brachiaria mutica. Common names: paragrass, californiagrass, panicumgrass, buffalograss

Description: Sprawling grass with rooting runners to 18 ft long, reaches upward to 5 ft tall, hairy. Stems branched, smooth, with hollow internodes. Sheath longer than internodes, more or less hairy, ligule membranous. Leaves to 10 inches long by 0.6 inches wide.

Distribution: A desirable forage in high-rainfall and marshy lands; origin unknown, distributed throughout the tropics. Occurs in wet areas and extends into open water, including brackish ponds, on Kauaʻi, Oʻahu, Lānaʻi, Maui, and Hawaiʻi. First collected on Oʻahu in 1924.

Environmental impact: Interferes with stream flow and poses a nuisance to marine navigation when rafts of the grass float out to sea. Forms monotypic stands in forest openings and marshes, displacing native plants and destroying bird habitats.

Management: A weed in wet open forests and aquatic environments. Drizzle applications of glyphosate at 1 lb/acre with a good surfactant.[3]

Caution: Pure glyphosate is low in toxicity to fish and wildlife, but some products containing glyphosate may be toxic because of the other ingredients in them.[4]

Kāko'o 'Ōiwi does not use herbicides such as glyphosate, so California grass must be dug out by hand or by machine. Because California grass dominates the wetland, it must be removed in order to rebuild the water gardens into which kalo will be planted. Their removal will also improve water flow and quality.

Again, on a practical level, weeds such as California grass have to be removed in order to restore lo'i. This process is important because wetland taro farming addresses capacious problems facing Hawai'i: as a 'Ōiwi (Native Hawaiian) food system this project takes up the problem of food insecurity and access while simultaneously addressing current and future issues around water as it also reflects an Indigenous approach to watershed management. Additionally, by restoring the ecological balance among plants, animals, and humans, Kāko'o 'Ōiwi staff are working to also restore the spiritual and familial relationship among kānaka and our other-than-human kin, such as kalo, that live in the ahupua'a.

Part 2: "That One's No Good"

The University of Hawai'i Indigenous Politics program and the Indigenous Governance program at University of Victoria held our seventh exchange in December 2016. We spent one week in seminar exploring the gendered dimensions of Indigenous resurgence, Indigenous futurity, and Indigenous futurism, and a second week on Hawai'i Island where our former student and the Pa'auilo community in Hāmākua were our hosts. While on Hawai'i Island we would visit Pele and Hi'iaka at Kilauea and we would visit Mauna a Wākea. I wanted to offer a ho'okupu (tribute) to present to these akua (gods, deity). On the Saturday before we left for Hawai'i Island, I attended a community workday with my daughter and two IGOV students. As we were cleaning up after pulling weeds and planting kalo, I asked the executive director if I could offer kalo from the lo'i as ho'okupu to our akua on Hawai'i Island. He said, "Sure, go huki [pull up] the one that speaks to you," and pointed to the adjacent lo'i where the kalo was more mature. I climbed out of lo'i #6 and into lo'i #5 and started walking up and down the rows, pulling weeds as I went, waiting for the kalo who wanted to come with me to Hawai'i Island to make themself known. I stopped beside a group of kalo whose purple huli (stalks) were strong and whose dark green lau (leaves) were blowing in the breeze. "This is the one I will bring with me," I thought. After I huki-ed the kalo, I took it to the ʻauwai (the irrigation canal) to clean. Shawn, a staff member, came by and Koa, the executive director of Kākoʻo ʻŌiwi, explained what I was doing. He replied, "Why did you choose that one? It's no good. Let me get you a Hawaiian variety." He walked off towards loʻi #6 and started looking for a "good one." I kept cleaning the kalo.

When he returned, he was carrying a kalo whose huli was light green and the ʻiʻo (corm) was the size of the nerf football my kids left in the back of the car. The leaves were green with specks of white, and the piko (the centre) was chartreuse. He told me this was a Pikokea variety and this one would be better to take than the one I chose. Apparently, I chose a Lehua variety, which is a hybrid between a Palauan and Hawaiian variety used by a lot of the commercial taro farms because they produce a larger yield than some of the "Hawaiian variety." Poi companies mix the Lehua variety with other Hawaiian varieties when they make commercial poi. Koa explained that while I was free to take both kalo with me, the folks on Hawaiʻi Island would probably accept only the Hawaiian variety. I was unsettled by the conversation but didn't say anything. I decided to bring them both and see what happened.

Because I am not trained in Hawaiian protocol I asked two former students (who came with us as kōkua – helpers) to help me prepare the kalo for hoʻokupu. I explained that I had two varieties: Pikokea and Lehua. Their response was different from Koa's and Shawn's. Kaleo, a mahi ʻai kalo (taro farmer), said that it would be best to give the Pikokea as hoʻokupu when we went to Mauna Kea since this variety was named for Wākea. He then added that the Lehua was also important because it feeds our people. He suggested we give it as a gift, makana, to our hosts, who could plant it in their māla (garden) where it would feed the people of Paʻauilo. On Wednesday, I presented the huli (the stalk) on the ahu (altar) to honour Wākea. In that moment, I felt spiritually and genealogically connected to ʻāina (land, that which feeds) and akua.

While I was initially taken aback by Shawn's statement, I have since come to understand this interaction as a gesture of aloha – an example of his respect and gratitude for me and the time and effort I had given to the project. As Kanaka Maoli scholar Stephanie Nohelani Teves so eloquently explains, aloha has come to be a fraught concept. Aloha is simultaneously a cherished cultural value and practice that evokes great love and affection for our land and our people while also being misappropriated and commandeered by settler colonialism.[5] My interactions with Shawn evoked these same tensions – between what is a culturally appropriate tribute and what is "no good." The crux of this tension are racial logics of blood dilution and deracination that continue to be perpetuated within our communities and used against each other through discourses of authenticity, tradition, and cultural expertise.

What I cannot stress enough is that staff members work with Kākoʻo ʻŌiwi because it as an opportunity to participate in restoring ʻŌiwi land, our knowledges, and our people. Until recently, I fully and completely bought into the power and symbolism of removing invasive weeds and how this practice could be used as a metaphor for deconstructing settler colonial institutions. In presentations, I too described the work we do as a direct response to colonial invasion by plants, animals, institutions, and ideologies. I embraced the metaphor of removing non-native, invasive species/institutions because I was excited by the possibility of being able to turn my analytical skills from critiquing the colonial invaders to doing something to physically remove them. As Linda Tuhiwai Smith explained, we Indigenous academics are trained to be critical: we sharpen our analytical knives and go at it.[6] But what remains? What parts of the structure have we really dug into and eviscerated and what parts of it have gone relatively untouched? Also, once we have taken the structure apart, what do we replace it with? My motivation in this chapter is not to criticize the staff. Rather, I offer these moʻolelo as a critical reflection on the analytical work we do in academe. While the metaphor of removing invasive species feels liberatory because it ignites passion to remove colonial impositions on our land, bodies, and minds, we must pause and reflect on the larger implication of the rhetoric that we use to make our case for liberation. I argue that there are rhetorical and tactical limits to the metaphor that all non-native plants, institutions, and people are invasive and thus must be removed. This over-generalization can be dangerous and cause harm unwittingly to others and to our own movements.

Thus, while we must remove weeds – those plants that do not contribute to the health of the land and water, and the abundance of edible food plants – we need to be mindful of how we frame this work. As the second story illustrates, we proceed with caution and care so as not to overextend our metaphors. Smith's questions are provocative because they push us to consider the afterlife of critique. The second story also illustrates the transformative possibilities that come from restoring our relationships with ʻāina. Every fibre in my being tells me this project is a game changer. The process – the work of clearing the land, digging out the loʻi and ʻauwai (irrigation canals that draw water from the stream through the taro ponds and back to the stream), and maintaining the taro patches – is not a one-off event but must to be repeated day after day, and generation after generation in order to bring about ea.[7]

In very material, practical ways, the work of restoring loʻi kalo requires the removal of non-native plants, including pesky California grass. And then we have to continue to pull weeds because California grasses keep coming back and new weeds pop up once we get the others under control. This is not glamorous work; it is backaching, repetitive work. Every month at community workdays volunteers pull weeds. I argue that it is through work – labouring with and for ʻāina, day after day and generation after generation – that we restore our Indigenous relationships with our human and other-than-human kin.

Even with the transformative work taking place at Hoi, racial logics continue to structure who and what has value at the loʻi. When Shawn said the hybrid was "no good" he unwittingly made two racializing and authenticating moves simultaneously. The first evoked the logic of blood racialization. As J. Kēhaulani Kauanui argues, "blood racialization" works to "construct Hawaiian identity as measurable and dilutable." She locates this logic within the blood quantum rule, which "operates through a reductive logic in both cultural and legal contexts and undermines expansive identity claims based on genealogy. While some assume genealogy is a proxy for race, [Kauanui] argues that blood quantum racial classification is used as proxy for ancestry, with destructive political consequences for Indigenous peoples."[8]

The second racialization is related to hybridization in which the Hawaiian variety was cross-pollinated with a Palauan variety of kalo. The result was a "diluted," presumably less Hawaiian variety of kalo. Kanaka Maoli scholar Maile Arvin's work is particularly instructive because she traces the colonial and racial discourses produced by "ethnologists, physical anthropologists, and sociologists from the mid-nineteenth through the mid-twentieth century" who frame Polynesians as "almost white," Melanesians as Black, and Micronesians as somewhere in the middle, "and could swing either way, racially – sometimes it was seen as related to Polynesia, and other times it was more akin to Melanesia."[9] When he declared the Lehua was "no good" it is hard not to read Shawn's statement as a form of anti-Micronesian racism, which is pervasive in public discourse in Hawaiʻi.[10] I also know that Shawn did not intend any malice or harm. In my interactions and interview with him, he was quite cognizant of the racial logics that differentially position Hawaiians in relationship to purity and authenticity. In fact, during our interview he named the discourses that mark him as not Hawaiian enough – he was not born in Hawaiʻi, he does not speak Hawaiian, he did not graduate from Hawaiian studies, and he had no training in growing kalo before being hired to work at Hoi. During our interview he described two Hawaiian communities. One has cultural knowledge, speaks the language, and graduated from Hawaiian studies, and everyone else. He put himself in the category with everyone else. And here was where racial logics become articulated with notions of authenticity and tradition.[11] As

Teves argues, "Our performances of culture can thus function as a tool or weapon of the dominant culture, which forces Indigenous people to perform within limited and often negating frames it sets in order to be seen or recognized as subjects (read Native/Indigenous)."[12]

Aileen Moreton-Robinson stages a critically important conversation about the need for Indigenous studies to take seriously and interrogate the ways in which "patriarchal white nation-states and universities insist on producing cultural difference in order to manage the existence and claims of Indigenous people. In this way," she argues, "the production of knowledge about cultural specificity is complicit with state requirements for manageable forms of difference that are racially configured through whiteness."[13] She argues, along with other Indigenous studies scholars, for the need to move away from Indigeneity as an object of study towards "analyzing both the conditions of our existence *and* the disciplinary knowledges that shape and produce Indigeneity."[14] For better or worse, the conditions of our current existence are caught up with and entangled in the disciplinary knowledges of race, whiteness, and gender. Indeed, the moʻolelo featured above illustrate how we reproduce racializing logics through our interpersonal interactions and by the frames we use to make sense of our work.

Drawing on the insights from Brendan Hokowhitu, Teves also notes, "We must be critical of the representational apparatuses in which this 'authentic' culture is promoted and aware of what is foreclosed in the process ... some expressions of Indigenous precolonial pride – and I would add, cultural revitalization – require the death of Indigenous subjectivities that threaten strategic traditionalism."[15] Teves's caution is critically important. Unless we interrogate our assumptions about "authenticity" and "tradition" we risk perpetuating settler colonial practices of elimination by killing off aspects of Indigenous communities that do not conform to and thus threaten "strategic traditionalism."

In this chapter, I am pushing back against these racializations because I am deeply concerned about the kind of future we are planning for if we cannot make space for those deemed not-Native or not Native *enough*. I do *not* suggest that it is the kuleana (responsibility) of Indigenous peoples to make space for settlers so they can feel good about themselves. I also recognize that "making space" often results in the settler unsettling the Native, yet again. But that is not my goal. My point is that, when we normalize, racialize, and essentialize identity positions, cultural performances, and Indigenous revitalization based on notions of purity or according to a limited set of criteria, then we only reinforce and replicate the settler colonial structures we are trying to break down and replace. But what will we replace these structures with?

Part 3: Planting Piko

In November 2016, Kaʻiulani, a new Kākoʻo ʻŌiwi staff member, was in charge of the community workday. The objective was to prepare loʻi #1 for planting kalo. The loʻi had been weeded the month before and left fallow to rest before replanting. Because there is so much water in this wetland, we use the puʻe method of mounding mud into long rows approximately eighteen inches wide and at least one foot above water level. In these rows, kalo will be planted. But on this day, Kaʻiulani had an idea. She wanted to shape the rows in a spiral pattern so that in the centre of the spiral the piko variety of kalo would be planted. I thought this was brilliant – a perfect pattern for this particular loʻi because it is triangular, roughly shaped like a kalo leaf. The centre of the kalo leaf is also called the piko.

Piko is the place on the plant where the leaf is attached to the stem. Piko is also a common type of kalo, with many different varieties all sharing the characteristic of the leaf blade indented from the stem. And piko is a site of convergence.[16] Piko is often translated as "navel" or "belly button" but in Hawaiian we have four piko – the poʻo (the fontanel on the top of the head), the ōpū (belly button), the maʻi (genitals), and the wāwae (base of the foot). Each piko connects us to our ancestors – the past, the present, the future, and the ʻāina. When Kaʻiulani suggested we shape the puʻe into a piko I was excited because we did not just clear and prepare the ground for planting, we prepared the ground with a very clear intention – to create convergence.

The next time I visited the loʻi I went to loʻi #1 and counted at least a dozen different variety of kalo planted in the piko. Seeing the diversity of varieties reminded me that these are only a small fraction of the eighty varieties in cultivation today across the pae ʻāina (archipelago).[17] These eighty varieties are also only a fraction of the three hundred varieties that were in cultivation in the times of my ancestors. This diversity reminds me that mahi ʻai kalo were masters of farming and bio-engineers. They skilfully and intentionally cross-pollinated and carefully cultivated different varieties of kalo for specific qualities and characteristics. They created kalo that was purely decorative and others that could be used as food. They created kalo with different sizes, shapes, colours, textures, hardness, and growing time to meet their many needs. They grew kalo that had different flavour profiles to satisfy different palettes and pair with different foods. They grew kalo for the corm and for its leaves.[18] And with over three hundred different varieties, I can only imagine what other purposes those mahi had in mind for the kalo they cultivated.

I feel confident that my ancestors considered all of these varieties of kalo our ancestor, our elder sibling. I believe that they valued each and

Figure 3.1.   Preparing the piko. In November 2016 we prepared loʻi #1 in the shape of a taro leaf with the piko at its centre. Photograph taken by author.

every one for their special gifts and celebrated the uniqueness they contributed to the world. Over the next seven months I watched the diversity of kalo flourish in this piko. I remain hopeful that racial logics are not intractable and that we can work from alterNative frameworks that allow us to value all our relations for the gifts they bring to this project.

Mahalo: Giving Thanks

I think often about the relationship between Indigenous hosts and our responsibilities as guests and the words that are written and spoken on Indigenous lands. This chapter was first presented at the symposium "Indigenous Resurgence in the Age of Reconciliation" at the University of Victoria on Lukwangen territory. Mahalo to Cheryl Bryce for introducing me to her territory and for being a caretaker of the kwetlal (kamas). I also presented a revised version of the paper at the Race, Whiteness, and Indigeneity International Conference on the sovereign territory of the

Figure 3.2. Valuing all our relations. In January 2017, loʻi #1 had been planted with a wide variety of kalo. The different colours of leaves and stems indicate the number of different varieties of kalo planted in this loʻi. Photograph taken by author.

Kombumerri Nation, Queensland, Australia. Mahalo to Uncle Graham Dillion for welcoming us to his country. This research was funded in part by a grant from the University of Hawaiʻi Sea Grant Program.

NOTES

1 J. Kehaulani Kauanui, *Hawaiian Blood: Colonialism and the Politics of Sovereignty and Indigeneity* (Durham, NC: Duke University Press, 2008).
2 For a discussion of how blood logics are racialized and then used by Native Hawaiians as authentication technologies against each other, see Rona Tamiko Halualani, *In the Name of Hawaiians: Native Identities and Cultural Politics* (Minneapolis: University of Minnesota Press, 2002).
3 "Brachiaria mutica," College of Tropical Agriculture and Human Resources, https://www.ctahr.hawaii.edu/invweed/WeedsHI/W_Brachiaria_mutica.pdf.
4 "Glyphosate," National Pesticide Information Center, http://npic.orst.edu /factsheets/glyphogen.html.
5 Stephanie Nohelani Teves, *Defiant Indigeneity: The Politics of Hawaiian Performance* (Chapel Hill, NC: University of North Carolina Press, 2018).

6   NIRAKN "Race, Whiteness and Indigeneity" Conference, Gold Coast, Queensland, Australia, 6–8 June 2017.

7   Here I am referring to Noelani Goodyear-Kaʻōpua's definition of *ea* (breath, sovereignty): "Ea can be seen as both a concept and a diverse set of practices.... Ea refers to political independence and is often translated as 'sovereignty.' It also carries the meaning of 'life' and 'breath,' among other things.... Ea is based on the experiences of people on the land, relationships forged through the process of remembering and caring for wahi pana, storied places.... Ea is an active state of being.... Ea cannot be achieved or possessed; it requires constant action day after day, generation after generation." Noelani Goodyear-Kaʻōpua, Ikaika Hussey, and Erin Kahunawaika'ala Wright, eds., *A Nation Rising: Hawaiian Movements for Life, Land, and Sovereignty* (Durham, NC: Duke University Press Books, 2014), 3–4.

8   Kauanui, *Hawaiian Blood*, 3.

9   Maile Arvin, "Possessions of Whiteness: Settler Colonialism and Anti-Blackness in the Pacific," *Decolonization* (blog), 2 June 2014, https://decolonization.wordpress.com/2014/06/02/possessions-of-whiteness-settler-colonialism-and-anti-blackness-in-the-pacific/. See also Arvin, *Possessing Polynesians: The Science of Settler Colonial Whiteness in Hawaiʻi and Oceania* (Durham, NC: Duke University Press, 2019).

10 For a vivid and provocative example of anti-Micronesian racism in Hawaiʻi see Kathy Jetñil-Kijiner's poem "Lessons from Hawaii," https://www.kathyjetnilkijiner.com/videos-featuring-kathy/.

11 For a critical discussion of how notions of tradition work to divide Native nations see Joanne Barker, *Native Acts: Law, Recognition, and Cultural Authenticity* (Durham, NC: Duke University Press, 2011).

12 Teves, *Defiant Indigeneity*, 5–6.

13 Aileen Moreton-Robinson, *The White Possessive: Property, Power, and Indigenous Sovereignty* (Minneapolis: University of Minnesota Press, 2015), xvii.

14 Moreton-Robinson, *White Possessive*, xviii.

15 Teves, *Defiant Indigeneity*, 5.

16 I was introduced to the notion of piko as convergence of people, places, and practices during a collaborative graduate seminar between the University of Hawaiʻi Indigenous Politics program and the Indigenous Governance program from the University of Victoria. The ideas explored during that educational exchange are collected in Jeff Corntassel, et. al., eds., *Everyday Acts of Resurgence* (Olympia, WA: Daykeeper, 2018).

17 Leo David Whitney, *Taro Varieties in Hawaii* (Honolulu: Hawaii Agricultural Experiment Station, 1939).

18 James R. Hollyer, Jennifer L. Sullivan, and Margaret E. Josephson, eds., "Taro, Mauka to Makai: A Taro Production and Business Guide for Hawaiʻi Growers" (Honolulu: College of Tropical Agriculture and Human Resources, 1997).

4 (Ad)Dressing Wounds: Expansive Kinship Inside and Out

DALLAS HUNT

Last year I attended an event centred upon Indigenous knowledge and wisdom. The meeting had panel presentations, visits to neighbouring Indigenous communities, as well as small breakout sections wherein a group of Indigenous thinkers/scholars/artists gathered around a table and talk about a specific topic or problem. During one of these gatherings, a well-known Indigenous artist expressed his concern that "the problem with feminist, socialist academia is that it does not know how to deal with masculine energies." Most around the table nodded in agreement.

I bring up this specific instance as emblematic of a larger pattern within Indigenous intellectual conversations to make a few observations. One: contrary to the speaker's claim, academia has always been interested or preoccupied with "masculine energies," overly so. Two: at this meeting about Indigenous knowledges, masculinity was foregrounded and framed as something that is, or should be, central to our communities, our gatherings, and our wisdom. To put it simply, what I am concerned with in this instance, but also within Indigenous studies generally, is how masculinity is tethered to wisdom and thereby helps to set and arbitrate the terms of what is intelligible and consequential to Indigenous studies and its practitioners. I am concerned with how masculinity constructs and/or orients Indigenous politics and how it might configure imaginaries that direct us away from our relational obligations in the contemporary moment and thus foreclose on the possibility of liberatory futures premised on an ethics of care for all of our relations.

Or, to paraphrase Black studies scholar Denise Ferreira da Silva, we need to live *now* like we are living in the future. By this I mean to say that the aspirational political horizons governing dominant modes of thought in Indigenous studies, such as the macro-political project of "getting the land back," can sometimes serve as a protective shield deployed by Indigenous men who proclaim to do "the serious work" of decolonization or resurgence on the one hand, but who ultimately enact harmful, violent, and/or extractive relations in the present on the other. This future horizon, premised on the return of land through decolonization, can absolve men from engaging in good relations in the present, especially with regard to how they interact with Indigenous women, queer, trans, and two-spirit peoples. While on the one hand, having one eye fixed on the wider goals of decolonization, which would be a radical redistribution of lands and the end of settler colonialism as we know it, is crucial, we also need to be attuned to how we relate to one another in the process, in the now. What if we understood that fostering respectful, reciprocal, non-coercive, and non-violent relationships is central to the work of decolonization, rather than something that has to wait until the "real" work of decolonization is done? That is to say, what if we related to one another in a good way, instead of deferring these good intentions for good relations until after the decolonial project is complete? What use is decolonization if, when we get the land back, we are still shitty to each other, and Indigenous men (continue to) engage in predacious or violent behaviours?

Taking these questions as its starting point, this chapter concerns itself with the everyday and the often derided or delegitimized knowledges that the everyday attends to. This chapter does not propose the abdication of larger, macro-political projects, but rather suggests the need to challenge false distinctions between the macro- and micro-political, while simultaneously outlining how the intimate spaces we inhabit are worthy sites of analysis and action in Indigenous communities. Kwagiulth scholar Sarah Hunt challenges this macro-/micro- distinction when she asks, "What would happen if every time an Indigenous woman had her personal boundaries crossed without consent, we were moved to act in the same way as we've seen to the threat of a pipeline in our territories?"[1] Indigenous peoples' critical and literary engagements with the "everyday" and the primacy of our relational obligations receive little sustained interest or engagement from wider academic circles outside of Indigenous feminists and Indigenous queer studies scholars, and especially in comparison to issues like policy interpretation or land tenure. This economy of attention and engagement is highly gendered. It often favours masculinist conceptualizations of the political and relies on the labour of Indigenous women, queer, trans, and two-spirit peoples to nurture and theorize everyday relations, even as it values this labour less than other forms of Indigenous political action and knowledge production. A focus on everyday life and kinship can help us to outline, navigate, and denaturalize the colonial dimensions and parameters of what is currently called Canada. This focus also underscores the need for Indigenous peoples to remain accountable to each other (and to our other-than-human kin) as we struggle together against colonialism and towards the possibility of other worlds. Using the methodological framework I have just described, I will consider how the interventions of Indigenous feminist, queer, and two-spirit authors have challenged notions of Indigeneity that are rooted in masculinist ideals that reproduce cis-hetero-patriarchy and the colonial gender binary, and thereby violate reciprocal kinship obligations and prevent more expansive notions of kinship from flourishing. In particular, I address these issues through the critical writings of Griffin Poetry Prize winner, and Cree queer Treaty 8 poet Billy-Ray Belcourt.

(Re)Orientations: Mapping Modes of Thought

In 2018 I taught a course titled "Contemporary Indigenous Scholarship," and I structured the syllabus of the course to begin with notions of Indigenous feminism(s), then proceeded to teach units on queer Indigenous studies and two-spirit studies, deciding to conclude the course by devoting my last week of classes to "Indigenous masculinities." I thought that one week would be enough to address the major themes, arguments, and ideas in the field of Indigenous masculinity studies, and also might help me avoid prolonged conversations over damaged masculinities and how inordinate time should be apportioned to fixing or recuperating these masculinities. For the readings that week, I paired an interview with Taiaiake Alfred[2] with Billy-Ray Belcourt's provocative blogpost "Can the Other of Native Studies Speak?"[3] My intention was to provide a representative – or, perhaps more appropriately, symptomatic – example of Indigenous masculinities with Alfred's interview (and the ideas it espouses) and to challenge, contest, or put this in conversation with Belcourt's meditative critiques of the field of Indigenous masculinities.

In a frustrating but simultaneously not at all surprising way, Indigenous masculinities began to seep and infiltrate into the other units I had scheduled as news of Taiaiake Alfred's interpersonal violences began to receive greater attention both in Indigenous contexts and the "mainstream" media. And since Alfred had been a central figure within Indigenous political studies, these violences have had a profound and reverberating effect within Indigenous studies more broadly.

I address Alfred here primarily because I am interested in the implications of his role as an intellectual leader of one of the most revered and influential institutions of Indigenous political thought and modes of governance at a national, and perhaps even global scale for many years.

Though, to be clear, I am less interested in Alfred as an individual or public figure and rather am interested in him as someone who was once at the helm of a hub of Indigenous "wisdom" in Canada. In short, the focus on Alfred here has less to do with him as a person and more with how his actions are a symptom of larger, dominant, and dominating systemic issues within Indigenous studies and in the way we as Indigenous peoples relate to one another. Additionally, while I acknowledge that making room for the internal complexities of Indigenous communities risks potentially affirming narratives put forth by settler imaginaries that Indigenous men are "barbarians" and that settlement was and is, in some ways, a benevolent project designed "to save" Indigenous women and children from those men, I think it is also incumbent on us not to attribute masculinist violence in Indigenous academic circles and non-academic communities as *always* and/or *only* a product of settler colonial white supremacy. At what point does "internalization" of colonial patterns become constitutive or consolidation? Or, put another way, is it possible for Indigenous masculinities to "right the wrongs that brought them into being"?[4] Indeed, we need to think of and practise more generative and generous ways of being with one another, which is to say ways that do not reproduce recapitulate the same formative logics upon which our worlds are structured.

If the field of Indigenous masculinity studies (and, by extension, Indigenous studies more generally) continues to defer or relegate the issues of (toxic) masculinity to an external imposition, a white supremacist outside, then we will fail to account for its wild permutations within our communities (which Belcourt takes pains to articulate in his poetry as well as his critical work). Indigenous masculinity studies often relies on a romanticized version of Indigenous communities or "tradition" that puts forth the assertion that Indigenous communities historically have had few (or zero) problems with masculinist domination. If we can acknowledge the complexity of Indigenous communities – their governance structures, their varied and nuanced articulations of gender – should we not also be hesitant to cast a homogenizing view of masculinity as it has manifested in communities historically and as it exists today?

Wounded Worlds: Indigenous Masculinities' (Dis)Contents

In an interview with Sam McKegney, Taiaiake Alfred ruminates on the issues facing Indigenous men, asking, "What's the role of the Native male?... There's no channel, I guess, for productive masculinity in a productive way. You still constantly reproduce the image of all of those four ... the absentee, the drunk, the tough guy, the warrior – and those are all anti-family messages."[5] While Alfred appears to recognize the dominant models of masculinity imposed upon Indigenous men, he still ascribes masculinity to bodies willing (or bodies that *should be* willing) to (re)produce "families." "To recover something *meaningful* for Natives," Alfred suggests, "is to put the image of the Native male back into its proper context, which is in the family" – and it is not a stretch to surmise that Alfred means "at the head" of the family here.[6]

Alfred ends his discussion of masculinities with a disparaging comment about feminism(s), relegating it to the realm of liberal Canadian polite society: "I think most art is capitalist today, and most literature is very mainstream: it's a typical kind of navel-gazing, middle-class, either feminist or politically correct multicultural Canadianism."[7] Alfred here lumps all feminisms together, dismissing them wholesale, including, implicitly, Indigenous feminisms. Not only this, but he also attributes (Indigenous) feminisms to a solely "individualistic" enterprise or project, instead of a valuable mode of thought that engages with everything from Indigenous governance, to politics, history, medicine, law, and justice. This conflation of feminism, especially Indigenous feminism, with individualism robs Indigenous feminisms (and their practitioners) of the wider, communal impulses and orientations of this work. In many ways, modes of thought that do not solely preoccupy themselves with "masculine energies" are marginalized as "individualist" efforts that putatively do not concern themselves with broader collectivist politics and, as such, should be relegated to the margins or dustbins of Indigenous political thought and action. Framing feminist writings/theories in this way (as either highly "individual" or in no way "collective") does not attend to the full complexity of what Cree scholar Gina Starblanket has referred to as the "network of relationships between people and places interacting not only in the present, but also the past and future."[8] Providing a scene that runs counter to this "individualizing" impulse projected onto Indigenous women, Mohawk scholar Audra Simpson writes how Iroquois women have "advised men on what to do in terms of the formal politics of the community."[9]

Many of the critiques, dismissals, and erasures of Indigenous feminisms are also directed at queer Indigenous studies. Queer Cree poet and scholar Billy-Ray Belcourt has described Indigenous studies' engagement (or lack thereof) with queer Indigeneity: "[Queer Indigenous peoples] are not interpellated into Native Studies' Native, but, instead, into the token minoritarian interlocutors tasked with complaining about things … complaints that are too often met with cold shoulders."[10] Speaking to the strategic inclusion or instrumentalization of queer Indigeneity, Belcourt continues: "There might be collections written and scholars researching under the rubric of 'Queer Indigenous Studies,' but this does not mean that our work is being taken up in ways that recklessly generate radically new ways of being in the world."[11] In his lyrical poetry and critical writing, Belcourt problematizes the notion that "Indigenous men ... must be healed in order to later govern as Sovereigns" to ultimately "achieve" or reach decolonization.[12] He addresses the rising tendency to emphasize the victimization of Indigenous men because it often positions men's issues in opposition to (or competition with) those of women, queer, trans, and two-spirited individuals, thereby monopolizing the limited space and resources that these minority groups are already forced to vie for. For Belcourt, the ultimate goal is not simply "being included," since a decolonizing strategy that invests so heavily in the notion of masculinity – healthy or otherwise – binds the future of Indigenous studies and Indigenous decolonization to the maintenance of a gender binary that has largely been harmful to those who are not cis-straight men. Rather, Belcourt gestures to a world wherein all of our relations are accounted for, in the present, and signals for new worlds that are possible if we disrupt the continuous ongoings of Native/Indigenous studies as a discipline (and its potential inherent harms).

Belcourt's ideas, as they came in up in my class, stood in stark contrast with the representations of masculinity that we had engaged with in the course, particularly those offered by Alfred and others. And given his helming of a program that cultivated an air that had "little tolerance for LGBTQ and two-spirited individuals,"[13] the class became interested in how the immensely influential Alfred (and the ideas he represents) figures into Belcourt's critique of Indigenous masculinities and "Native Studies' Native." That is to say, we were concerned with whether or not "Native Studies' Native" is always conceptualized as the profoundly masculine "man-on-the-land" that Belcourt attributes to this configuration.

In an illustrative interview, shortly after stepping down as head of the Indigenous Governance Program, Alfred attempted to clarify his position and thoughts on the accusations brought against him and the program. Speaking to a contributor to the *Two Row Times*, Alfred declared, "If you're asking me if I'm hyper-masculine, well, I'm Mohawk from Kahnawake ... I'm a Mohawk from Kahnawake and that's who I am."[14] A few things are at work in this paradoxical statement (or, perhaps more accurately, admission): the first is the explicit tethering of "(hyper-)masculinity" to Indigeneity here – a speech act that is doing more work than Alfred appears to realize. Alfred was not asked if he was "Indigenous or non-Indigenous," or what nation/community he hails from, but rather he was pressed about the accusations of the masculinist culture of the program. Alfred's response, illuminatingly, is to reassert his "Nativeness," and how a particular manifestation of "Nativeness" (in this instance, Mohawk), should be properly read as always already male or masculine. The answer to the question, Alfred appears to suggest, is clear; it is embedded in the very question itself and its evocation of masculinity. Here I want to stress that my intention is not to position Alfred and Belcourt as individual foils for one another, but rather to consider how their contrasting approaches challenge us to reconsider how we conceive of taken-for-granted notions of everything from being (properly) "Native," to what is legible to Indigenous studies and its practitioners as forms of (or worthy of being) Indigenous knowledge.

To return to our class discussions, we arrived at the conclusion that the notions of Indigenous masculinity currently in vogue and/or circulation in academic and community discourses are impoverished, to say the least, and that they constrict the possibilities for ethical relations in Indigenous studies, and within Indigenous communities more generally. As a result, we need to think critically about these discourses and how they might foreclose on more radical futures offered by the work undertaken by queer, trans, and two-spirit Indigenous peoples. For the remainder of this chapter, I focus on this work and how it manifests in the everyday and in relation to the reciprocal obligations, or the lack thereof, enacted or enabled by Indigenous masculinities, and how these manifest in Belcourt's writings.

This Process of Worlding and Thinking Otherwise

Billy-Ray Belcourt is Cree from the Driftpile Cree Nation in Treaty 8 territory in Northern Alberta. Belcourt's multiple award-winning first book of poetry, *This Wound Is a World* (2017), addresses a variety of issues, from embodied knowledges, to the conditions of reserve life, to the processes of making a world or world-making. In an interview surrounding the release of his text, Belcourt proclaimed that he was "trying to figure out how to be in this world without wanting it" and suggested that "perhaps this is what it is to be Indigenous."[15] He is specifically interested in how queer Indigenous peoples are compelled to inhabit a world that regularly harms them and is thus, paradoxically, uninhabitable. Belcourt writes at the disciplinary boundaries of Indigenous studies and queer studies, proclaiming that he is "*of* but not *in*" either field.[16] This theoretical dexterity, or promiscuity, allows Belcourt to exist at the intersection(s) of queerness and Indigeneity, and to ask important questions about how both fields of study, as well as ways of being, can relate, influence, inhabit, and/or prohibit one another. Belcourt's work is especially generative for addressing "the rise" of Indigenous masculinity studies, and indeed Belcourt himself has explored how queer Indigenous studies allows, and in some ways demands, a critical examination and calling to account of Indigenous masculinities and the socialities they offer and foreclose.

Critical Indigenous masculinities, as defined by two influential texts released in relative proximity to each other, *Masculindians* (2014) and *Indigenous Men and Masculinities: Legacies, Identities, Regeneration* (2015), are complex and varied. According to Canadian literature scholar Sam McKegney, Indigenous masculinity "is a tool for describing the qualities, actions, characteristics, and behaviours that accrue meaning within a given historical context and social milieu through their association with maleness, as maleness is normalized, idealized, and even demonized within a web of power-laden interpenetrating discourses."[17] Speaking to this, Innes and Anderson, in their introduction to *Indigenous Men and Masculinities*, write that a study of Indigenous masculinities can produce an "understanding of how race and gender bias intersect to disadvantage Indigenous men, and how this disadvantaged position has had negative ramifications for Indigenous communities."[18]

At times, however, Indigenous masculinities appear to be configured or conceptualized only in relation to their perceived "opposite," which is to say Indigenous femininities or feminisms. As McKegney writes, a "recent report for Indian and Northern Affairs Canada (INAC) ... demonstrate[s] that the conditions of Indigenous men are improving at a much slower pace than those of Indigenous women in Canada."[19] My intention here is not to diminish the potential violences that Indigenous men face, but rather to point to the ways in which the study of Indigenous masculinities appears to constitute itself always *in opposition to* or even in competition with the violence faced by Indigenous women, and rarely, if ever, discusses in any significant detail the violence faced by trans or two-spirit peoples within Indigenous communities. Further, while some Indigenous scholars and critics, such as Alfred, are quick to foreground reproduction and the Indigenous "family" in nation-building/resurgence efforts, I follow Leanne Simpson's assertion that "creating life comes in many forms, not just from the womb, and it creates a space where all genders can have valuable, ethical, consensual, meaningful, and reciprocal relationships with all aspects of creation."[20]

For Billy-Ray Belcourt, the issues foregrounded by Alfred are evidence of "the grammar of Indigenous studies misapprehend[ing] the tumult of everyday life."[21] Belcourt recognizes the often-maligned status of the everyday in Indigenous studies, as efforts are normally put in service of larger macro-political issues like "the land" and "sovereignty," in forms that are largely masculinist. What is often lost in these orientations,

however, are not only the daily violences and resistances faced and enacted by Indigenous peoples (and bodies), but also the ways in which
the macro-political and micro-political are intertwined and in conversation. Regularly omitted in discussions of macro-political issues are the
ways in which embodied knowledges influence macro-political orders,
as well as the ways in which two-spirit or queer Indigenous community
members are often excluded from narratives about mass movements in
the contemporary moment, even as they shape these movements and
have shaped them historically. As Sarah Hunt writes, "Recounting and
reclaiming this history [has] been central to validating the lives of di-
versely gendered Indigenous peoples today as integral to the sociocul-
tural and governance practices of Indigenous nations."[22] Further to this
point, Qwo-Li Driskill remarks that Indigenous "Two-Spirit/queer people position ourselves and our identities as productive, if not central, to
nationalist, decolonial agendas,"[23] particularly given the role of colonialism in naturalizing hetero-patriarchy and the gender binary. Arvin, Tuck,
and Morill write that as "settler nations sought to disappear Indigenous
peoples' complex structures of government and kinship, the management of Indigenous peoples' gender roles and sexuality was also key in
remaking Indigenous peoples into settler state citizens."[24] Speaking to
this fact as well, and the way it effects everyday modes of kinship, Belcourt argues that "settler colonialism is fundamentally affective: it takes
hold of the body, makes it perspire, and wears it out ... it is an *epistemic
rupturing of our attachments to life, to each other, and to ourselves.*"[25] Belcourt
points to vulnerability as a potential site of cohesion, against these epistemic ruptures, since "[vulnerability] is also an affective of commons and
we are in it with one another, which enables us to dream up a future in
which vulnerability is not about being subject to the actions of racist
others, but is about falling apart in a good way."[26] Belcourt, then, inves-
tigates the ways in which Indigenous peoples can "fall apart" together in
a "good way" –in a way that acknowledges our reciprocal obligations to
each other in their full complexity.

In his poem "Something like Love," Belcourt articulates how, for queer
Indigenous peoples, there "are days when being in life feels like consent-
ing to the cruelties that hold up the world."[27] One tangible way these
cruelties manifest is through the prism of (Indigenous) masculinities. If,
as Innes and Anderson remark, Indigenous masculinities are about "the
ways in which Indigenous men, and those who assert Indigenous masculine identities, perform their identities, why and how they perform them
and the consequences to them and others because of their attachment
to those identities,"[28] then Belcourt is interested in how in "attach[ing]
masculinity to the decolonial future," this "might mean ... repudiat[ing]

queer life as such – queerness being that which germinates all over the place, without or beyond the aegis of gender."[29] Belcourt writes, "If masculinity is an object we attach to, because we think we need it to keep going, I want to know what that object stands in for because no attachment is neutral."[30] Belcourt echoes this in his critical writing when he states that "to approximate indigeneity, you must approximate tradition in this way and not that, *or else.*"[31] Such romantic narratives can not only erase or minimize actually existing homophobia within contemporary Indigenous communities, but, as Sarah Hunt also points out, "It is important to avoid generalized statements that idealize pre-contact Indigenous societies as uniformly balanced, accepting, and appreciative of" all genders and sexualities. For Belcourt, acts of queer Indigenous refusal provide space for the flowering of new Indigenous lifeworlds, ones wherein the prisons of imposed heteronormative masculinity do not hinder or prevent nascent forms of being in the world and being with one another.

The trope or narrative – that men have to be saved or redeemed in order for things to improve or not deteriorate further – in many ways recentres cis-heteronormative, masculinist formations of being in the world. White masculinity is often positioned as distinct from (healthy/traditional) Indigenous masculinities. However, as Belcourt views it, "that masculinity becomes an object of inquiry – indeed, one that can remedy the social – is symptomatic of a kind of shortcutting whereby the future is thought vis-à-vis the analytics of the present, a present that, by all means, isn't good for most of us."[32] Put more simply, the "normative project of 'Indigenous Masculinities,'" to Belcourt, is "to make a healthy masculinity for Indigenous men in order to repair the social."[33] The field of Indigenous masculinity studies is invested in a movement that repositions or reifies "Man as sovereign" at the forefront of broader Indigenous collectives. Belcourt, recognizing the bereft sites open to other forms of being (particularly queer or non-normative ones) when masculinity is prioritized and re-prioritized, stages his creative and critical work as an intervention into these reifications that position Indigenous masculinities at the forefront of Indigenous communities. We should value the expansive and alternative forms of kinship relations, for, as Belcourt notes, the "crows and flies ... don't care about gender" and the normative relationships its binary prescribes.[34]

As Qwo-Li Driskill writes, "Instead of seeing decolonization as something that has a fixed and finite goal, decolonial activism and scholarship ask us to radically reimagine our futures," and ultimately to continually enact those futures.[35] One way to do this is to focus on or centre good kinship relations *now* and not wait for the perpetually-always-in-the-offing worlds offered by healthy masculinities. What would our reciprocal

obligations to each other look like if we did not have to wait on the re-
cuperation of Indigenous masculinities and we were able to hold each
other accountable in meaningful ways? If Indigenous women, queer, and
two-spirit peoples have been foundational to Indigenous communities
and their survivance historically, why must the futurities we imagine for
ourselves be conscribed by the re-emergence of a masculinity that can
be mobilized in a variety of harmful ways (often against these vary same
foundational bodies)? Anishinaabe scholar Dory Nason asks "all of us to
think about what it means for men, on the one hand, to publicly profess
an obligation to 'protect our women' and, on the other, take leadership
positions that uphold patriarchal forms of governance."[36] Perhaps we
can take this one step further and ask why the only forms of governance
(supposedly) available are so dependent on the eminence of a "healthy
masculinity," one that reifies cis-normative notions of the gender binary.

Kinship Now: Other Ways of Being in the World

In describing macro-political concerns as "masculinist," my intention
here is not to say that Indigenous women, queer, and two-spirit peoples
are not preoccupied with or engaged in these issues as well; rather what
I am positing is that they often focus on these issues in different ways,
and alongside (rather than in opposition to) the whole host of other
entanglements they have with other beings, be they their familial kin,
other-than-human kin, or more expansive notions of kinship including
the cosmos. With that said, I am also wary of attributing or ascribing
the formulation and eventual flourishing of these new forms of expansive kinship relations solely to Indigenous women, queer, and two-spirit
peoples – too often these groups are tasked with saving the world from
the ills created by extractive, kin-obliterating, predominantly masculine,
harmful activities. Rather, what I want to suggest is that the (renewed)
focus on Indigenous masculinities can delimit or foreclose on our horizons of imagining things differently, and that queer Indigenous political
thought and practice offers one possible pathway for shifting away from
"repair and toward Indigenous flourishing."[37]

Belcourt writes that "investment is the social practice whereby one
risks losing it all to be a part of something that feels like release."[38] This
"losing it all" opens up a world of thriving as opposed to simply surviving,
as Belcourt states elsewhere that "survival is an impoverished goal."[39] Belcourt, then, is against a rhetoric or mode of being in the world that takes
"survival" as its telos, and rather is interested in cultivating worlds that are
good for all of us, ones wherein "no one is falling apart in a bad way."[40]
Indeed, Belcourt advocates for new ways of operating that account for

all of our entanglements with one another and that do not foreclose on queer Indigenous futurities through the prism of Indigenous masculinities. In so doing, we might be able to "build our own communities of care and love."[41] Through the critical and creative writing of Belcourt, Indigenous peoples can potentially glimpse a world wherein all of their kin are accounted for and cared for, and where their futures are not tethered to the ascension of healthy masculinities that reinscribe cis-heteronormative notions of the gender binary – indeed, a world wherein we can be undone by one another, in a good way. The question remains, especially for those of us socialized into hegemonic forms of Indigenous masculinity, whether we are willing to "lose it all" and "fall apart" generatively, so that these other possibilities for collective well-being can thrive.

NOTES

1 Sarah Hunt, "Embodying Self-Determination: Beyond the Gender Binary," in *Determinants of Indigenous Peoples' Health: Beyond the Social*, ed. Margo Greenwood, Sarah de Leeuw, and Nicole Marie Lindsay, 2nd ed. (Toronto: Canadian Scholars, 2018), 8–9.
2 "Reimagining Warriorhood: A Conversation with Taiaiake Alfred," in *Masculindians*, ed. Sam McKegney (Winnipeg: University of Manitoba Press, 2014), n.p.
3 Billy-Ray Belcourt, "Can the Other of Native Studies Speak?," Decolonization: Indigeneity, Education and Society Blog, February 2016, https://decolonization.wordpress.com/2016/02/01/can-the-other-of-native-studies-speak/.
4 Vincent Mousseau, "Material for Worldbuilding: In Conversation with Billy-Ray Belcourt," *Articulation Magazine*, 7 April 2018.
5 Sam McKegney, "Introduction," in *Masculindians*, 79.
6 McKegney, "Introduction," 70 (italics mine).
7 McKegney, "Introduction," 86.
8 Gina Starblanket, "Complex Accountabilities: Deconstructing 'the Community' and Engaging Indigenous Feminist Research Methods," *American Indian Culture and Research Journal* 42, no. 4 (2018): 6.
9 Audra Simpson, *Mohawk Interruptus: Political Life across the Borders of Settler States* (Durham, NC: Duke University Press, 2014), 60.
10 Belcourt, "Can the Other of Native Studies Speak?"
11 Belcourt, "Can the Other of Native Studies Speak?"
12 Belcourt, "Can the Other of Native Studies Speak?"
13 Barrera, "Enrolment Suspended."
14 Alfred, "Reimagining Warriorhood."

15 Billy-Ray Belcourt, "The Body Remembers When the World Broke Open," *Arts Everywhere Musagetes*, 8 February 2017, https://www.artseverywhere.ca /body-remembers-world-broke-open/.

16 Belcourt, "Can the Other of Native Studies Speak?"

17 McKegney, "Introduction," 3.

18 R.A. Innes and K. Anderson, eds., *Indigenous Men and Masculinities* (Winnipeg: University of Manitoba Press, 2015), 4

19 McKegney, "Introduction," 6.

20 Leanne Betasamosake Simpson, *As We Have Always Done: Indigenous Freedom through Radical Resistance* (Minneapolis: University of Minnesota Press, 2017), 121.

21 Billy-Ray Belcourt, "Indigenous Studies beside Itself," *Somatechnics* 7, no. 2 (2017): 182.

22 Hunt, "Embodying Self-Determination," 107.

23 Qwo-Li Driskill, "Doubleweaving Two-Spirit Critiques: Building Alliances between Native and Queer Studies," *GLQ: A Journal of Lesbian and Gay Studies* 16, no. 1–2 (2010): 69–92.

24 Maile Arvin, Eve Tuck, and Angie Morrill, "Decolonizing Feminism: Challenging Connections between Settler Colonialism and Heteropatriarchy," *Feminist Formations* 25, no. 1 (2013): 15.

25 Billy-Ray Belcourt, "A Poltergeist Manifesto," *Feral Feminisms* 6 (2016): 25 (italics mine).

26 Jessica Johns, "Everything Is Something Else: In Conversation with Billy-Ray Belcourt," *Prism International*, 12 April 2018.

27 Billy-Ray, Belcourt, *This Wound Is a World* (Calgary: Frontenac House, 2017), 41.

28 Robert Alexander Innes and Kim Anderson, eds., *Indigenous Men and Masculinities: Legacies, Identities, Regeneration* (Winnipeg: University of Manitoba Press, 2015), 4.

29 Belcourt, "Can the Other of Native Studies Speak?"

30 Belcourt, "Can the Other of Native Studies Speak?"

31 Belcourt, "Poltergeist Manifesto," 29 (italics mine).

32 Belcourt, "Can the Other of Native Studies Speak?"

33 Belcourt, "Can the Other of Native Studies Speak?"

34 Belcourt, *This Wound Is a World*, 9.

35 Driskill, "Doubleweaving Two-Spirit Critiques," 70

36 Dory Nason, "We Hold Our Hands Up: On Indigenous Women's Love and Resistance," *Decolonization: Indigeneity, Education & Society*, 12 February 2013.

37 Belcourt, qtd. by Mousseau, "Material for Worldbuilding," 31.

38 Belcourt, *This Wound Is a World*, 31.

39 Belcourt qtd. by Mousseau, "Material for Worldbuilding."

40 Belcourt, *This Wound Is a World*, 13.

41 Belcourt qtd. by Mousseau, "Material for Worldbuilding."

PART TWO

Claiming Our Relationships to the Political

5 Beyond Rights and Wrongs: Towards a Resurgence of Treaty Relationality

GINA STARBLANKET

It was a rude diplomacy at best, the gross diplomacy of the rum bottle and the material appeal of gaudy presents, webs of scarlet cloth, silver medals, and armlets. Yet there was the heart of these puerile negotiations, this control that seemed to be founded on debauchery and licence, this alliance that was based on a childish system of presents, a principle that has been carried on without cessation and with increased vigilance to the present day – the principle of the sacredness of treaty promises. Whatever has been written down and signed by king and chief both will be bound by so long as "the sun shines and the water runs"....

The treaty policy so well established when the confederation of the provinces of British North America took place has since been continued and nearly all civilized Canada is covered with these Indian treaties and surrenders. A map coloured to define their boundaries would show the province of Ontario clouted with them like a patchwork blanket; as far north as the confines of the new provinces of Saskatchewan and Alberta the patches lie edge to edge.[1]

The Beginnings and Ends of Treaty-Making with the Crown

I include Duncan Campbell Scott's epigraph from 1906 to highlight the association between treaties and the creation of Canada.[2] This association may seem straightforward, with the negotiation of the numbered treaties commonly understood as bringing Indigenous peoples and territories under the legal and political jurisdiction of the newly confederated Canadian nation state, authorizing westward expansion on a fixed set of written terms that Indigenous people willingly negotiated and consented to.[3] Yet the function of treaties in relation to the creation/continuity of the settler state is complex and often contested, giving rise to inquiries about the role of treaty relative to contemporary Indigenous political projects.

Selectively represented as non-violent means of incorporating Indigenous peoples into the Dominion of Canada, popular accounts of treaty as
transaction contribute to the maintenance of colonial mythologies about
the ways in which Canada came to be, but also narratives that inform false
understandings of Indigenous peoples' contemporary political location relative to Canada.[4] In Scott's 1906 description, the patchwork blanket represents frontiers – geographical and political – that incrementally extend the
boundaries of "civilized Canada" with the signing of each subsequent treaty.
These frontiers are conceived of as rigid because settler and Indigenous
ways of life are incommensurable, suggesting that social, legal, and political
orders, and relationships with the land are antithetical and cannot co-exist.

In the creation of Canada, representations of treaties as land transactions are, to use the framing of Patrick Wolfe, both eliminatory and
productive.[5] They are eliminatory in their finality, intending to ensure
the end of Indigenous political authority and jurisdiction over the land
and to what Campbell Scott describes as "rude and costly" diplomatic
practices. Tasked with addressing outstanding Indigenous claims to land
following the "purchase" of Rupertsland and the North-West Territories
from the Hudson's Bay Company, Canada's assertion of sovereignty and
jurisdiction remained incomplete, even if already presumed. Treaties
thus served a crucial role in what Wolfe refers to as the "inchoate" stage
in the formation of the settler state – the point between the theory and
realization of territorial acquisition.

While Indigenous practices of treaty-making with settlers long
preceded Canadian Confederation, the realization of Canadian sovereignty depended upon the reduction of Indigenous peoples' political
status to that of subjects through the extension of a legal order that
would fully "consummate" and thus promise to maintain the structure of
settler-colonial society. Heidi Kiiwetinepinesiik Stark argues that treaties
provided an ideal vehicle for settler states to negotiate this transition,
as they involved recognition of Indigenous political status necessary to
effect the "cessation" of rights to the land, while also providing a mechanism for Indigenous political subordination.[6] Stark observes that efforts
to assert the continuity of Indigenous jurisdiction or political authority
following treaty-making with the Crown were subsequently framed as
criminal acts against the settler state. This framing pitted even the most
modest assertions of rights or authority under treaties as contrary to the
national interest, which in turn justified, normalized, and softened state
violence against Indigenous peoples.

If we return to Scott's writing, we can see how the parameters of "civilized Canada" were understood to have been incrementally extended as
the "treaty policy" effected the extinguishment of Indigenous lifeways.

Even if some Indigenous peoples survived in these spaces, they were to think, behave, and act in ways that conformed with the dominant social, political, and intellectual orders. Thus the success of the treaty policy is illustrated by how it transformed Indigenous lands into "civilized Canada," which produced a settler state with claims to complete jurisdiction and a cohesive national identity, or at least a national identity that transcended the differences that constituted it.

Treaties, then, represent a foundational axis of settler colonialism. As the originary "land transactions" that purportedly allowed Canada to claim jurisdiction across vast tracts of land, they could not be discarded by the state, as that would undermine the legitimacy of its legal and political formations and invalidate its cultural and moral claims.[7] Rather, the story of treaties as land transactions must be selectively and strategically retold in order to sustain Crown claims to legal and political authority over Indigenous people, to jurisdiction over treaty territories, and to the virtue of non-Indigenous Canadians as contemporary "treaty people."

Like any story, Campbell Scott's isn't the only version. As many Indigenous and non-Indigenous peoples are well aware, the transactional interpretation stands in direct contrast to the meaning and intent of treaties recorded and passed on by Indigenous knowledge-holders.[8] The negotiation of treaties with the Crown followed a tradition of treaty-making with other living beings as a way to negotiate land use. These practices predate the arrival of Europeans, helping to mediate the relationships between Indigenous populations and other living beings in shared spaces.

According to Indigenous knowledge-holders, treaties represent the creation of a relationship that allows Indigenous people and newcomers to live together in shared spaces under the laws of the Creator.[9] As living agreements, they represent much more than the exchange of material items for land. They represent a legal and political arrangement where forms of difference coalesce to create "[an] enduring and lasting relationship" of "mutual ongoing caring and sharing" between treaty parties,[10] representing a continuity and the initiation of a new relationship, but not an ending. By invoking the sun, water, rivers, grass – and even in some treaties, the rocks and mountains – Indigenous peoples positioned the relationship between treaty partners as dynamic, always growing, and demanding care and attention into the future. Importantly, treaty entails much more than the terms recorded by the Crown; the sacred laws, doctrines, and teachings of Indigenous people serve as the foundation for new relationships to be created under treaty.[11]

Like European newcomers, Indigenous people understood treaties as a beginning of sorts. But this beginning was not intended to supplant what came before. It was a beginning based on continuity; that is, the continuity of Indigenous ways of being, laws, political systems, languages, ways of knowing, and relationships with the land and other living beings. Returning to Campbell Scott's description of treaty territories as a patchwork blanket, one might juxtapose the purported "blanket extinguishment" of Indigenous rights and title that flows from a transactional understanding with the image of fabric created by weaving together Indigenous peoples' ways of life and the new skills and teachings that settlers brought with them.

Rather than positioning difference as a threat to be eliminated, treaty-making follows from a deep respect for and appreciation of the value of difference. While living beings have distinct roles and responsibilities, no single contributions are more important than any others. The ethic of relationality embodied in treaties gives rise to practices that facilitate the co-existence and mutual growth of treaty partners through a legal, political, and spiritual arrangement that allows groups to retain their ways of being. At the same time, treaty partners learn from one another and rely on one another in times of need, becoming stronger as they gain new knowledge and skills. The relational world view expressed in treaties defies the antagonism inherent in settler colonial logics, allowing for a vision of the future based on multiplicity and balance, not hierarchy or domination. Importantly, treaties are intended to guarantee the survival, well-being, and continuity of all Creation, not of one nation at the expense of another. They are about generating something healthy and liveable from the tensions between ways of life that seem irreconcilable, and believing that out of those tensions new possibilities can be born that are greater than deteriorating, harmful, or violent relations.

Upon even a cursory comparison of Indigenous and settler understandings of treaties, several issues quickly appear: the seemingly insurmountable contradictions between continuity and finality, pluralistic and antagonistic approaches to difference, relationships with and cession of land, and the affirmation or elimination of Indigenous life. These incongruities form a paradox for Indigenous people working towards resurgence; that is, what are we to do with these intergenerational relationships, negotiated by our ancestors in our collective name, when their vision of relationship has continually been overwritten by Canadian institutions in ways that have functioned to perpetuate violence and dispossession?

The Remains of Treaty

When I write on treaty, I refer to the diplomatic practices that Indigenous people utilize to negotiate the sharing of land with other living beings. Contemporary analyses of treaty relations with the Crown that employ this understanding are often steeped in a sense of deficit or lack, wherein the types of treaty relationships that Indigenous peoples envisioned in agreeing to share the land with settlers are nowhere to be found aside our past (and in some respects, future) aspirations.

In the contemporary political and economic climate, state commitments to renew the "nation-to-nation relationship" between treaty nations and the Crown have seldom been accompanied by a demonstrated commitment to address issues that remain outstanding under treaties (such as jurisdiction and resources), or to undertake structural changes such as the redistribution of power, land, and revenues that would be required to substantially improve the political status of treaty First Nations relative to Canada. Indeed, advocacy for treaty implementation can seem to be leading nowhere in light of the disparity in political and economic power between Indigenous and settler governments in the present day.[12] Far from improving Indigenous political subordination, rhetorical commitments to facilitate treaty implementation can be shorthand for new forms of political domination, incorporation, and co-optation by and for the settler state that promises only to sustain, even if masking, violence and dispossession against Indigenous peoples.

For these and other reasons, some argue in favour of writing off treaties as historical agreements that were entered into and have been rendered irrelevant as a result of the ways in which they have been dishonoured or "broken." Jill St. Germain grapples with the "broken treaties" tradition of treaty interpretation, explaining how analyses that are preoccupied with the actualization of the fixed terms of treaties can give the impression that treaties are meaningless, given state habits of breaking them.[13] This line of thought can position treaty-making with a finality, or at least situate it as irrelevant, as it provides a "persuasive rationalization for relegating treaties and treaty relations to the dustbin."[14] She argues for the need to assess treaties beyond the realm of policy, encouraging appreciation of Indigenous partners as active agents rather than passive subjects or recipients in the treaty relationship.[15] While it may be a stretch to situate Indigenous people as active agents in contemporary Indigenous-state relations (at least unaccompanied by acknowledgment of the ways in which that agency is delegated and heavily circumscribed by the state), St. Germain draws our attention to the implications of analyses that situate Indigenous parties as non-agential, and/or that gauge the relevance of treaty to contemporary Indigenous political projects through reference to the potential for their implementation by the state. Such approaches obscure the political significance of the meaning of treaty as understood by Indigenous people, and importantly, the principles and doctrines embodied in our practices of treaty-making. When evaluating the relevance of treaty to contemporary Indigenous political projects, it is crucial that we distinguish between treaties with the Crown and between treaty-based modes of relating that have been practised by Indigenous people long before treaties negotiated with European newcomers.

I can think of no worse fate than for Indigenous peoples to lose sight of our own political traditions, such as of treaty-making, because they have been mis-inhabited by settlers and sometimes by Indigenous people ourselves. This would endow the Crown with even greater power to over-write how we understand our practices of diplomacy and relationality, constituting another form of elimination (and one that generations of treaty activists have worked to refuse). Since their signing, Indigenous peoples have asserted treaties as relationships that are as important to-day as they were 100 years ago if, for nothing else, to act as a reminder of the outstanding nature of issues that the Crown has deemed to be "settled." Harold Cardinal explains that while there is "much to quarrel with in the treaties as they were signed," they remain important "not so much for their content as for the principles they imply in their very existence."[16]

Cardinal frames treaties as the Indian "Magna Carta," in that they in-form the legal and political order that all partners agreed to live under as well as the associated responsibilities of both settler and Indigenous pop-ulations. While he acknowledges many limitations inherent in the pro-cess of negotiating treaties and in the content of written treaties, he also redirects our attention to the costly risks of letting them go.[17] He shifts discussion from how they have been misinhabited by settlers, towards the importance of treaties as they are understood by Indigenous peoples:

> We cannot give up our rights without destroying ourselves as people. If our rights are meaningless, if it is inconceivable that our society have treaties with the white society even though those treaties were signed by honoura-ble men on both sides, in good faith, long before the present government decided to tear them up as worthless scraps of paper, then we as a people are meaningless. We cannot and will not accept this. We know that as long as we fight for our rights we will survive. If we surrender, we die.[18]

Here Cardinal associates treaties directly with survival, depicting the "fight for our rights" as a process that is constitutive for Indigenous peo-ple. In contemplating this association, we must recall that he was writ-ing when Canada's Indian policy was leaning towards elimination of the Indian Act, Indian status, and our distinct political location under the treaties. His words should not be interpreted strictly as a desire to se-cure recognition of our rights, but instead as speaking to the importance of the continuity of a treaty-based politic that manifests differently over time and in the face of different social and political contexts. Treaties are not understood here in the ways they have been interpreted by Canada (as scraps of paper), or as agreements that give rise to a narrow spectrum of cultural rights, but rather as vital to Indigenous peoples' continuity. They embody a refusal to die, not just physically but also in our social, cultural, and political survival as peoples. Perhaps the most important part of Cardinal's approach is the way in which he prompts us to consider what dimension of our lifeways as Indigenous people we might be giving up while eschewing a treaty-based politic.

Here we arrive at a familiar place in the theory on decolonization: the crossroads between political pragmatism and imagination. It is a place where we must contend with the often prohibitive choice between immediate needs and long-term political visions. Yet this framing is a false dichotomy, as political decisions are often more complex and nuanced in practice. The decision to "make or break" treaty relations is not a new juncture, and we would be wise to recall that our ancestors faced a similar challenge: they had to make decisions that involved conditions necessary to ensure their immediate, material survival but also entailed long-term visions for future generations to thrive and prosper.

Unlike our ancestors, however, we have different resources to draw on in theorizing contemporary approaches to treaty politics. We can gain insights from the ways in which they traditionally sought to make political decisions while recognizing that we have additional information on which to draw. We can look to the history of treaty implementation in Canada and utilize these insights to better understand the possibilities and pitfalls of varying approaches to treaty. In the next section, I argue that treaties can have an important role in the contemporary political climate, in what they can elucidate in the operations of settler colonialism, and what they can mean for Indigenous political projects in resurgence.

The Rhetoric of Treaty as a Technique of Settler Governance

Let us return to the association between treaty-making and the creation of Canada described at the outset of this chapter. I described how in undertaking treaty negotiations, settler officials understood treaty-making as a form of diplomacy that extended the boundaries of settler societies over and above Indigenous people and our relationships with Creation. Campbell Scott acknowledges that Indigenous people regard treaty with a sense of continuity, and the settler acknowledgment of continuity as a treaty principle indicates that treaties were to provide settler society with certainty in perpetuity. While I have situated treaty as having a role in the establishment of the settler state, it did not merely facilitate a one-time instance of Indigenous subordination by and for the settler state, but an enduring one. Thus, one reason treaties remain important is that examination of the rhetoric surrounding treaty can elucidate the inner workings of settler colonial structures and of Indigenous oppression over time. Rather than enacting a critique of the ways that treaties *have been neglected* by the state in the past and present, I am arguing for a critique of the ways that *treaties are invoked and operationalized* by settler governments in present contexts of colonialism to facilitate further dispossession through the language of "treaty implementation."

Today we might turn our attention to the violence that settler governments are committing when drawing on the importance of treaty relations while narrowly interpreting and infringing on them. The characterization of contemporary relations between treaty First Nations and the Crown as "nation-to-nation" is set against a backdrop of evolving settler colonial violence that has involved the continuous political subordination and dispossession of treaty First Nations (even if differently masked over time). Today, Indigenous political subordination is concealed by the rhetoric of treaty implementation and of rights recognition, which all too often results in Indigenous political mobilizations that advocate for robust conceptions of the fixed terms of treaty as recorded by the Crown.

Mobilizing a critical treaty politic involves more than just turning to the "spirit and intent of treaty" as understood by Indigenous knowledge-holders. It involves being continually mindful of the politics surrounding *how* Indigenous understandings are invoked and operationalized in movements towards change. For instance, some might draw on Indigenous understandings of treaty in order to advocate for more robust readings of written terms. Yet these efforts have a tendency to contain the breadth of treaty to compartmentalized policy areas and can inadvertently reproduce a fixed-term understanding in our efforts to work towards "actual" or meaningful treaty implementation. Theorizing through the broadest conception of treaty possible can enable a treaty politic that exceeds a fixed-term approach and can give rise to more robust critiques surrounding the role of treaty relative to contemporary settler colonial structures.

Far from historical land transactions, treaties can be understood as active relations that are continually operationalized by Canada to contain the exercise of Indigenous political orders while legitimating its own claims to sovereignty in response to shifting socio-political climates. Understanding these processes can help bring forward a more nuanced understanding of treaties, not just as agreements that were broken or dishonoured, but ones that have been selectively invoked and employed to sustain conditions of Indigenous dispossession, marginalization, and vulnerability. This is particularly true within the current era of recognition and reconciliation, where Indigenous visions of treaty relationships can be invoked as potential pathways to reconciliation. When we start from a different understanding of treaty, we are better situated to interrogate the limits of such invocations. For instance, it allows us to evaluate if the relatively recent scholarly "turn to treaty" within discourses on reconciliation hold the transformative potential its advocates claim.[19]

While a "nation-to-nation" relationship between Indigenous and Canadian governments has never materialized, it remains a crucial part of Canadian identity. Repeated calls from settler governments for "renewal" of the nation-to-nation treaty relationship are at once a suggestion that a nation-to-nation treaty relationship was once a defining feature of Canada and that, despite its lengthy record of repressive and eliminatory policies aimed at Indigenous peoples, treaties continue to be invoked by Canada as a symbol of the idealized ethnic and political plurality that Canada will strive to be yet again. Here we might understand the contemporary role of treaties as part of a broader conciliatory project that Miranda Johnson describes as bound up with ideas of re-founding of the nation.[20] She writes that such movements may have little to do with transformations of political power but rather are about grafting settler belonging onto a "postcolonial" nation. The story of treaties, then, can be understood as playing a crucial role in the beginning of Canada for settlers, but also in Canada's rebirth in a neoliberal era of recognition and reconciliation. As settler governments seek to obtain "certainty" surrounding jurisdictional questions and legal obligations through the creation of modern "treaties" and negotiated "self-government" agreements, these rebeginnings are themselves also contingent on the elimination of ongoing threats posed by Indigenous political life – that is, the uncertainty occasioned by the potential assertion of an Aboriginal or treaty right, or by a title claim or jurisdictional dispute. These inquiries stand to clarify our understanding of the function of treaty in contexts of settler colonialism, which, in turn, can help inform the direction of Indigenous political projects.

Such critical conversations can help shed light upon the role that transactional understandings of treaties have played not just legally and politically, but also in the construction of what Linda Tuhiwai Smith refers to as the discursive fields of knowledge that imperialism produces. Part of "writing back" and "theorizing back" against these Western modes of knowledge-production involves working within our own theories, knowledges, and ways of seeing the world.[21] This can help in the development of a treaty politic that is illegible to Canadian institutions and geared towards purposefully disorienting Canadian interpretations of treaty rights in law and politics, while also grounding the political actions of Indigenous treaty partners in the dimensions of treaties that remain important and significant to us.

At the same time as critiques of colonial violence and abuses, including those masked by the guise of treaty implementation, can elucidate the logics of oppression responsible for Indigenous peoples' suffering, we must also be cautious not to allow the state's invocations of treaties to direct the entire configurations of our political movements.

This would limit our capacity to theorize strategies of political change that are grounded upon our own visions of what treaties are and what they can entail. It is particularly important that Indigenous peoples do not internalize interpretations of treaties as fixed-term transactions that give rise to a narrow spectrum of cultural rights, and remain mindful that these processes inevitably shape our political vocabulary and strategy. This means that we must make concerted efforts to critically reflect upon the ways in which our own understandings of treaties as Indigenous peoples have been changed and contained by colonial narratives of treaty-making and implementation.

While critiques of the Crown's interpretation of treaties are important, Indigenous people should also be weary of focusing the bulk of our time and energy in seeking justice for the many ways in which treaties have been and continue to be misinhabited by the state, as this may take away from our capacity to pursue other political projects. As Dian Million writes, struggles for justice and self-determination are not the same and cannot necessarily be achieved through the same avenues for change.[22] An oppositional treaty politic may distract from the need to build an alternative treaty politic instead, as oppositional approaches can run the risk of limiting movement and self-transformation and can contain our ability to engage in alternative theorizations that might break free from, instead of just being differently configured by, colonial power relations.[23]

When we Indigenous peoples constitute ourselves through oppositional politics rather than what we aspire to be, we inadvertently allow our own political projects to be shaped by external sources rather than our own philosophical traditions. Indeed, Indigenous peoples' ability to theorize in a way that is not reliant on Western traditions of thought is severely constrained when we focus our resources and capacities on addressing the sources of injury rather than actualizing our own political norms and objectives.[24] This severely restricts the scope of dialogue and theorization around how political action may be conceived of in a way that reflects our traditional practices and allows for change and adaptation to present and future contexts.

Towards a Resurgence of Treaty Relationality

As Indigenous peoples contemplate how to imagine alternative ways of drawing upon practices of treaty-making within contemporary political engagements, a treaty-based ethic of relationality may help shift the focus away from articulations of treaty rights "claims" against the settler state and towards a community-driven engagement with our own intellectual resources and knowledge of treaties. Such a focus is in no way intended to harden boundaries or cultivate an internal unity or sense of homogenous political norms, but instead to invite conversation and critique around competing collective imaginations. This could strengthen the capacity for dialogue and engagement with a variety of perspectives within communities, allowing the space for individual contestation and involvement in governance while cultivating a more inclusive and participatory atmosphere for political engagement. When the politics of treaty implementation are grounded in Indigenous peoples' own visions of what treaties represent, rather than in opposition to the many ways that treaties have been neglected by the state, we Indigenous peoples can broaden our collective political involvement and engage in crucial conversations about how we want to relate to other living beings.

This also means engaging in critical dialogue about the power relations and internal logics that are at play in treaty advocacy. Such conversations, in turn, can help mitigate the ways that treaty implementation can be promoted in delegated self-government structures or economic development initiatives that are so frequently presented to Indigenous people as opportunities for treaty implementation. As I see it, one of the most important possibilities for a critical treaty politic is to push back against the tendency among Indigenous leaders and organizations to internalize and/or reproduce neoliberal, capitalist understandings of treaty implementation, such as initiatives grounded upon commoditive or possessory understandings of land and that threaten our ability to carry out our responsibilities to the living earth or to remain accountable to future generations. Rather, a critical treaty politic might look to treaties as a way of drawing out broader notions of responsibility and accountability that can allow us to contemplate the impacts of the decisions we make today on the many relations we inhabit now and into the future.

Perhaps the most transformative part of this approach is the process of renewing and redefining our understandings of our own legal and political practices within Indigenous communities. An important way of avoiding approaches that have been frozen in time and instead engaging treaties in a more creative and future-oriented way is to shift the character of political discourse away from a focus on the Crown's record of treaty implementation and towards the question of what treaties mean to us as Indigenous people. Moving towards the reconfiguration of collective political pursuits, Dian Million emphasizes the importance of social and political imagination and of embodying the transformations we envision for our communities through processes that we know are relevant and important to us. She situates Indigenous philosophies of relationality as distinctly political and explains that they can contribute to the development of a future-oriented political vision by positioning Indigenous people to constitute our political selves not through opposition to colonial violence but by doing what we have always been doing. Similarly, Leanne Simpson writes that focused rebuilding using Indigenous processes "enacts an Indigenous presence that has the ability to give life to an Indigenous future and changes not only the actors involved in the focused rebuilding" but also the power dynamics between involved actors both internal and external to the community.[25] My understanding of these interventions relative to the topics taken up in this chapter is that implementation of the terms of treaty should not be an end goal (even if treaty is understood in a robust way), but that we can look to treaty as a process that can inform a better model of organizing, living together, and constituting ourselves politically, not just in external relations, but perhaps most importantly, internally, within Indigenous communities.

Resurgence may prompt us to direct greater attention to the role of our everyday interactions in defining and pursuing our political objectives and priorities. A focus on the everyday positions of treaty relations as dynamic and ongoing comprise a multiplicity of relations and are open to dialogue and interpretation. While treaty implementation requires change to macro structures of power, we can engage subversive practices grounded in treaty relationality in small but meaningful ways. In this way, we can work to transform, move, renew, and honour our relationships as we understand our responsibilities within them and importantly, on terms that we created and agree to.

Conclusion

To some, contemporary treaty implementation can mean advancing Indigenous political imperatives through "claims" that require us to shape our political identities and movements through terms imposed by the settler state. The limits of such approaches have become abundantly clear over the years, leading some to question to relevance of treaty to contemporary Indigenous political movements and, particularly, Indigenous political movements that are external to the settler political structure. In my view, treaties are not irrelevant to Indigenous movements towards resurgence and can have an important role in contemporary Indigenous political projects generally; however, the transformative potential of this role is heavily contingent on the way in which treaties are interpreted and the contexts in which they are deployed.

When treaties are dismissed because of the way they have been inhabited by settlers, we stand to centre a transactional approach whereby the state is the provider and Indigenous peoples are the recipients of treaty rights, while also reproducing notions of boundedness and hierarchy between communities. Moreover, if we ultimately discard our own practices of treaty because of the way they have been violated in our engagements with settlers, we stand to lose some of our most important resources for how to enact a relational world view and actually begin to attend to living our interrelatedness in practice.

Dismissals of treaties as irrelevant to the contemporary context continues to give the state the authority to determine or delimit the ways in which we theorize about the future and can lead Indigenous peoples to overlook the possibilities that treaty-based modes of relating can contribute to the development of alternative political arrangements. Instead, employing a relational understanding of treaties can facilitate the resurgence of values and principles inherent in our customary ways of relating with other communities and the world we live in.

Theorizing and working towards change through an alternate vision of treaties that seeks to revitalize the relational ethics and practices embedded in their spirit and intent can represent an empowering shift in Indigenous politics. It can inform a politic that is critical of the ways in which the rhetoric of treaty implementation used by settler governments can bolster the appearance of reconciliation and/or transformation while sustaining Indigenous political subordination. And while critical analyses of the Crown's record of treaty implementation can help deconstruct and challenge the power relations underlying settler colonialism, Indigenous people also require an organizing framework that can help us work towards the restoration of our ways of life through political action and discourse that is meaningful to and that has space for involvement and contestation within our communities. To this end, a critical and relationally oriented treaty politic stands to engage continuous, future-oriented governance practices as affirmed in the treaty relationship, governing through a renewal of our own resources – those values and principles that flow from practices of treaty-making that, prior to those negotiated with settlers, sustained our inter-relatedness. The principle of continuity does not mean that we cannot critique and disengage from oppressive relations with the state; it means that we should take care to bring new life to our own governance practices precisely because of the ways they have been damaged by the state. The renewal of treaty-based modes of relating represents a crucial form of resurgence – a politics not oriented by or against the state, but driven and mobilized by Indigenous peoples' own laws and philosophies.

NOTES

1 Duncan Campbell Scott, "The Last of the Indian Treaties," *Scribner's Magazine* 40 (1906): 573–83.
2 Note that this association isn not exclusive to historical contexts. For instance, Judge Arnot (former treaty commissioner for Saskatchewan) describes treaties as "building blocks for our country."
3 The treaty mythologies of Indigenous cession and surrender of land and political authority that are outlined in this chapter are also reproduced by many Indigenous peoples in many contexts, particularly by Indigenous peoples who are not parties to the numbered treaties.
4 See G. Starblanket, "The Numbered Treaties and the Politics of Incoherency," *Canadian Journal of Political Science* 52, no. 3 (2019): 443–59.
5 Patrick Wolfe, "Settler Colonialism and the Elimination of the Native," *Journal of Genocide Research* 8, no. 4 (2006): 387–409.
6 See Heidi Kiiwetinepinesiik Stark, "Criminal Empire: The Making of the Savage in a Lawless Land," *Theory & Event* 19, no. 4 (2016).
7 Stark, "Criminal Empire."
8 As Michael Asch writes, "The interpretation provided by the contemporary Elders and leaders of the Indigenous parties to the negotiations more accurately reflects *the shared understanding of both parties* as it is reflected in the record of what transpired than does the representation contained in the written text." Michael Asch, *On Being Here to Stay: Treaties and Aboriginal Rights in Canada* (Toronto: University of Toronto Press, 2014), 82 (emphasis in the original). See also René Dussault and Georges Erasmus, *Report of the Royal Commission on Aboriginal Peoples* (1996), 2, 43; Cardinal and Hildebrandt, *Treaty Elders of Saskatchewan;* Walter Hildebrandt, Dorothy First Rider, and Sarah Carter, *True Spirit and Original Intent of Treaty 7* (Montreal and Kingston: McGill-Queen's University Press, 1996).
9 Cardinal and Hildebrandt, *Treaty Elders of Saskatchewan,* 15.
10 Cardinal and Hildebrandt, *Treaty Elders of Saskatchewan,* 15.
11 Cardinal and Hildebrandt, *Treaty Elders of Saskatchewan,* 15.
12 Harsha Walia, "'Land Is a Relationship': In Conversation with Glen Coulthard on Indigenous Nationhood," rabble.ca, 21 January 2015, http://rabble.ca/columnists/2015/01/land-relationship-conversation-glen-coulthard-on-indigenous-nationhood.

13 John L. Tobias, "Canada's Subjugation of the Plains Cree, 1879–1885," *Canadian Historical Review* 64, no. 4 (1983): 519–48.

14 Jill St. Germain, *Broken Treaties: United States and Canadian Relations with the Lakotas and the Plains Cree, 1868–1885* (Lincoln: University of Nebraska Press, 2009), xix.

15 St. Germain, *Broken Treaties*, xviii.

16 Harold Cardinal, *The Unjust Society: The Tragedy of Canada's Indians* (Edmonton, AB: M.G. Hurtig, 1969), 30.

17 Cardinal, *Unjust Society*, 24.

18 Cardinal, *Unjust Society*, 26.

19 Corey Snelgrove, "Treaty and the Problem of Colonial Reification" (paper presented at Socialist Studies Conference, Regina, SK, 26 May to 1 June 2018).

20 Miranda Johnson, "Reconciliation, Indigeneity, and Postcolonial Nationhood in Settler States," *Postcolonial Studies* 14, no. 2 (2011): 197.

21 Linda Tuhuwai Smith, "Decolonizing Methodologies: Research and Indigenous Peoples" (1999), 21.

22 Million writes, "The international law that enables Indigenous trauma to appeal for justice is the same sphere in which we articulate political rights as polities with rights to self-determination," which, in her view, are not "necessarily compatible projects." Dian Million, *Therapeutic Nations: Healing in an Age of Indigenous Human Rights* (Tucson: University of Arizona Press, 2013), 3.

23 Million, *Therapeutic Nations*, 102.

24 Wendy Brown, *States of Injury: Power and Freedom in Late Modernity* (Princeton, NJ: Princeton University Press, 1999).

25 Leanne Simpson, *As We Have Always Done: Indigenous Freedom through Radical Resistance* (Minneapolis: University of Minnesota Press, 2017), 245.

6 Thawing the Frozen Rights Theory: On Rejecting Interpretations of Reconciliation and Resurgence That Define Indigenous Peoples as Frozen in a Pre-colonial Past

AIMÉE CRAFT

> *Resurgence*
> *Revitalization*
> *Reclamation*
> *Reconciliation*
> *Regret*

"Re" as a prefix means "to go back or backwards."[1]

This chapter considers and problematizes two key concepts that brought together a group of Indigenous scholars in March 2017: *resurgence* and *reconciliation*.[2] Like other nouns, *resurgence* and *reconciliation* carry deep normative baggage that describe an occurrence, state, or action. Each has a diversity of meanings, applied and defined differently in various contexts and by different interveners, including scholars and activists, both Indigenous and non-Indigenous, as well as courts and governments. Their definitions and applications have been a site of contestation and celebration.

While the concepts of resurgence and reconciliation have been applied in ways that advance Indigenous thought and practice, at times these terms have been applied (including as used by courts in jurisprudence) in ways that anchor and fix Indigenous identities, cultures, and political and legal expressions in a distant pre-colonial past. Beginning with the concept of reconciliation, as applied in law, this chapter aims to problematize the adoption of reconciliation into Canadian law and political discourse. It is used in a way that is confused and multiple, and ultimately perpetuates and promotes the view that Indigenous expressions and ways of life exist only in relation to what we can collectively salvage from a past version of our collective selves. Resurgence, however, has remained anchored outside Canadian legal discourse, being assumed mostly by Indigenous activists and academics as a form of resistance married with reappropriation of culture, language, ceremony, lifeways, etc. I argue that since both terms have been adapted from colonial language and thought, and most explicitly as concepts derived from the English language, they can crystallize an assimilative (at best) or extinctionist (at worst) approach, while sounding very polite and conciliatory.

The language of reconciliation has been taken up by Canadian courts to define the relationship between Indigenous peoples and Canada in the "history of Canada's relationship with its Indigenous peoples." The Supreme Court of Canada has stated multiple times that the purpose of section 35 of the Canadian Constitution is to *reconcile* the prior occupation of lands by Indigenous people with asserted and assumed Canadian sovereignty. Justice Abella recalls that "the "grand purpose" of section 35 is "the reconciliation of Aboriginal and non-Aboriginal Canadians in a mutually respectful long-term relationship."[3] In addition, the court has invoked reconciliation in a variety of permutations to explain the reconciliation between Aboriginal culture, peoples, traditions, rights, perspectives, societies, prior occupation, and Crown and non-Aboriginal interests (the assertion of Crown sovereignty, Crown interests, other interests, broader society, the rest of Canadian society, the interests of all Canadians ...).

Beginning with the early section 35 jurisprudence on Aboriginal rights, in *Sparrow* and *Van der Peet*, the Supreme Court of Canada has contained the application of Aboriginal rights protection to practices and customs that are integral to the distinctive culture of groups. By distancing the doctrine of Aboriginal rights from self-determination, self-governance, inherency, and practices that emanate and derive from relationships with the land, the Court has limited the scope of constitutionally protected rights to the pre-contact and pre-colonial state of Indigenous peoples in Canada. While they admit that there is space for the "logical evolution" of a right, they limit the evolution to one that anchors itself in a pre-contact practice, with no room for an evolving and modern Indigenous practice without its past manifestation. This in turn supports the idea, often applied to Indigenous people by the state, that the only way to be authentically Indigenous is to return to the past. In turn, when the concepts of resurgence and revitalization of Indigenous life ways are used in the context of returning to ancestral ways, this lends support the law's preference for practices, customs, and traditions that existed prior to European contact, and subsequently more violence is done to Indigenous peoples' futurities.

To understand the law and interpret it, legal scholars look to linguistic understandings that illustrate the normative value contained in the word (known also as the plain meaning rule of interpretation). Put differently, the word tells us the law. For example, in Canadian constitutional law we invoke principles like federalism, the rule of law, or democracy, and the body of law follows the word. We consider plain language meanings and legislators' original intent in using certain terms. The law is also considered through purposive interpretation, an evaluation of the law's purpose and evolution of its enactment. The same interpretive method applies in an Indigenous context. We contemplate the use of particular words and consider their purpose and implications. Elder D'Arcy Linklater tells us that "law is in the language."[4] Words are important and they carry deep normative meaning. Referring to the use of legal concepts, Elder Harry Bone reminds us that "as long as you know the spirit of the law, that's what's important. The Supreme Court does that. That's the way it should be done."[5]

The use of the term *reconciliation* in common law jurisprudence effectively freezes Indigenous rights, thought, and practice in an idealized historical pre-colonial past. Correspondingly, the concept of resurgence can be misunderstood to invoke romanticized and essentialized ideas of Indigenous present and future, as a reflection of what can be reclaimed from this same static past. This is precisely why caution is required in applying colonial languages to the concepts that frame an Indigenous past, present, and future. Elder Harry Bone suggests that reconciliation should be defined within Indigenous nations as an articulation of our relationships with the Creator, our Mother the Earth, and with the people, as illustrated by the prayer in the pipe ceremony.[6]

To avoid the dangers that this use of language produces, Indigenous scholars, activists, and allies must exercise restraint in using state- (and court-) appropriated terminology to define our identities, cultures, governance, and law. I suggest that breathing life into our own languages allows Indigenous people to claim present and future *mino-bimaadiziiwin* (collective well-being), coupled with a forward-thinking pre-surgence that grounds itself in the emergence of contemporary Indigenous identities, thought, and practices that are inherently anti-colonial in their rejection of frozen identities and rights.

Reconciliation: Courts and Their Impoverished Understanding

When asked how to translate or frame reconciliation in Indigenous languages, the Elders explained to the Truth and Reconciliation Commission of Canada over the course of many days that there was no single word or concept that could equate with reconciliation as described in the English language. In part, the inability to adequately translate reconciliation into Indigenous languages is related to the inability to agree on the full normative implication of the term. For example, the TRC defines reconciliation as a long-term process of establishing and maintaining mutually respectful relationships, which requires "real societal change."[7] However, the Supreme Court of Canada's vision of reconciling is about the reconciliation of prior Indigenous occupation with the Crown's assumed sovereignty, while attempting to balance the interests of society as a whole with the interests of Indigenous peoples. This "balancing equation" has often resulted in the benefit to broader society outweighing Indigenous interests. Responding to the equational illogic, D'Arcy Vermette has explained, "Aboriginal systems must do all the reconciling."[8]

In a chapter I wrote for an edited volume on reconciliation,[9] I considered reconciliation from three perspectives, each of which would attach a range of normative obligations to a substantive duty of reconciliation. In contrasting the TRC's view, the Supreme Court of Canada's interpretation of reconciliation, and Indigenous conceptions,[10] it became evident that there was no agreement on what should constitute reconciliation.

As the SCC characterized Parliament's reconciliation agenda,

> The constitutional changes, the apologies for historic wrongs, a growing appreciation that Aboriginal and non-Aboriginal people are partners in Confederation, the Report of the Royal Commission on Aboriginal Peoples, and the Final Report of the Truth and Reconciliation Commission of Canada, all indicate that reconciliation with all of Canada's Aboriginal peoples is Parliament's goal.[11]

In its final report, the TRC explained that there are conflicting views between Crown perspectives and Indigenous understandings of reconciliation:

> Aboriginal peoples and the Crown have very different and conflicting views on what reconciliation is and how it is best achieved. The Government of Canada appears to believe that reconciliation entails Aboriginal peoples' accepting the reality and validity of Crown sovereignty and parliamentary supremacy in order to allow the government to get on with business. Aboriginal people, on the other hand, see reconciliation as an opportunity to affirm their own sovereignty and return to the "partnership" ambitions they held after Confederation.[12]

Through Supreme Court of Canada cases, the Canadian common law has characterized reconciliation as a project,[13] goal,[14] objective,[15] principle,[16] promise,[17] and something to be "achieved"[18] between Indigenous people and non-Indigenous communities. However, the Court does not

Table 6.1. Phrasing permutations of the SCC's use of the term *reconciliation*[19]

Reconciliation of Aboriginal	Culture Peoples Traditions Entitlements Interests Territorial claims Rights Perspectives Societies Prior occupation of North America	with	Assertion of Crown sovereignty Crown sovereignty over (Canadian) territory Crown interests Other interests Non-Aboriginal interests Non-Aboriginal peoples Common law perspective Arrival of Europeans Broader political community Broader society Larger Canadian society of which they are a part Rest of Canadian society Broader social, political, and economic community Other societal rights Interests of all Canadians Canadian sovereignty

explicitly define reconciliation in any of its decisions. Table 6.1 illustrates how the Court has used the concept of reconciliation to attempt to legally justify assumed sovereignty over Indigenous peoples and lands and render assumed sovereignty complete.

As I have previously argued,[20] the SCC's characterization of reconciliation arises from jurisprudence on treaty and Aboriginal title and rights claims, more particularly in the context of justifying the infringement of those rights. The doctrine of justification balances Indigenous rights against "broader societal interests," and Indigenous interests are often seen as subordinate to potential "interference" with Crown sovereignty. This approach is problematic because it continuously subjects Indigenous peoples to "Canada's ongoing exercise of achieving reconciliation between its Aboriginal peoples and the broader population,"[21] to the detriment of long-term collective Indigenous interests. In fact, it allows for a continual doctrinal slippage away from the recognition of rights and betrays a progressive judicial orientation against Indigenous sovereignty in Canada. Unpacked, the SCC's approach to reconciliation is centred on the things that Indigenous people must compromise, in favour of non-Indigenous societal, political, economic, and legal interests. By employing these colonial legal concepts and values, a narrow interpretation of reconciliation emerges, which positions Indigenous people and their "cultural rights" (the lens through which the SCC has defined

Aboriginal rights) at a significant disadvantage, without a constitutionally explicit limitation clause.[22]

Section 35 of the Constitution Act 1982 recognizes and affirms existing treaty and Aboriginal rights. But as interpreted by the courts, only those rights that were not extinguished by unilateral actions of the Crown (provincial or federal) prior to 1982 and are grounded in practices, customs, and traditions that date prior to contact received constitutional protection. In practice, this means three things. First, that the premise of extinguishment of rights (meaning the culture, practices, and traditions of Indigenous people) were subject to unilateral extinguishment by the Crown prior to 1982 and the enshrinement of rights in the constitution. Second, only practices that date back prior to contact can be afforded constitutional protection. Third, these rights are frozen in time and in scope, allowed to evolve only in accordance with a "logical evolution" of the original practice, without regard to how the practice had evolved prior to contact. Snyder, Napoleon, and Borrows have expressly rejected originalist interpretations of law that freeze and romanticize the past at the expense of discourse.[23] They alert us to the universal recognition that tradition is not neutral and can be purposefully deployed to discipline and morally police Indigenous women.[24]

The test for proving an Aboriginal right, for example, requires that the right be a practice, custom, or tradition that is integral to the distinctive culture of the Indigenous group, at the time of contact. This has been termed the "frozen rights" theory. This strict framing of rights has been relaxed slightly to allow for "logical evolution" of the right. However, this evolution is limited to what is connected to a pre-contact practice. "Logical evolution means the same sort of activity, carried on in the modern economy by modern means. This prevents aboriginal rights from being unfairly confined simply by changes in the economy and technology. But the activity must be essentially the same. 'While treaty rights are capable of evolution within limits, ... their subject matter ... cannot be wholly transformed'" (*Marshall 2*, at para. 19).[25] Furthermore, the framing of these rights generally recognizes men's practices and excludes the important work of women as past and ongoing dimensions of Indigenous economies and ways of life.

Similarly treaties have been interpreted into a narrow, pre-treaty conception of practices (like hunting, trapping, and fishing) that governments were able to extinguish or unilaterally modify, without the consent of treaty partners. I think, for example, of the SCC's decision in the *Badger* case that the 1930s Natural Resources Transfer Agreements with the Prairie provinces merged and consolidated any commercial rights that might have been contained in the numbered treaties.[26]

Furthermore, where historic treaties were entered into that preserved a commercial right, the modern interpretation of the right is limited to a moderate livelihood. The right is limited in its commercial dimension to working "for a living through continuing access to fish and wildlife to trade for 'necessaries.'"[27] This illustrates the bias in colonial interpretations of law that would make it impossible to equate a historic right to a modern right of Indigenous people to become wealthy. It limits the conception of a right to one of "survival."

In essence, the constitutional law that is meant to "recognize and affirm," further distilled, is about bringing Indigenous people back to time before European contact or sovereignty. It romanticizes an Indigenous past that often remains beyond the reach of contemporary Indigenous aspirations. It subjects the protections articulated by section 35 to the underlying theory that what is to be protected existed only before settlement, "sovereignty," and contact, as though Indigenous people were not already and constantly evolving and adapting prior to contact with Europeans.

Thus this application of reconciliation in Canadian law is a concept that enhances state sovereignty and confirms only the historic nature of the exercise of Indigenous lifeways. When used by the state and/or Indigenous peoples, it risks the unintentional adoption or replication of a frozen rights theory onto Indigenous futures. The concept of reconciliation, as applied in a Canadian context, does not emanate from Indigenous thought or practice. It is a legal, academic, and social construction that propagates the undercurrent of political and legal colonial thought in Canada that aims to freeze Indigenous rights to the point of contact, assumed Crown sovereignty, or, in the case of the Métis, after the moment of effective political and legal control. Reconciliation, as applied, assumes that the state of being Indigenous is defined by contact with settlers and that the core of an Indigenous person's ongoing experience in the world must replicate what that person's ancestors were doing at the time of that contact.

Resurgence: Indigenous Thought and Practice as a Pre-contact Relic

It is difficult to draw a direct analogy between reconciliation and resurgence, since the term *resurgence* has not been used by courts in relation to Indigenous peoples. However, the current discourse in legal scholarship picks up both terms.

John Borrows has argued, "There is persuasive precedent in Canadian law recognizing the pre-existence of Aboriginal rights and their associated laws. Furthermore, the courts have created an opportunity to receive these laws into Canadian law by analogy and through *sui generis* principles. These principles must be allowed to influence the development of law in Canada. When First Nations laws are received more fully into Canadian law, both systems will be strengthened."[28]

More recently, Borrows and Tully have described reconciliation and resurgence as having become "ways of describing the field of activities, relationships, and possible futures between Indigenous and settler people," while acknowledging that the terms themselves "are continuously contested and reformulated in practice, policy, and academic research. Thus practice-based struggles over reconciliation and resurgence are also struggles over the meanings of the terms themselves."[29] Borrows marries the concepts of Indigenous legal resurgence to a process of facilitating reconciliation with the earth.[30]

Leanne Simpson, a leading author and thinker in resurgence, admits "the word resurgence is now used in all kinds of ways, some of which feed nicely into discourses around reconciliation and neoliberalism, and others that remain in critical opposition to both."[31]

While the SCC does not build resurgence into the construction of section 35, Chief Justice McLachlin (as she then was) spoke to the concept of resurgence in the context of civil liberties and the potential for the state to infringe upon those liberties in a justified manner.

> To lose our liberties is to lose our sense of who we are. Our civil liberties are not accidental accretions borrowed from foreign civilizations. They are deeply rooted in Canada's own unique history. We cannot deny them without denying our history and ourselves. From time to time in our histories, these values have been challenged. Sometimes, for years at a time, they have been put aside. Yet they have always resurged. They have survived the tests of time, and define what we are – peoples of a free society possessed of rights that can be limited, yes, but only if the state can justify the limitation in terms of the greater public good.[32]

McLachlin's speech promotes the idea that we can bring historical practices back and then subject the exercise of those practices to the state's ability to infringe upon them, for the greater public good. This bears a conceptual resemblance to the SCC's approach to reconciliation as an instrument to justify infringements of section 35's constitutionally protected rights and to the approach to the constitutional protection of only historical practices that are integral to the pre-contact practice of Indigenous peoples.

The discourses of resurgence emerging from scholarly literature and grassroots movements are aimed at reclamation and revitalization of

Indigenous ways of being and knowing. Particular focus has narrowed onto language, land-based practices, harvesting, culture, ceremonies, laws, and governance, etc. My comment is less on the practices of re-surgence, reclamation, and revitalization and more about how we *frame* them using English terms that essentialize and reify a state of Indigenous "pastness" as a current standard that Indigenous people have internalized or weaponized against each other.

By taking up state and legally sponsored narratives of resurgence, re-vitalization, and reclamation, we risk framing our existence as retrospective and frozen in a past idealized sense of indigeneity. Too often the "authenticity" of our actions (or words) is weighed against how closely tied our practice is to the "way things used to be done" or "what our ancestors did." This has been used as a means to exclude our own, and sometimes ourselves from being, living and evolving as Indigenous people. In some cases, our acts of reclamation through learning, experiencing, and discovering are used to position us against the other, through claims of superiority and authenticity. We (often unwittingly and unwillingly) replicate systems of oppression that have been transmitted through systems of assimilation that were imposed on us. In this way, we risk adopting an assimilationist agenda that promotes keeping all that is Indigenous in the past, or like the past, which helps to legitimize state claims over Indigenous territories.

While acts of resurgence can be framed as important political demonstrations that support and affirm Indigenous jurisdiction, self-determination, and self-governance, a collective intellectual consciousness must shine a light on the potential danger of framing resurgence and revitalization as a reclamation of the past. Some might not agree with this view, claiming that the only way to make up for what was *taken* from Indigenous people is to *reclaim* it. But I ask, Was it every really *owned?* Was Indigenous thought, language, song, ceremony ours to barter or trade, kept to the exclusion of others? Or has all of it always belonged to creation?[33] Colonial thought has treated and continues to treat Indigenous *giikendaasowin* (knowledge, values, and ways) as something that can be removed or discarded, in favour of non-Indigenous knowledge values and ways. And where it serves a colonial, economic, or aesthetic purpose, it can be appropriated. By responding to what colonization has attempted to take from Indigenous people by simply taking it back as though it was a possession perpetuates the violence inflicted by colonialism itself.

Indigenous Conceptions of Pre-surgence

Indigenous thought, practice, and way of life is always subjected to the "Re." As demonstrated throughout this chapter, the concepts of reconciliation and resurgence are derived from colonial languages that allow for the malleability of the normative obligations and responsibilities that flow from their interpretation and understanding. These terms and their associated etymology are not Indigenous, and while we may invest in their redefinition or appropriate them for Indigenous purposes, there is reason to be cautious. Elder Isbobel White reminds us of the cautious approach, "*weweni.*" We sometimes think of this term as a call to act cautiously or to do things in a good way. However, at its core, it reflects a fundamental Anishinaabe instruction to walk gently in this world.

Cree political science scholar Kiera Ladner refers to reconciliation as understood and operationalized in Indigenous conceptions such as *miyo pimat'siwin* or "living collectively in accordance within an ecological contextuality, or an ethical relationality, like what grounds Nehiyaw (Cree) teachings, practices, ethics and philosophy."[34] Given the problematic nature of the use of reconciliation by courts, and the potential to import that political and legal baggage into the concept of resurgence and revitalization, I suggest that we should use Indigenous languages to frame practices that are relational and responsive to our current circumstances. Mary Deleary proposes that "we are talking about our relationship, our relationship to one another and our responsibilities as Anishinaabe people first because that's our first responsibility is to ourselves, our nations of people. And then we have another responsibility because we are responsible too for this land, our land and all of our relatives on this land."[35]

Rather than using English terms, which import normative baggage that does not serve Indigenous future interests, we should utilize Indigenous languages to ground practices and thought. They must be accompanied by a focused construction of Indigenous futures that are responsive to the past and deeply engage with what it means to be well in a modern Indigenous sense, while rejecting the colonial weight of being defined by pre-contact or pre-colonial identities. In conversation with Elder Sherry Copenace, we were imagining what Anishinaabemowin words could replace the concepts of reconciliation, resurgence, revitalization, and reclamation, while keeping their best intent. She suggested *kaanwayiing*, which is our breath, or the sound of our language. In this way, our language gives us the tools to explain more fully what we mean when we wish to live well collectively into the future.

The purpose of using reconciliation and resurgence as concepts is ultimately to ensure a future way of life for Indigenous people. In reflecting on radical resurgence and grounded normativity, Leanne Simpson states, "Indigenous futures are entirely dependent upon what we collectively do now as diverse Indigenous nations, with our Ancestors and those yet unborn, to create Indigenous presences and to generate the conditions for Indigenous futures by deeply engaging in our nation-based grounded normativities. We must continuously build and rebuild Indigenous worlds. This work starts in motion, in decolonial love, in flight, in relationship, in biiskbiyang, in generosity, humility and kindness, and this is where it also ends."[36]

Similarly, Elder Mary Deleary explains that creating balance is the objective: "Reconciliation must continue in ways that honour the ancestors, respect the land, and rebalance relationships."[37] Responsibilities do not begin and end with human relationships, and balance needs to be restored with the land and all other beings in creation with whom we are related. Elders continue to teach us that reconciliation has to take place with the earth, our mother, before it can happen between people. We find guidance for this within many Indigenous legal systems.[38] When reflecting on the importance of water, Elder Peter Atkinson remarked, "We are responsible to each other and the land."[39]

No Elder, knowledge-keeper, or *gitizi-m'inaanik* has ever said to me that we should try to be the exact way we used to be. To the contrary, all wisdom that I have been gifted has encouraged evolution, assuming responsibility and relationships. This is at the foundation of our legal orders. In addition, Anishinaabe Elders have expressed that Anishinaabe law is not a theory. It is a way of life.[40]

Elder Allan White shared that law is about living it and sharing it with each other: "We are actually living it. It's very important to give every little bit of what we know. Law is all around us."[41] This affirmation is at the core of the discord between the intellectual exercise of theorizing about resurgence and reconciliation and roots itself in a relational paradigm that calls for a deep humility of thought, practice, and expression. We are simply living, in response to our relationships, as multiple and complex as they are. I think here of relationships with our families (biological, extended, ceremonial, chosen, etc.), to our land and waters, with our ancestors and our histories, with our languages, to those who are yet to come and who sit and watch us as we prepare what we will leave for them.

Conclusion

The claim I make in this chapter is bold. Its purpose is to dispel the myth of the past tense. I am rejecting "re" language as it applies to Indigenous thought, actions, bodies, politics, and language in ways that constrict Indigenous people to the past, as defined by colonial contact as the time in which Indigenous identities are validated. As argued above, the adoption into Indigenous thought of the prefix *re* can generate a fixed notion of time and identity. It supports the ways in which Canadian law grasps at the past as the marker of what Indigenous rights are and should be.

However, what *used to be* is not an Indigenous benchmark. The frozen rights approach was imposed through a system of thinking that was designed to assimilate or exterminate Indigenous peoples in Canada. Yet it seems to have been (at least partially) internalized in Indigenous political thought. To try to live in an ahistorical frozen past is to be complicit in cultural genocide.

However, as I have argued elsewhere, "The substance and scope of reconciliation remains contested by many Indigenous people who argue that genuine reconciliation must be anchored in revitalization, resurgence, resistance, and reclamation, through grounded normativity and practices that revalue Indigenous ways of knowing and being. This includes living and rebuilding Indigenous legal traditions, which are embedded in profound understandings of relationship."[42] I see now how much "re" language I used in this one paragraph. And I do not intend to discard the concepts and application of the terms *reconciliation* or *resurgence*, as properly defined, with Indigenous futures firmly embedded in their legal and political normative.

The TRC concludes, "Aboriginal peoples need to become the law's architects and interpreters where it applies to their collective rights and interests."[43] Reconciliation must make space for Indigenous resurgence outside the parameters of the relationship with non-Indigenous Canada. One mechanism for that resurgence is the revitalization of Indigenous legal principles, through Indigenous languages. These laws were part of forging the original relationships between Indigenous people and settlers to this territory, and confirmed by making treaties. This resurgence must support the dismantling of colonial systems of oppression and the rebuilding of Indigenous nations' legal systems. Maria Campbell has said, "I don't believe that it should be about them anymore. Every single time we get together it's always about them, we have to figure out how we are going to forgive them, how we are going to reconcile with them, how are we going to do all of these things with them. If they care about where we are at, they will help support and nurture the work that we are doing."[44]

Acknowledging and applying Indigenous laws and systems of thought is not just about exploring or discussing them, but rather about being able to actually put them into practice. Anishinaabe law is not a full code of laws but a body of principles for living a good life. The constitutional principles attached to that law are found in our drums, songs, stories, and pipes.[45] While we may not realize our values perfectly, they underlie our systems of thought, views of the world, and responsibilities that we have towards one another.

We are instructed to *apply*, not theorize, so as to live a way of life. This does not mean only framing and understanding our identities on the basis of the past but to be future-thinking. Like everything, the application of law must be balanced with awareness, knowledge, and lived experience. We cannot voluntarily or implicitly freeze ourselves in the past. No person or nation has achieved wellness by replicating the past (although admittedly, the past is an important consideration when thinking about the future – it just cannot define or constrict it).

Our late Uncle Charlie sang a beautiful resiliency song of a horse rider whose family and community has been devastated by war. With everyone dead around him, his horse he tells the rider to walk with him and to only look forward. I take this song to mean that in the face of the most devastating experience (the loss of family), we must think of what we will build for the future. The horse and the rider did not stay and rebuild around their loss, but rather rode together, towards what they would build. The rider had with him a bundle of ceremony, language, knowledge, and love. These were his tools of building.

Today we are standing with the horse. My hope is that we can break free of interpretations and concepts that limit us to a pre-colonial past. I also hope that we can continue to breathe life into our collective wellness as our defining ethos as we create our desired futures.

NOTES

1 Merriam-Webster online.
2 In March 2017, the NCTR partnered with the University of Victoria to hold a symposium co-chaired by Heidi Stark and me. This was an opportunity to think through some of the challenges to developing resurgence discourse in an era of reconciliation. We gathered Indigenous scholars in Indigenous studies, political science, and law to have meaningful and frank discussions about the concepts of resurgence (which have begun to emerge in the scholarly literature and grassroots movements), and contrasted it with systemic and institutional approaches that aim to submerge society into a state of reconciliation.
3 *Daniels v Canada* 2016 SCC 12, [2016] 1 SCR 99 at para 34.
4 D'Arcy Linklater, Harry Bone, and the Treaty & Dakota Elders of Manitoba, with contributions by the AMC Council of Elders, *KA'ESI WAHKOTUMAHK ASKI, Our Relations with the Land: Treaty Elders' Teachings*, vol. 2 (Winnipeg: Treaty Relations Commission of Manitoba and Assembly of Manitoba Chiefs Secretariat, 2014), 11.

5 Anishinaabe nibi inaakonigewin, *Report on Elders Gathering* (Winnipeg: Centre for Human Rights Research, 2014), 13.

6 See Aimée Craft, "Neither Infringement Nor Justification: The SCC's Mistaken Approach to Reconciliation," in *Renewing Relationships: Indigenous Peoples and Canada*, ed. B. Gunn and K. Drake, 59–82 (Saskatoon: University of Saskatchewan Native Law Centre, 2019).

7 Truth and Reconciliation Commission of Canada, *The Final Report of the Truth and Reconciliation Commission of Canada* (Montreal and Kingston: McGill-Queen's University Press, 2015), 6:11–12.

8 D'Arcy Vermette, "Dyzzing Dialogue: Canadian Courts and the Continuing Justification of the Dispossession of Aboriginal Peoples," *Windsor Yearbook of Access to Justice* 29 (2011): 61.

9 A. Craft, "Neither Infringement Nor Justification: The SCC's Mistaken Approach to Reconciliation," in *Renewing Relationships: Indigenous Peoples and Canada*, ed. B. Gunn and K. Drake (Saskatoon: University of Saskatchewan Native Law Centre, 2019), 59–82.

10 In most Indigenous languages, there is no singular word that would translate or relate the concept of reconciliation. Elders and knowledge-keepers told the TRC that "there are many words, stories, and songs, as well as sacred objects such as wampum belts, peace pipes, eagle down, cedar boughs, drums, and regalia that are used to establish relationships, repair conflicts, restore harmony, and make peace. The ceremonies and protocols of Indigenous law are still remembered and practiced in many Aboriginal communities." Truth and Reconciliation Commission of Canada, *What We Have Learned: Principles of Truth and Reconciliation* (Ottawa: TRC, 2015), 12.

11 *Daniels v Canada*, at para 37.

12 Truth and Reconciliation Commission of Canada, *Final Report*, 6:9.

13 *Manitoba Metis Federation v Canada (AG)* 2013 SCC 14, [2013] 1 SCR 623 at para 99 [*MMF*]; *Tsilhqot'in v British Columbia* 2014 SCC 44, [2014] 2 SCR 257 at para 23; *Ktunaxa Nation v British Columbia* (Forests, Lands and Natural Resource Operations), 2017 SCC 54 at para 89 [*Ktunaxa Nation*].

14 *R v Van der Peet*, [1996] 2 SCR 507 at para 310 [*Van der Peet*]; *Haida Nation v British Columbia (Minister of Forests)* 2004 SCC 73, [2004] 3 SCR 511 at para 35; *Mikisew Cree Nation v Canada (Minister of Canadian Heritage)* 2005 SCC 69, [2005] 3 SCR 388 at para 33; *Rio Tinto Alcan Inc v Carrier Sekani Tribal Council* 2010 SCC 43, [2010] 2 SCR 650 at para 34; *MMF* at paras 137 and 140; *Tsilqot'in* at para 82.

15 *Mikisew* at para 50; *Beckman* at paras 91, 103, 107, and 203.

16 *MMF* at para 143.

17 *R v Kapp* 2008 SCC 41, [2008] 2 SCR 483 at para 121 [*Kapp*].

18 *Ktunaxa Nation*.

19 Reproduced from Craft, "Neither Infringement Nor Justification," 59–82.

20 Craft, "Neither Infringement Nor Justification."
21 *Alberta (Aboriginal Affairs and Northern Development) v Cunningham* 2011 SCC 37, [2011] 2 SCR 670 at para 86.
22 Vermette, "Dyzzing Dialogue," 59.
23 Emily Snyder, Val Napoleon, and John Borrows, "Gender and Violence: Drawing on Indigenous Legal Resources," *UBC Law Review* 48 (2015): 593; John Borrows, "(Ab)Originalism and Canada's Constitution," *Supreme Court Law Review* 58 (2012): 360.
24 Snyder, Napoleon, and Borrows, "Gender and Violence," 593.
25 *R v Marshall*, [1999] 3 SCR 533 [*Marshall 2*] at para 19; *R v Bernard*, 2005 SCC 43, [2005] 2 SCR 220 at para 25.
26 *R v Badger* [1996] 1 SCR 771.
27 *Marshall 2* at para 4.
28 John Borrows, *Recovering Canada: The Resurgence of Indigenous Law* (Toronto: University of Toronto Press, 2002), 27.
29 Michael Asch, John Borrows, and James Tully, eds., *Resurgence and Reconciliation: Indigenous-Settler Relations and Earth Teachings* (Toronto: University of Toronto Press, 2018).
30 John Borrows, "Earth-Bound: Indigenous Resurgence and Environmental Reconciliation," in Asch, Borrows and Tully, *Resurgence and Reconciliation*, 50.
31 L. Simpson, *As We Have Always Done: Indigenous Freedom through Radical Resistance* (Minneapolis: University of Minnesota Press, 2017), 48.
32 "Remarks of the Right Honourable Beverley McLachlin," Symons Lecture, Charlottetown, PEI, 21 October 21, 2008.
33 For a discussion on my views of cultural appropriation, see my chapter "Look at Your 'Pantses': The Art of Wearing and Representing Indigenous Culture as Performative Relationship," in *Cultural Appropriation and Indigenous Issues*, ed. Kent McNeil and John Borrows (Toronto: University of Toronto Press, 2022).
34 Kiera Ladner, "Proceed with Caution: Reflections on Resurgence and Reconciliation," in Asch, Borrows, and Tully, *Resurgence and Reconciliation*, 243.
35 Mary Deleary, "Statement to the Truth and Reconciliation Commission of Canada," TRC Forum on Reconciliation, Elders and Knowledge-Keepers, Winnipeg, June 2014.
36 L. Betasamosake Simpson, *As We Have Always Done* (Minneapolis: University of Minnesota Press, 2017), 246.
37 Truth and Reconciliation Commission, *What We Have Learned*, 5.
38 Doris Pratt, Harry Bone, and the Treaty and Dakota Elders of Manitoba, with contributions by the Assembly of Manitoba Chiefs Council of Elders, *UNTUWE PI KIN HEntuwe: Who We Are: Treaty Elders' Teachings*, vol. 1 (Winnipeg: Treaty Relations Commission of Manitoba and Assembly of Manitoba Chiefs, 2014); Linklater, Bone, and Treaty and Dakota Elders of Manitoba,

KA'ESI WAHKOTUMAHK ASKI; Joe Hyslop, Harry Bone, and the Treaty and Dakota Elders of Manitoba, with contributions by the Assembly of Manitoba Chiefs Council of Elders, *Dtantu Balai Betl Nahidei: Our Relations to the Newcomers,* vol. 3 (Winnipeg: Treaty Relations Commission of Manitoba and Assembly of Manitoba Chiefs, 2015).

39 Aimée Craft, *Anishinaabe Nibi Inaakonigewin Report,* 2014, 9. https://papers.ssrn.com/sol3/papers.cfm?abstract_id=3433235.

40 Craft, *Anishinaabe Nibi Inaakonigewin Report,* 9.

41 Craft, *Anishinaabe Nibi Inaakonigewin Report,* 8.

42 Aimée Craft, "Broken Trust: Finding Our Way out of the Damaged Relationship through the Rebuilding of Indigenous Legal Institutions," in Law Society of Upper Canada, *Canada at 150: The Charter and the Constitution* (Toronto: Irwin Law, 2017), 380.

43 Truth and Reconciliation, *Final Report,* 6:51.

44 Maria Campbell, "Statement to the Truth and Reconciliation Commission of Canada," TRC Forum on Reconciliation, Elders and Knowledge-Keepers, Winnipeg, MB, June 2014.

45 A. Craft, "Giving and Receiving Life from Anishinaabe Nibi Inaakonigewin (Our Water Law) Research," in *Methodological Challenges in Nature-Culture and Environmental History Research,* ed. Jocelyn Thorpe, Stephanie Rutherford, and L. Anders Sandberg (New York: Routledge, 2016), 116, 118.

7 Nêhiyaw Hunting Pedagogies and Revitalizing Indigenous Laws

DARCY LINDBERG

Then after ... we use the moose's brain, from the moose's head.... [W]e stir that brain vigorously.... We don't stop stir[ring].... [A]t long last it begins to cook.... Then I spread that entire brain of his all over; I move it all around. I work the whole hide around so that that will be enough.

Omushkego Nêhiyaw elder Sophie Gunner, teaching how brains make things soft – in this case, tanning hides[1]

Peyak (One): Methodologies of Harvesting Moose

There are many *nêhiyaw*[2] ways to hunt moose. There are very old required legal teachings, each passed down through families and communities, learned through the patient experience of preparing to take a life. Just as these ways depend upon the repetition of footsteps on prairies and through muskeg and bush, they also rest upon the recollection of songs and stories, and upon the guidance of ceremonies. For those who continue to practise these legal practices, the hunt starts long before the bush. It is initiated through offerings and dreams[3] as the people begin to come to terms with harming a relative. All of this is entering into a relationship of reciprocity. All of this is continuing a relationship with nêhiyaw law, with similar application to harvesting our *paskwa-mostos* (buffalo), *amisk* (beaver) or *kinisew* (fish) relations.[4] Proper adherence to these laws teaches how to respect the moose's life and how to continue on with our lives in *kwayaskosowin* (doing things in a correct way), fulfilling obligations towards *miyo wicehtowin* (good relations).

Once a moose has given its life to you – for you[5] – there are many nêhiyaw ways to prepare moose. The initial frenzy of dressing a moose (removing its organs and guts, quartering and removing the meat, and skinning) dissipates and gives way to the slow, hard work of making the most of the life you just took. You have become obligated.[6] Making use of the meat and the organs is the easier and exciting work. The bones are harder. They can be cracked open for marrow, filled with grease from the fatty parts of the moose, or saved for soup. The very committed convert the bones into tools for scraping. The moose hide – seemingly growing heavier by the hour with your responsibilities – must be stretched until it is almost as taut as a drum. The tighter it is, the easier the scraping becomes. Scraping moose hide is tough work. The older ones have developed a hidden strength for this hardest work – a strength they have built through hours of clutching and moving scrapers on rough rawhide, convincing tufts of hair that it is okay to fall away. Eventually it relents and gives way to its new life, maybe as a drum, part of a *mikiwap* (teepee), or a pair of moccasins.

And then there is the process of using the brain to tan the hide. The old ones know the best tricks, how to use the brain to make hard things soft. It is just like in law or in academia: "the brain is the magic ingredient ... that makes everything happen."[7] After the brain is cooked it is smoothed all over the hide, it is worked in slowly yet persistently until, as experienced hands know, the transformation is complete. Young hands (no, young minds) are easily defeated in this process and are prone to slowing or giving up entirely. It is the old ones who bring us back to this work and teach us that learning to grasp these old tools and these laws is form of resistance, a ceremony. And slowly but surely, we eventually become those old ones.

There are many other, non-nêhiyaw ways to hunt and to harvest a moose. In Alberta, you are required to buy a licence and can hunt moose only when they are in season.[8] You are required to remove and care for the edible portions of the moose from its body, except those that are damaged in the hunt. You must use weapons that ensure that a moose dies quickly. You must report your successful hunt to provincial authorities. So there too are obligations. These obligations are silent on any requirement regarding the hide, the bones, or the brain. There is no indication that story or song is contemplated, no ceremonies are required for those taking a life, according to Alberta law.

Niso (Two): Only the Best Cuts – Resisting the "Supermarket" of Indigenous Legal Orders

Reflecting on these older ways of nêhiyaw life, I acknowledge that force is sometimes necessary in *nêhiyaw pimatisiwin* (Cree way of life), as it is in the day-to-day lives of people within all societies. We use it every day for survival. We kill to ensure our needs for sustenance are met. We kill the moose we hunt, and the slaughterhouse attendant kills far away from our eyes long before the chicken, cow, or pig shows up on our grocery shelves. Force touches the cedar, the cottonwood, and the oak felled to make our walls, our tables, and our centre poles. It touches the stone crushed to make our pavement, or carved to make our pipe bowls.

Of course, more force is used in our world than necessary. When I claim that it is necessary, I do not promulgate the use of force (or violence). Rather I acknowledge its presence and have a clear vision of the forces that mediate it in our lives: to better account for it; to relate to those who are subject to our force and to recognize its effects;[9] to fully contemplate the use of our ceremonies as relational tools to seek consent for these transformations; and to teach how we can include our animal, plant, and other relatives in our deliberations on their uses. Developing practices of *wahkotowin* (kinship) in this manner requires understanding the limits of our need to take the lives of our non-human kin. Contemplating this necessity, I also think about power relations, ideas of volition and consent, and when such transformational acts become violence. I think about whether the violence is necessary to live. I think of how our ceremonies seek consent for the forceful transformations of the relations that will nourish us, and how our obligations to our animal relations after we have taken their lives fulfils the promise of our ceremonies.

All of these contemplations relate to the implications of the transforming relationship between Indigenous legal orders and Canadian legal institutions, specifically law schools and Canadian courts. The remainder of this chapter will explore this relationship with these two institutions specifically, and how nêhiyaw harvesting pedagogies offer an avenue to advocate how law schools and court processes can approach Indigenous laws generally. Just like the differences in obligations to moose found within nêhiyaw and Alberta law respectively, the Western socio-legal approaches to Indigenous legal orders have a myopic view of reciprocal obligations to the people, beings, and institutions inspirited with law that it relies upon for its legal processes to operate.[10] One cause of this this myopia is its tendency to recognize the legal principles and processes within Indigenous law that mimic approaches of Western legal systems, while failing to recognize those that share little or no commonalities. Further, because Canadian jurisprudence tends to decontextualize law from the social practices and events in which it arises, it seeks similar decontextualization within Indigenous law. As John Borrows notes, Canadian jurisprudence often overlooks "the broader social function of Canadian law" by unmooring legal reasoning from its "cultural contexts," thus providing the false notion that Canadian law exists almost primarily within a positivistic, declarative field.[11] Thus, obtaining and gifting for the use of knowledge is a foreign concept within the Canadian legal system, let alone a commitment to engaging in the nuances of such processes like that within nêhiyaw harvesting pedagogies.

While Indigenous legal orders and constitutionalism have not gone anywhere since European contact and the colonization of Indigenous territories within Canada, this generation of Canadians may be the first to *think* of Indigenous laws in a widescale manner. This raises significant issues in how Indigenous law is received, translated, implemented, and, at its most basic, theoretically understood.[12] A product of the growth of Indigenous legal orders within the academic and professional spheres of a non-Indigenous Canadian public is the natural tendency and temptation to use only the "best meat" of Indigenous laws. When this temptation is indulged, it results in law schools using only the legal principles that are easily translatable into Canadian legal processes, relying only on ones that are simple to understand from the Western pedagogical perspective, or being drawn to legal processes that fit within the idealization of Indigenous peoples and cultures generally as always healing or restorative.

Indigenous communities face this temptation when bringing legal knowledge into these institutions. They need the non-Indigenous Canadian public to consider, understand, and take Indigenous laws seriously, but while maintaining the integrity of legal systems and processes, practitioners and teachers of Indigenous legal orders must be vigilant that their work does not feed into this temptation. Nêhiyaw harvesting pedagogies offer one pathway to guide law professors, lawyers, judges, and researchers towards deeper understandings of the workings of Indigenous legal knowledge systems. Essential to this guidance is an understanding that nêhiyaw legal processes operate according to protocol and obligation, which ensure that law remains intertwined with other social institutions such as stories, songs, ceremonies, bundles, artistic renderings, kinship ordering, land/water relationships, and elders. "Engaging robustly and respectfully with Indigenous legal traditions ... clearly requires more than just identifying and articulating legal principles"[13] so there is an obligation for Canadian law to recognize Indigenous legal institutions alongside the utilization of Indigenous law within its reasoning. Without the use of the full institutional process that resides within Indigenous legal orders, legal principles used within law school or Canadian courtrooms may just become "a superficial resemblance to the original."[14] While it is instinctive for outsiders of an Indigenous legal order to gravitate towards the translatable portions of legal principles, there needs to be a commitment to understanding and upholding the deeper obligations to the systems of legal knowledge with Indigenous societies.

Avoiding the Temptation of "Taking Only the Best Meat" in Law Schools

In September 2018 the inaugural cohort of the combined common law/ Indigenous legal orders degree (the JD/JID) began studies at the University of Victoria. Students were provided introductions to Indigenous legal orders, alongside traditional common law teachings. The launch of the JD/JID is occurring during the extensive growth of Indigenous law teachings in law schools generally, with law faculties at University of Victoria, University of Alberta, University of British Columbia, University of Saskatchewan, Lakehead University, Osgoode Hall, University of Toronto, University of Ottawa, and Dalhousie University (amongst others) teaching Indigenous legal orders.[15] The demography of law schools generally provides an additional challenge to course development and class pedagogy. The overwhelming majority of law students enrolling in these courses are non-Indigenous.[16] Aside from intelligibility and translatability, issues of quite simply understanding Indigenous histories, norms, and practices arise in these teaching situations where they rarely arise within common and civil law courses. As law remains moored to cultural and social norms, while Indigenous legal principles may be easily comprehended by law students, the underpinning social norms that give Indigenous law vitality may remain hidden, or worse, discounted by law students because of different forms of reasoning that give rise to law. A common example is the use of origin or creation stories by many Indigenous societies to set out constitutional or legal principles. As such stories often contain fantastical elements, beings with magical or mystical qualities, or story arcs that are folklore-like (from a Western gaze), legal reasoning based on origin stories may be questioned.[17] Further, the "outsider-in" approach that law schools must take means that law sourced from spiritual, sacred, and natural elements is largely diminished or distorted in academic pedagogies.

Thus the ability to access legal resources from Indigenous social practices remains a challenge in the academic study of Indigenous law. Hadley Friedland identifies three general categories of legal resources according to their accessibility and availability: "(1) resources that require deep knowledge and full cultural immersion; (2) resources that require some community connection; and (3) resources that are publicly available."[18] Resources that require deep knowledge and full cultural immersion include laws embedded within a "language, dreams, dances, art, beadwork, pots, petroglyphs, scrolls, songs, natural landscapes, ceremonies, feasts, formal customs and protocols."[19] Resources that require some community connection include laws embedded in "stories, communally owned oral traditions, information from knowledgeable community and family members ... as well as personal knowledge and memories."[20] Resources that are publicly available include "published resources" such as "academic works, and works of fiction by community members, descriptive academic work by outsiders ... published court cases, [and] trial transcripts."[21] Thus "the most ideal resources" – those intertwined with ceremony, songs and language – "are likely the least available at this time, while the least ideal resources," such as stories and published resources, "are the most available."[22]

The initial trend within law schools is to rely upon a few methodologies (all three that overlap each other) to teach Indigenous legal principles. An initial avenue has been the modified case-brief method that has been developed and utilized by the Indigenous Laws Research Unit at the University of Victoria. This methodology relies on the synthesis of case analyses of stories to identify and restate legal principles within Indigenous social orders. Understanding that multiple analyses are needed, researchers immerse themselves within the stories of the community. This strategy aims to have researchers discover trends within the normative practice of the community, leading them to a thicker frame of legal analysis. This methodology is favoured because it requires mostly publicly accessed knowledges (published stories) and is tailor-made for the pedagogical environment of the law school. The largest drawback from the adapted case-brief method is that it decontextualizes legal principles from the lifeworlds they relate to and requires a light relationality with Indigenous communities without a natural onus for researchers to engage with a community or seek feedback on their conclusions. It requires institutions to apply internal accountability mechanisms that require community feedback on the results of their synthesis.[23]

The broader challenge highlighted by the adapted case-brief methodology is that, under the wrong guidance, it can be employed in a way that is unmoored from the other social institutions, where story is only one point in a constellation of locations where legal process and legal reasoning are found. While stories can be used to identify and begin to describe legal principles, other legal institutions like ceremonies and language can offer deeper knowledge of the legal principles and can help describe specific obligations attached to the legal principle. The word for law in nêhiyawewin is *wiyasiwêwin*, translated as "the act of weaving."[24] There is strength in weaving; stories on their own are bereft of the cross patterns of other legal resources to give them pattern and strength. Further, Indigenous legal methodologies always work against traditional academic methodologies in the lifeworlds of Indigenous peoples, often come from an anthropological frame, and have involved rendering to make Indigenous legal knowledge translatable for study.[25] Leanne Simpson observes that, during research, Indigenous knowledge can be "stripped of its dynamism and its fluidity and confined to a singular context. It is void of the spatial relationships created between elder and youth. It becomes generalized and depersonalized. It is separated from the land, from the worlds of spirits, from its source and its meaning, and from the methodologies for transmission that provide the rigor that ensures its proper communication."[26]

Academic methodologies and pedagogies are implicitly extractive. Some may even bristle at discussing Indigenous legal principles as *resources*, as the term's contemporary connotation aligns itself with neoliberal positions on education and knowledge. While I agree that the commoditization of Indigenous legal knowledge is an implicit threat in academic studies, I am also drawn back to nêhiyaw harvesting methodologies, which recognize that transformations may sometimes be necessary. In this way, the reality of the resurgence and revitalization of nêhiyaw law requires us to engage in these transformations. By accepting this fact, we can also begin to accept the obligations that arise from our *resourcing* of legal knowledge from lifeworlds to academia. Entering into this more nuanced dialogue, we become aware of when this use turns into a relationships of bald extraction or exploitation.

Canadian law schools can reflect nêhiyaw harvesting pedagogies in this manner by committing to deeper relationships with the communities where the resources and systems of knowledge. As John Borrows states, the teaching of Indigenous laws is "best facilitated by understanding and working through Indigenous legal epistemologies" to "develop an understanding of how Indigenous peoples create and justify what they think they know to be true in their own terms," including the "sources and limits of [Indigenous] knowledge."[27] For example, as a part of the changing environment forthcoming with the JD/JID program, the University of Victoria is designing a space to facilitate legal teaching beyond the traditional lecture/seminar style within law schools, including ceremonial spaces. Further, many schools have developed in field schools where land-based education is a priority.[28] Finally, while not affiliated with a law faculty, Dechinta Center for Research engages in land-based teaching socio-cultural practice, which forms the basis of the on-the-land university.[29] As starting points, committing to the harder obligations that come with harvesting the "best meat" of Indigenous legal knowledge requires learning and respecting protocol and procedures within

Indigenous social/legal/ceremonial ordering; ensuring legal teaching is done in the proper venue, situation, and season; ensuring that the work has been vetted and is accountable to Indigenous communities and societies; compensating and generally valuing people and organizations that provide knowledge and teachings; being open to critical guidance from Indigenous peoples on their legal methods and pedagogies. Larger goals, like the recognition of Indigenous sovereignties, nationhood, and human rights must underpin the use of their respective legal orders for academic study.

The Best Cuts in Canadian Law

Where academic institutions attempt to include social processes integral to the function of law within Indigenous communities, the use of Indigenous legal principles and procedures within Canadian courts remains a significant challenge. While Canadian jurisprudence has affirmed a need for Indigenous laws to be considered in disputes, there has been little application of Indigenous laws within the Canadian courts.[30] Further, Canadian-state legal processes dominate such proceedings.

The result is that it can still be difficult for Indigenous legal ordering when a community uses it to approach the courts to advance freedoms, as Indigenous communities generally must distort legal principles and cosmological beliefs to fit within the common/civil law–dominated court system. As much of litigation between Indigenous nations and Canadian-state governments surrounds rights and title to lands, these processes are doubly violent, as often after Indigenous legal principles are rendered into distorted versions of themselves, court decisions often enable or affirm state-sanctioned violence to Indigenous territories. The most recent reminder came on 2 November 2017, when the Supreme Court of Canada released its decision in *Ktunaxa Nation v. British Columbia (Forest, Lands, and Resources Operations)* [2017] 2 SCR 386, upholding the British Columbia Supreme Court's trial decision to allow a ski resort to be developed in Qat'muk (as known by the Ktunaxa) or the Jumbo Valley (as known by British Columbians).[31] The Ktunaxa sought court intervention into the development partly on the grounds that development in the valley violates their freedom of religion, as Qat'muk was home to Kławła Tukłułak?is or the "Grizzly Bear Spirit" and its development would cause it to vacate the valley. Although the majority of judges found their belief in Kławła Tukłułak?is was reasonably held, the freedom of religion set out in section 2(a) of the Canadian constitution does not protect the object of a religious practice.[32]

While the decision is troubling for its treatment of Ktunaxa spirituality and what that means for other Indigenous societies and nations seeking court protection of sacred areas, it also warns against future use of section 2(a) to bring Indigenous spirituality into the Canadian legal process. In order to make the appeal, the Ktunaxa were forced to reveal sacred knowledges of Qat'muk and Kławła Tukłułak?is, that otherwise would have remained secure within Ktunaxa legal processes.[33] As knowledge of Qat'muk and the Grizzly Bear Spirit was held by elders of the community, it was revealed as an exception. Once out in the world, knowledge of Qat'muk and the Grizzly Bear Spirit went from the internal protections of Ktunaxa socio-legal practices into the blunt and distorting rendering of the Canadian legal system. Further, Ktunaxa beliefs became publicly litigated in the minds of Canadians with the publication of the decision. As Aimee Craft notes, the Ktunaxa's decision to hold back information until the appeal factored into the SCC deciding against Ktunaxa interests, "including in the consultation and accommodation analysis."[34]

The Ktunaxa choice to publicly reveal knowledge of Qat'muk was forced by the valley's continuing development. Indigenous nations are often forced into making backfooted legal manoeuvres to protect territories, rights, and practices. The narrow scope of section 2(a) made the Ktunaxa claim difficult from the outset. Section 35 of the Charter theoretically offers a more assertive avenue for Indigenous nations to advance Indigenous laws as a method for territorial governance. However, judicial interpretation of section 35 on broad self-governance rights has not been realized.[35] This narrow interpretation is meaningless in terms of recognizing Indigenous law. Aside from specific claims where Indigenous nations are able to satisfy the *Van Der Peet* analysis[36] attached to a specific right, the recognition of legal ordering underpinning general governance will require fundamental shifts in the doctrines set by section 35 jurisprudence. Reimagining Canadian constitutionalism in a manner that formalizes room for Indigenous constitutional and legal orders requires constitutional amendment, formal broadening of the limits of section 35 through parliamentary action, or day-to-day incremental movement. While section 35 provides for "a recognition of inherent jurisdiction and sovereignty which exists as sui generis within the Canadian constitutional order,"[37] its narrow interpretation,[38] the inability of the courts to recognize governance rights in a general manner,[39] and the "cultural approach" to Aboriginal rights[40] have made section 35 extremely limiting in court recognition of Indigenous law.

A large challenge of using the court system to advance Indigenous law as an avenue to freedoms is the mediation by lawyers in the process. While the numbers of Indigenous lawyers is growing in Canada, law firms are similarly challenged in understanding and utilizing Indigenous law in their practice. Thus, the same pedagogical concerns that are raised in law school are applicable to lawyers and judges as well. Further, there are practical concerns in how Indigenous legal principles, legal ordering, and legal processes are utilized within the courts. This is not limited to Aboriginal law litigation. Aside from the pleadings, or the evidence or "authorities" used to persuade judges, Indigenous legal ordering can influence the Canadian court system in a multitude of ways. This potential exists at every step of the legal processes within all areas of Canadian law. Human rights complaints can be addressed through Gitksan law,[41] harms to individuals can be addressed through nêhiyaw wahkotowin practices,[42] and so on. Legal education about Indigenous legal orders is crucial, as it provides introductory teachings on how future lawyers will engage within Indigenous communities when standing up for their laws in formal court proceedings.

Nourishing Canada: Revitalizing Indigenous Legal Pedagogies

The resurgence of Indigenous laws within Canadian-state legal forums will require a shift in the relationship between the Canadian state and Indigenous nations. Despite reconciliation rhetoric, it is trite to say that colonial strategies of the Canadian state continue to have substantial negative impacts on the operation of Indigenous legal ordering. I offer the above not as a magic bullet for decolonization and Indigenous sovereignty, but as temporary protections of territories and rights that serve Indigenous freedoms. As Indigenous nations, polities, and legal systems revitalize in spite of the pressures of colonization, inter-societal legal discourse is inevitable. As *Ktunaxa* shows, whether Indigenous nations are ready for it or not, we must all engage in critical research of Indigenous laws and prepare for the transformations in the academy and the Canadian legal system generally. Development into spiritually significant areas of Indigenous territories will continue. As part of a strategy to protect Indigenous spiritual practices, thinking critically how these knowledges will be accessed and used and what processes will guide their transformations are needed before these questions are forced upon Indigenous nations and societies. Although it is not the first choice as an avenue of revitalization and resurgence of Indigenous law, academic research is also necessary in reformation of Canadian legal processes to account for the multi-juridical landscape of Canada. In response to continuing colonization pressures on Indigenous nationhoods, transformations (in some key situations) are necessary to sustain Indigenous legal systems.[43]

These spaces also provide an avenue to raise and address questions about the need to regenerate and strengthen historical practices within communities,[44] to revitalize law in the face of colonization,[45] and to acknowledge the gendered nature of some Indigenous legal orders.[46] The health of our legal orders depends upon Indigenous methods of critical theorizing as well.[47] Thus nêhiyaw hunting pedagogies provide nourishment in this revitalization of Indigenous law. They provide a referent for resistance against the decontextualizing approach of Canadian jurisprudence. In doing so they assure the maintenance of obligations to the inspirited beings and institutions that are subject to law. While it is not within the scope of this chapter to explore the depths of how this will practically affect the operation of Canadian-state law within *nêhiyawaskiy* (Plains Cree territory), harvesting pedagogies can teach us how to return to nêhiyaw concepts of community and kinship in our legal decision-making – concepts that include the consideration of non-human beings. In the transformational, critical, or even deconstructive work we do in Indigenous law, they provide a referent to how to approach transformations in a respectful and reciprocal way. In acknowledging the transformational force of using Indigenous legal knowledges within Canadian academic and legal systems, it is important to remember that these transformations do not automatically result in the irrevocable change of Indigenous knowledge systems. The use of stories to describe law in academic settings does not destroy the story. The song sung in a courtroom to describe law does not render the song unusable in its traditional settings. Our knowledge systems that hold legal information have always been more resilient than the pressure we can put on them. And like the *kohkômak* (grandmothers) who would hold sweats under kitchen tables when the ceremony was outlawed by the Canadian state, we can acknowledge that these acts are temporary ones of love and resilience. Ekosi.

NOTES

1 Sophie Gunner, "Tanning Moose-Hide," in *atalohkana nesta tipacimowin: Nêhiyaw Legends and Narratives*, ed. Douglas Ellis (Winnipeg: University of Manitoba Press, 1995), 295.
2 Meaning "Cree."
3 See Richard J. Preston, *Nêhiyaw Narrative: Expressing the Personal Meaning of Events* (Montreal and Kingston: McGill-Queen's University Press, 2002), 187, 216, for a description of the importance of songs and dreams in preparation for a hunt.
4 See John Borrows, *Indigenous Legal Traditions in Canada* (Ottawa: Law Commission of Canada, 2006), 7. Borrows observes that "laws can arise whenever interpersonal interactions create expectations about proper conduct." A

close look at the normative hunting practices within Nêhiyaw communities displays expectations of how hunters conduct themselves towards their prey.

5 For a critique of this view, see Calvin Martin, *Keepers of the Game: Indian–Animal Relationships and the Fur Trade* (Berkeley: University of California Press, 1978). Martin's position is that the idea that animals would give themselves for humans is harmful for the preservation of moose populations. While taken out of the web of related principles on moose-human relations this may seem so, I contend that this is a flat understanding of such a statement. It is tied up in a different ethos towards ecological relationships that many Nêhiyaw continue to practise towards animals. Such refrains reinforce kinship with the moose; in doing so it attempts to remove a mediating force between humans and moose (that the moose as a different species is a "resource") and causes further reflection and care in our obligations to moose populations in our kinship with them. For a greater exploration of the benefits of moose populations for ecological practices that engage in relational, anthropomorphic dialogue, see Elizabeth Anderson, "Benevolent Grandfathers and Savage Beasts: Comparative Canadian Customary Law," (2010) 15 Appeal L J (20100): 1. For another contribution that explores a relational approach to environmental conservation, see Charlotte Cote, *Spirits of Our Whaling Ancestors: Revitalizing Makah and Nuu-chah-nulth Traditions* (Seattle: University of Washington Press, 2015).

6 For a greater description of obligations in hunting within the normative practices of the Nêhiyaw, see Elizabeth Anderson, *Benevolent Grandfathers and Savage Beasts: Comparative Canadian Customary Law* (2010) 15 Appeal 3.

7 Bruce Hoye, "'Magical Ingredient': Hunters Learn to Tan Hides Using Animal Brains in Winnipeg," CBC News, 2 April 2016, http://www.cbc.ca/beta/news/canada/manitoba/animal-hide-brain-tanning-winnipeg-1.3518106.

8 Alberta's hunting regulations can be found at https://albertaregulations.ca/huntingregs.

9 I argue that the ceremonies that occurred/occur before events like the hunt in nêhiyaw communities are actions of such relations. To offer something in return for the lives taken reframes (or works against) the commodification of game. Such ceremonies are part of a different ecological practice.

10 Thinking of the relationship between law and society in a nêhiyaw context, obligations arise to the beings and institutions that teach law (elders, animals, stories, ceremonies, songs, etc.) by virtue of nêhiyaw beliefs of their being subject to a spirit. Thus the term *inspirited.*

11 John Borrows, *Canada's Indigenous Constitution* (Toronto: University of Toronto Press, 2010), 109.

12 John Borrows, "Heroes, Tricksters, Monsters & Caretakers: Indigenous Law and Legal Education," *McGill Law Review* 61, no. 4 (2016): 22.

13 Hadley Friedland, "Reflective Frameworks: Methods for Accessing, Understanding, and Applying Indigenous Laws," *Indigenous Law Journal* 11, no. 1 (2012): 12.

14 Friedland, "Reflective Frameworks," 79.

15 See John Borrows, "Outsider Education: Indigenous Law and Land-Based Learning," *Windsor Yearbook of Access to Justice* 33 (2016): 1, for a survey of law schools using land-based learning specifically in teaching about Indigenous legal orders.

16 One exception is Akitsuraq Law School Program in Nunavut, where a large portion of students are Inuit.

17 See Darcy Lindberg, "Miyo nêhiyâwiwin (Beautiful Creeness): Ceremonial Aesthetics and Nêhiyaw Legal Pedagogy," *Indigenous Law Journal* 16/17, no. 1 (2018): 51.

18 Friedland, "Reflective Frameworks," 11.

19 Friedland, "Reflective Frameworks," 11.

20 Friedland, "Reflective Frameworks," 11.

21 Friedland, "Reflective Frameworks," 11.

22 Friedland, "Reflective Frameworks," 12.

23 UVic's Indigenous Law Research Unit works on this model, working only with communities that request this work, and engage in community feedback sessions once conclusions are drawn in their research projects.

24 See Sylvia McAdam, *Nationhood Interrupted: Revitalizing Nêhiyaw Legal Systems* (Saskatoon, SK: Purich, 2014), 104.

25 I share this reflection in my own research of nêhiyaw law in preparation for this chapter. I have scoured transcripts of interviews that anthropologist David Mandelbaum conducted in his research of Plains Nêhiyaw people. Often within these transcripts were researcher notes on the "uselessness" of some of the narratives he used. In them I found a wealth of nêhiyaw legal knowledge, disregarded by Mandelbaum as "confused."

26 Leanne Simpson, "Anticolonial Strategies for the Recovery and Maintenance of Indigenous Knowledge," *American Indian Quarterly* 28, no. 3–4 (2004): 375.

27 Borrows, "Heroes, Tricksters, Monsters & Caretakers," 22.

28 Borrows, "Outsider Education."

29 See Dechinta Center for Research, https://www.dechinta.ca.

30 See Alan Hanna, "Spaces for Sharing: Searching for Indigenous Law on the Canadian Legal Landscape," *UBC Law Review* 51 (2018): 105. In *Tshilqot'in Nation v British Columbia*, 2014 SCC 44, the SCC reaffirms that the Aboriginal perspective must be taken into consideration in the determination of Aboriginal rights and title.

31 *Ktunaxa Nation v British Columbia (Forest, Lands, and Resources Operations)* [2017] 2 SCR 386.

32 *Ktunaxa Nation* at paras 70–2.

33 Or as the Ktunaxa Nation provided to the Supreme Court of Canada, "Ktunaxa doctrine of secrecy regarding their spirituality includes strictures on sharing their communal religious beliefs and sacred sites with non-Ktunaxa persons, and prevents persons who have gained sacred knowledge from widely revealing it." See Appellants' Factum in *Ktunaxa Nation*, https://www.scc-csc.ca/WebDocuments-DocumentsWeb/36664/FM010 _Appellant_Ktunaxa-Nation-Council.pdf, 9.

34 Aimee Craft made this observation in reviewing a draft of this chapter. For the SCC's characterization of the timeline of claims raised by the Ktunaxa, see *Ktunaxa v British Columbia*, paras 23–43, 101–8.

35 For the judicial treatment of self-governance claims through section 35, see *R v Pamajewon* [1996] 2 SCR 821. The SCC held that the claimants' governance rights (on gambling within their First Nations) were limited to the right to participate in and regulate the activity, rather than the right to manage their lands broadly.

36 See *R v Van der Peet* [1996] 2 SCR 507, where the "integral to a distinctive culture" test is set out by the SCC to determine the existence of an Aboriginal right. As John Borrows notes, the test instils a "frozen rights" approach to Aboriginal rights, where "aboriginal is retrospective. It is about what was, 'once upon a time,'" failing to acknowledge the living, breathing legal lives of Indigenous peoples. See John Borrows, *Recovering Canada: The Resurgence of Indigenous Law* (Toronto: University of Toronto Press, 2002), 60.

37 Kiera Ladner, "(Re)creating Good Governance, Creating Honourable Governance: Renewing Indigenous Constitutional Orders" (paper, Annual Conference of the Canadian Political Science Association, Ottawa, May 2009), 2, https://www.cpsa-acsp.ca/papers-2009/Ladner1.pdf.

38 Ladner, "(Re)creating Good Governance," 6.

39 *R v Pamajewon*.

40 See *R v Van der Peet*.

41 See Indigenous Law Research Unit, "ILRU Case Note: Human Rights in Indigenous (Gitxsan) Law," University of Victoria, https://www.uvic.ca/law /assets/docs/ilru/ILRU%20Case%20Note%20-%20Human%20Rights %20FINAL%20OCT%2026%202016.pdf.

42 See Harold Cardinal, "Nation-Building as Process: Reflections of a Nêhiyow (Cree)," *Canadian Review of Comparative Literature* 34, no. 1 (2007): 74–5.

43 I am working on the belief in the necessity of academic work in the revitalization and resurgence of Indigenous legal orders.

44 For example, see John Borrows, "Stewardship and the First Nations Governance Act," *Queen's Law Journal* 29 (2003): 103–11; Val Napoleon, "Thinking about Indigenous Legal Orders," in *Dialogues on Human Rights and Legal Pluralism*, ed. René Provost and Colleen Sheppard (New York: Springer,

2013), 239–41; Emily Snyder, Val Napoleon, and John Borrows, "Gender and Violence: Drawing on Indigenous Legal Resources," *UBC Law Review* 48, no. 2 (2015).

45 For example, see Aimée Craft, *Breathing Life into the Stone Fort Treaty: An Anishnabe Understanding of Treaty 1* (Saskatoon, SK: Purich Publishing, 2013); Aaron Mills, "The Lifeworlds of Indigenous Law: On Revitalizing Indigenous Legal Orders Today," *McGill Law Journal* 64, no. 4 (2016): 847; Danika Billie Littlechild, "Transformation and Re-Formation: First Nations and Water in Canada" (LLM diss., University of Victoria, 2014).

46 For example, see Tracey Lindberg, "Critical Indigenous Legal Theory (PhD diss., University of Ottawa, 2007); Emily Snyder, "Indigenous Feminist Legal Theory," *Canadian Journal of Women and the Law* 26, no. 2 (2014): 600–28; Patricia Monture, *Thunder in My Soul: A Mohawk Woman Speaks* (Halifax: Fernwood Publishing, 2005).

47 See Gordon Christie, "Indigenous Legal Theory: Some Initial Considerations," in *Indigenous Peoples and the Law: Comparative and Critical Perspectives*, ed. Benjamin J. Richardson, Shin Imai, and Kent McNeal (Oxford: Hart, 2009), 195.

PART THREE

Narrating Reconciliation and Resurgence

8 Thinking through Resurgence Together: A Conversation between Sarah Hunt/Tłaliłila'ogwa and Leanne Betasamosake Simpson

SARAH HUNT/TŁALIŁILA'OGWA AND LEANNE
BETASAMOSAKE SIMPSON

This is a record of a conversation between Sarah Hunt/Tłaliłila'ogwa and Leanne Betasamosake Simpson in digital space in April 2018, loosely based on their conversation with Glen Coulthard during the "Resurgence in the Age of Reconciliation" symposium at the University of Victoria, 16–17 March 2017, Lkwungen territories. We are both Indigenous writers, academics, and activists who have engaged deeply with each other's works, and the body of literature and the resurgence movement. Even more, we are both committed to thinking through what it means to engage in community building in the context of resurgent organizing and question who gets to be a part of that struggle. Speaking and moving across diverse spaces in our daily lives and activism, we trace the movement of resurgent politics, theories, and practices through our own relationships and commitments.

Leanne: In *As We Have Always Done*, I wanted to "think through together" our experience of resurgence both as theorizing and organizing.[1] The political climate of the past few years, and the work of emerging 2SQ and trans writers and activists, presented an opportunity for me to think through whether resurgence in concept is still a useful Indigenous response to colonial domination. On one hand, the superficial engagement of neoliberal governments in Canada requires sharp and incisive critique and organizing, regardless of which political party is in power, and of course our nations' regeneration work will always be ongoing, whether we call it resurgence or not.

In taking stock of our collective work on resurgence, though, there were valuable critiques. Two-spirit and queer peoples and issues have often not been centred in resurgence work. Anti-violence work has not been present in resurgence work to the degree it must be.

The ongoing violence of heteropatriarchy replicated by some individuals within the movement have caused harm in our communities, to students, to Indigenous women, and to 2SQ and trans peoples, further weakening relational nationhood and hindering our collective freedom movements.

I worried that the term *resurgence* had much more resonance on the West Coast than it did in northern, central, and eastern Canada and much more resonance in the Western-educated urban community than in reserve communities. I worried that the work of resurgence can be too centred within educational institutions and is sometimes co-opted into institutions in general. I'm very drawn to intellectual projects that, as Ashon Crawley (following Stefano Harney and Fred Moten) writes about Black studies, "force of belief that blackness is but one critical and urgently necessary disruption to the epistemology, the theology-philosophy, that produces a world, a set of protocols, wherein black flesh cannot easily breathe."[2] His book *Blackpentecostal Breath* argues that "blackness is released into the world to disrupt the institutionalization and the abstraction of thought that produces the categorical distinctions of disciplinary knowledge."[3] To me, resurgent struggle is about world building, not just in the future, but in the present. It is about disruption and generative refusal: creation as disruption.

Sarah: Although I have been engaged in cultural practice for my entire life and in activist organizing and solidarity work since I was a teenager, resurgence is not a word that I started using until recently – like, very recently. Maybe in the last five years. As a 2SQ Kwagu'ł and Dzawada'enuxw woman who began my university education in the nineties and took courses on Indigenous issues throughout all of my degrees, this tells me something about how resurgence has been framed within the literature and how it has or has not translated into activist and community circles. I did not see myself in resurgence theory. And I did not see the need to use theories of resurgence to engage in decolonial scholarship and activism – to live my life as I always have in the diverse community spaces that have nurtured my activist scholarship.

For me, building community spaces in which to engage in cultural practice and activism has always been shaped by expressions of heteropatriarchy that have disciplined the way I could be in those spaces. Addressing predatory behaviour and intergenerational abuse has been a necessity of moving into and out of cultural and community spaces. As someone who is known to do work on violence, family, friends, and strangers alike have felt comfortable disclosing things to me they normally keep private, and I carry this responsibility with me into spaces that might be called "spaces of resurgence." The weight and labour associated with this responsibility often prevent me from engaging in resurgence practices that have thus far been out of reach for me, such as learning to speak my language of Kwak'wala or learning how to smoke clams or being a part of the annual canoe journey along our coast. I spend so much time and energy trying to filter violence, make sense of violence, fend off violence, support others in fending off violence, that it keeps me from being in the spaces imagined to be "on the land" or "on the water" – spaces where resurgent cultural work takes place.

Much of my own internal decolonial work has been realizing that the role I take up in intimate practices of care is also resurgence work, though I am still tentative to label it as resurgent because this is not how I have understood it up until now. Learning from my family members, mentors, and collaborators in anti-violence work, I have recognized the cultural teachings that are nurtured when we witness one another in our wholeness. There are so many examples of how we take this up in our everyday relationships as we counter the harms of colonialism, which manifest at every scale. I remember a friend sharing with me that their grandma was helping to find a word in their language to reflect their gender identity. This is resurgence work, countering transphobia and homophobia through creativity in language revitalization and making it possible for each individual to have a place of honour and importance.

These relational acts are carried out not in isolation but in connection, walking alongside one another and building spaces in which to see one another anew. Yet this work is often devalued or, worse, seen as a threat within certain ideas of traditionalism that perpetuate harmful expressions of power in which women, queer, trans, and two-spirit people, youth and children, and people with disabilities are devalued. So there is a necessity to politicize and value the intimate work of denormalizing violence – whether it be through spiritual, physical, and emotional healing work, supporting survivors through justice processes, working directly with people who are violent and abusive, teaching sexual and reproductive health, or other roles – in order to spread the work around. The more we integrate this intimate decolonial work of transforming our everyday relationships into our resurgent practices and theories, the more welcoming cultural and political spaces will be for all our relations. And we must continue asking ourselves who is at the centre of our community spaces. Whose voices are being held up? Because colonial heteropatriarchy dictates that there will be a tendency for cisgender men to be recognized in ways that the rest of us are not if they increasingly take up this work. The point isn't for any one person to be an "expert" or "leader" but for it to be the norm that anti-violence work is integrated into everyday resurgence practices at every scale. This is a responsibility we all carry with us, as the principles embedded in our ancestral and land-based teachings are manifest in how we conduct ourselves at the individual level.

Leanne: And of course a lot of our people who live in Indigenous communities don't use any of these terms, whether that's resurgence or decolonizing or anything else, yet they do the work, they live the work. When I was reading Christina Sharpe's *In the Wake* I was really taken by the energy she put into creating language and theorizing around describing her communities' experiences with violence and domination through slavery and anti-Blackness – "the wake," "the weather."[4] That generates a very rich body of theorizing. She reminded me that in Nishnaabeg thought we can't ever be too committed to a single concept or a word, in the action and the kinetics of how we live our lives both as individuals and together that disrupts and creates different spaces and different understandings. Maybe our writing in English needs to also reflect that.

I was also concerned that resurgence has failed to support and hold up the people in our communities that work to make the material lives of our peoples better through freedom schools, food programs, safe rides, in favour of more visible activist engagements. I'm thinking about food programs, freedom schools and child care, care of the elderly, support and organizing around the missing and murdered, safe ride programs, shelters, harm-reduction programs and safe street programs. I thought about all of the incarcerated people and those that work to support their cultural and intellectual lives.

I wondered how we as a movement are embodying solidarity with the peoples of Palestine,[5] the global anti-capitalist movement, or freedom fighters organizing in Black Lives Matter.

In the end, the concept of resurgence still held resonance, hope, and a path forward for me, particularly while the state's idea of reconciliation is taking up so much space, and because of the community of cultural workers and knowledge producers that are employing this radicalness in their work. Resurgence for me has provided a thinking and acting space that does not shy away from the *radical* politics my ancestors used to build their worlds – worlds that lived as part of the land forever. Those spaces are rare. Regenerating Nishnaabeg worlds – relational nationhood, politics, governance, education, gender relations is our freedom. If resurgence is to remain a useful theorizing and organizing tool, it would have to (continue to) be willing to destroy the pillars of white supremacy, heteropatriarchy, and capitalism. It would have to understand dispossession in an expansive way – including land, bodies, minds, and spirits. It would have to centre 2SQ people and anti-violence work. It would have to be concerned not just with the future, but with the present and be willing to organize to meet the social, cultural, and material needs of our communities, where they are.

It would have to be willing to be place-based and internationalist in scope and "think through together" with other movements and mobilizations. It would have to remain vigilant, intellectually and ethically rigorous, radical, and political. It would need to be a continual cycle of disruption and generation of life. *As We Have Always Done* is the result of me thinking through these questions. In the end, I wanted a radical space to think and write, and resurgence still provided that, particularly when I centred how 2S, queer, non-binary, trans, and women were using the concept.

Sarah: I am inspired by this desire to "think through together," both with an inward focus, situating my own body at the centre, and with an outward focus situating my body in relation to others. First and foremost, confronting heteropatriarchy means unpacking how I make sense of myself as I move through the world, carrying my ancestral obligations with me. No matter where I travel, my obligations arise from the shorelines of Kwakwaka'wakw territories – territories which are connected to those of our neighbours, which hold water and fish and other forms of life which flow into and out of other nations' territories, teaching us about the nature of governance on the coast. How can I think through together with these ancestral shorelines?

In my mind, I often visit the large (28 x 38 foot) pictograph cliff painting of a copper that Marianne Nicolson ('Tayagila'ogwa) created in Dzawada'enuxw waterways in Gwa'yi or Kingcome Inlet.[6] Created in 1998, it was the first such painting in over sixty years. The shoreline of Kingcome Inlet is across the waters from Kwagu'ł waterways, all part of the territories of our Kwakwaka'wkaw people. I think of the knowledge and spirit that is alive in those waters, the copper being seen from people passing by in boats or witnessed by whales or salmon below. In turn, the copper looks upon the caretakers of the lands and waters who continue the governance work of their ancestors. Our ancestors. The water below that copper holds words my mouth has yet to speak. In this place between water and earth, my name has a meaning that I do not yet fully comprehend. This is the place where I make sense as Tłaliłila'ogwa, but I only visit it in dreams. It is here that I can be embedded in relations in which I fully make sense as Kwagu'ł and Dzawada'enuxw. The name I carry from these territories emerges from within a set of responsibilities that long precede colonialism.

The violence of colonialism has prevented me not only from fully knowing the shorelines of Kwakwaka'wakw territories but of knowing myself in relation to these places and the knowledge and life that they hold. Talking to survivors over the years, I realize just how many of us are prevented from making sense of ourselves in the places and relations of our ancestors. What does it mean to our governance, our cultural revitalization, and our social movements if we are missing vast numbers of our relations from these spaces? This is the challenging internal work of rebuilding our nations and reconstituting good relations with our neighbours, as we have always done. Coming to terms with the fact that colonialism has made me incomprehensible to myself. And rejecting resurgence paradigms or cultural and traditional paradigms that actively work to suppress the ability of so many of us (particularly 2S, queer, trans, non-binary, and gender-diverse people, women, and youth) to witness and to be witnessed in relation to our ancestral places.

Leanne: Yes, expansive dispossession asymmetrically targets 2S queer, trans, non-binary people, children. women and youth. Our resurgence, cultural, traditional, and political paradigms cannot achieve Indigenous freedom while also replicating modes of expansive dispossession that remove us from intimate relationships with ourselves, our knowledge systems, our land, and Indigenous spaces. We cannot be nations born out of relationality while centring cisgenders, patriarchy, transphobia, while reinforcing the colonial gender binary and ignoring the concerns and needs of younger members of our nations. We need the very best of all of our people.

Working in my own family and territory, in Denendeh and in the land-based MA program at the University of Saskatchewan, I've learned on the land from some outstanding young survivors, 2S, queer, trans, and non-binary people, who are not only disrupting heteropatriarchy, traditional gender roles, and binaries, but also building learning communities that affirm the queerness of the land as our teacher.

This led me a lot of thinking about fugitivity, disruption, intervention, and this idea of generative refusal in the book. I am really drawn to the idea of unapologetic, uncompromising refusal of state and intimate violence, capitalism, ecocide, white supremacy, and heteropatriarchy as a starting point, and then centring the richness, the diversity, the brilliance of Indigenous thought in conversation with Black thought, for instance, or other bodies of disruption and world-building brilliance. From a theoretical standpoint and for Indigenous peoples, theory is always embodied and in motion, building a future that propels the life of this planet, means building a present that is continually giving birth to more life. And that is why this on-the-ground struggle our communities

are engaged in is so critical as an insertion of Indigenous life and freedom. Our blockades are never just blockades. We are always animating
our Indigenous political, spiritual, and social networks at the site of the
blockade. We are always reaching out and building solidarity with other
like-minded communities. We are always also engaged in building the alternative. Every time we do this, we generate more world-building theory.
We grow the disruption, and we grow Indigenous affirmation and joy. Indigenous spaces, whether they are at blockade sites, or in ceremony, on
the land, or in bars listening to Indigenous musicians, where I come out
feeling happy, where my bones glimpse the feeling of freedom, where I
feel proud and hopeful and *alive*, where I come out feeling slightly better
than when I went in – those are precious, powerful spaces for me.

What happens when Indigenous concepts of consent, diversity, individual and collective self-determination, ethics of non-interference and
deep relationality, ethics of care and kindness, and so on, once again
become the building blocks of our nations?

Sarah: As you say, it is the activation of these concepts that is key – not
simply theorizing but living, embodying, and collectively enacting the
principles and ethics that our nations require in order to become whole
again/anew. This brings to mind Tanana Athabascan scholar Dian Million's concept of felt theory or the necessity of emotional wisdom in theorizing power, violence, justice, and decolonization. Million says,

> Indigenous women have spoken and written powerfully from experiences
> that they have lived or have chosen to relive through the stories they choose
> to tell. Our voices rock the boat and perhaps the world. They are danger-
> ous. All of this becomes important to our emerging conversation on Indig-
> enous feminism, on our ability to speak to ourselves, to inform ourselves
> and our generations, to counter and intervene in a constantly morphing
> colonial system. To "decolonize" means to understand as fully as possible
> the forms colonialism takes in our own times.[7]

These dangerous theories are not straightforward – as Kaupapa Māori
scholar Leonie Pihama recently told me of her work on decolonizing
emotions, in the Māori language emotions are like waves.[8] They move
angrily at times, soft in other moments, lapping up against the shorelines
of our being in ways that are constantly in motion. So we must prepare
ourselves to make room for stories, teachings, and practices that are not
linear or that do not "make sense" of our lives in familiar terms but, like
navigating the ocean in a canoe, might seem choppy. This form of theorizing and living decolonization might require constantly finding new

reference points, letting go of old ones, and looking to, not one, but many points of reference on the shore and in the sky, to provide direction. Transformation requires letting go of certain norms; this is what I hear in your description of generating world-building theory. In building up anew, we must unhinge meanings around resurgence in order to generate theories which reflect the felt knowledge of youth, women, queer, trans, and two-spirit people, as well as peoples and communities we live alongside and in relation to. To me, this means embracing a productive confusion that opens up decolonial possibilities for comprehending our settler colonial present – this moment of resurgence in the face of "reconciliation" – in new ways. Part of that unhinging is, perhaps, letting go of definitions of resurgence that separate Indigenous struggles from other radical movements confronting racist heteropatriarchy, capitalism, and imperialism. Rather, as you say, situating the local place-based nature of our work in conversation and relationship with other movements for justice and freedom on our homelands as well as globally.

Leanne: I had the privilege of writing a lot of *As We Have Always Done* during the beginnings of Black Lives Matter becoming visible to white Canada. My territory is the north shore of Lake Ontario. Our communities have experience being together for four centuries. Robyn Maynard's *Policing Black Lives: State Violence in Canada from Slavery to the Present* came out at a similar time and is just such an incredibly important work for all of us. No one can ever again deny anti-Blackness as a foundational force in the creation of this country. This book is crucial because it was (in Robyn's words) "born out of movement work and is geared towards nourishing those same movements that have given me life over the years."[9] I felt nourished reading the book, even though I wasn't necessarily the intended audience, because I felt seen and affirmed even though my struggle is different, albeit linked to Black struggle. I think Robyn's book could lead to a deepening of the relationship between Black and Indigenous communities.

Policing Black Lives makes it very clear to me that I cannot possibly fully understand the impact of colonialism on my people (and all of life actually) without also understanding the historic, contemporary, and global *structure* of slavery and anti-Blackness – on one hand to work to not be complicit in it and to stand in solidarity with Black movements, but also because it is theoretically and politically imperative that I educate myself with this incredible body of work and action created by Black freedom fighters, writers, artists, and scholars so that I can fully understand how the forces of domination operate through white supremacy, heteropatriarchy, and capitalism.

Reading and thinking alongside *Policing Black Lives* has led me and my thinking in a direction where I'm continually deepening this work for myself. When I write about Michi Saagiig Nishnaabeg nationhood, I'm not talking about any Indigenous desire to be a nation state. I'm talking about dismantling the nation state. I'm thinking about how I can share space and land in deeply reciprocal and relation way with freedom fighters and diasporic communities in a way that supports each of our sovereignties and self-determinations, and I'm thinking about what relational solidarity might be like within Nishnaabeg thought.

I feel very, very grateful to the Black Lives Matter movement and to the contemporary radical Black art, activism, and theorizing that's happening right now and over the past several decades, because it challenges me to articulate my visions for an Indigenous future and Indigenous nationhood that categorically and unapologetically refuse white supremacy and challenge anti-Blackness in all forms.

During Idle No More, I was involved in a lot of conversations about allyship and about what tactics we should and should not use, about what strategies we should and should not use. I heard a lot of "we can't do that because we will lose the support of white people." Whiteness was so centred in our thinking towards solidarity. This moment that we're in right now offers brilliant alternatives to co-resistance without centring or bowing towards whiteness.

Sarah: I appreciate you bringing Robyn's work into this conversation because, to me, *Policing Black Lives* powerfully demonstrates how we can and should theorize from lived experience, rooted in community mobilizations, and accountable to those communities. Robyn shows us what is possible when persistent, systemic racist injustice is understood in relation to ongoing community mobilization by Black, Indigenous, and other racialized peoples, creating theories rooted not only in an incisive critique of violence but also an "affirmation of life" rooted in "an insistence that we must refuse to surrender our imaginations, even amid the backdrop of Black suffering and death that seems unstoppable."[10] Robyn not only holds up the everyday work of anti-racist organizers, but theorizes a different future through the possibilities they collectively foster.

Robyn Maynard's work is vital because as issues gain currency within academia, there is a danger in generating theoretical momentum that separates out discourse from the lived realities those discourses seek to represent. We see this with the police treatment of murdered and disappeared women from Vancouver's Downtown Eastside (DTES), and the subsequent uptake of MMIWG by academics, politicians, and activists not rooted in the local context. In conversation with many long-time DTES activists and support people who worked with families of murdered women, girls, and gender-diverse relations, it is clear that police violence and discrimination was not only towards Indigenous women, but women of colour, poor women and families, people who sell and trade sex, people who use drugs and alcohol, and others whose lives were devalued due to racism, classism, or stigma. However, MMIWG discourse has separated out anti-Indigenous racism from anti-Black racism and racism against Chinese and Japanese Canadians (an important point, given the proximity of the DTES to Chinatown and historically Japanese neighbourhoods) which were inherent to police neglect of missing women cases, and were also evident in the lack of public outrage over so many years. Robyn's work demands that we reject academic trends which separate where there should be complexity and connection, and demands that scholarly work be grounded in these complex expressions of power and resistance through which we have formed long histories of interdependence.

This causes me to reflect on the way my own activism around Indigenous issues was formed in relation to anti-racism movements from a young age, being raised on movies and books about the civil rights movement and stories of solidarity between diverse movements and peoples. In Grade 4, I wrote about the US civil rights movement and Black liberation struggles for a class assignment. Most of the other kids in my class had no idea what I was talking about, which made me realize how few of my peers had everyday conversations about racism, as we did in our house. In Grade 9, I went on a two-week exchange focused on anti-racism where I got to learn from a diverse group of youth and to strategize about doing anti-racism work while sharing cross-culturally. Through that experience, my own wisdom as an Indigenous youth was valued and I learned about the diverse ways that systemic violence and inequity impact young people. Importantly these conversations with other youth also allowed me to name the white privilege that I hold as a lighter skinned person of both white settler and Indigenous ancestry.

Raising children in diverse communities allows us to develop understandings of power via the people and places we have relationships to. Growing up, I didn't just hear about residential schools, the Indian Act, and Indigenous dispossession. I also learned about the internment of Japanese Canadians from our friends whose home and possessions were seized as their family was forcibly relocated and incarcerated during the war. I learned about the exploitative treatment of Chinese laborers who built the railway in BC – the railway my Ukrainian grandpa worked on. I learned about discriminatory immigration practices and heard of friends who had changed their last names to be more Anglicized so they could get jobs. From a couple who are Black and Japanese Canadian, I learned about the racist attitudes first expressed by their parents when they decided to get married, and then expressed in daily life by strangers. This taught me that anti-racism work happens in our own homes and families as well as in public spaces and institutions.

Encountering the whiteness of feminist academia as a young student, I also found solace in the writing, films, and creative works of feminist and queer scholars of colour as well as Indigenous women in other parts of the world, who provided a language in which to name my own experience. And I owe a great deal of my activist theorizing to the authors of books like *This Bridge Called My Back: Writings by Radical Women of Colour; All the Women Are White, All the Blacks Are Men, But Some of Us Are Brave: Black Women's Studies;* and *Making Face, Making Soul/Haciendo Caras: Creative and Critical Perspectives by Women of Color.*[11] In these texts, Indigenous women spoke alongside Black women and women of colour, queer women and straight women, linking our struggles and visions for change, bringing them into deeper dialogue. This was especially meaningful for me in my early twenties when urban Indigenous spaces made it difficult to be queer, and queer spaces were overwhelmingly white – I felt like I was always bridging these spaces, as *This Bridge Called My Back* so clearly reflected. In these collections and conversations, I saw room to collaborate with other queer, racialized, and Indigenous people in creating diverse spaces in which we could bring our whole selves to our anti-violence activism and creative work. Of course, there were significant gaps in some of these literatures, such as the lack of representation of trans people and gender-diverse relations, among others, but the assumption of cross-community dialogue about questions of power provided me with an understanding that our struggles – including the work to address transphobia and cissexism – are interwoven. It wasn't a matter of diversifying after the fact, as so many white feminist anti-violence groups seemed to do – rather, we needed each other in order to constitute a community to which we could fully belong.

Leanne: In the city, a relationship with the land can seem like a privilege that is unattainable, particularly for those fighting, organizing, and coping with state and intimate violence. In state schools, it is also pretty unattainable, and in prison a relationship to land is utterly unattainable. In rural areas, in the north, and in many reserve communities, people may have access to land, but far less resources for coping with state and intimate violence. Indigenous experience is diverse.

In my mind, all Indigenous practices are land-based practices – our songs and dances, our stories, our politics, and our ethics. Instead of a deficit model, focusing on what I don't have or what I can't do in my current situation, I try my best to focus on what I can contribute, what I can give to our collective struggle, whether I'm in the city or the bush. I try to live in the city in a way that my ancestors would recognize because they are always with me. There are many, many ways to affirm a diverse Indigenous presence. I don't see a need to build a hierarchy here, I see a need to undo hierarchy.

Land to me is everything. I will continue to prioritize a relationship with my homeland over other things in my life, and I won't apologize for that. Figuring out how to share space in an ethical way with other communities, how to make all of our practices as accessible and welcoming to where people are, is part of our collective struggle. *Violence on the Land, Violence on Our Bodies: Building an Indigenous Response to Environmental Violence* coming out of a collaboration between the Native Youth Sexual Health Network and Women's Earth Alliance is a wonderful resource in this regard.[12]

Saidya Hartman, in *Lose Your Mother: A Journey along the Atlantic Slave Route* deepened and complicated my understanding of land and my relationship to it. Hartman traces a slave route back to Ghana.[13] She writes about her experience being severed from her homeland, her family, her history and culture as a result of violence of three centuries of slave trade. There are both overlaps and radical differences in her work from my own experience and theorizing, and both were affecting for me. Within the concept of generative refusal, I'm so very interested in layers of Indigenous experience and theory rather than position different strains of our thought as competing.

Sarah: I want to thank you, Leanne, for this conversation which fosters interconnection, complexity, relationship, and theories of the present, which can hold the fullness of our communities. Rejecting harmful notions of resurgence, poetic and creative use of language is needed in order to honour our felt theories and to hold the nature of violence, which neither our languages nor the English language are able to fully represent. We have such a rich body of work to draw on in doing so – work which, as you have said, uses other language than that of resurgence or decolonization. The first book I read by an Indigenous woman was *I Am Woman* by Lee Maracle, which told the truths of heteropatriarchy without shame, reservation, or fear. As Lee writes, "By standing up and laying myself bare, I erased invisibility as a goal for the young Native women around me."[14] We have learned that that truth-telling means telling the truths about the limitations inherent to language. As Trinidadian Canadian poet Clarie Harris wrote in "No God Waits on Incense," "While babies bleed this is not the poem I wanted / it is the poem I could."[15]

Over the past twenty years, I have said these lines over and over to myself, as writing and speaking about violence seems so futile in the face of brutality. Reflecting on these vibrant genealogies, I am brought back to Dion Brand's book of poems *No Language Is Neutral*, which further opened up a new relationship to language where I could make a home for myself. I remember gathering in living rooms with other queers of colour to read aloud these intimately rendered scenes of violence, love, hope, movement, ancestry and desire: "You ripped the world open for me."[16] Ripping this world open, other worlds become possible.

NOTES

1 Leanne Betasamosake Simpson, *As We Have Always Done: Indigenous Freedom through Radical Resistance* (Minneapolis: University of Minneapolis Press, 2017).

2 Ashon T. Crawley, *Blackpentecostal Breath: The Aesthetics of Possibility* (New York: Fordham University Press, 2017), 3, 275; Stefano Harney and Fred Moten, *The Undercommons: Fugitive Planning and Black Study, Minor Compositions* (London: AK, 2013).

3 Crawley, *Blackpentecostal Breath*, 275.

4 Christina Sharpe, *In the Wake: On Blackness and Being* (Durham, NC: Duke University Press, 2016).

5 Steven Salaita, *Inter/Nationalism: Decolonizing Native America and Palestine* (Minneapolis: University of Minnesota Press, 2016).

6 A copper is a symbol of wealth and lineage that holds meaning for the Kwakwaka'wakw people. Nicholson's neo-petroglyph is an expression of unbroken Dzawada'enuxw jurisdiction. See images and more information at "Marianne Nicolson: Cliff Painting," Medicine Project, http://www.themedicineproject.com/marianne-nicolson.html.

7 Dian Million, "Felt Theory: An Indigenous Feminist Approach to Affect and History," *Wicazo Sa Review* 24, no. 2 (2009): 54–5.

8 See Leonie Pihama, Hineitimoana Greensill, Hōri Manuirirangi, and Naomi Simmonds, *He Kare-ā-roto: A Selection of Whakataukī Related to Māori Emotions* (Hamilton, Aotearoa: Te Kotahi Research Institute, 2019).

9 Robyn Maynard, *Policing Black Lives: State Violence in Canada from Slavery to the Present* (Halifax: Fernwood Publishing, 2017), xi.

10 Maynard, *Policing Black Lives*, 234.

11 Cherrie Moraga and Gloria Anzaldua, eds., *This Bridge Called My Back: Writings by Radical Women of Colour* (New York: Kitchen Table, 1981); Gloria T. Hull, Patricia Bell-Scott, and Barbara Smith, eds., *All the Women Are White, All the Blacks Are Men, But Some of Us Are Brave: Black Women's Studies* (New

York: Feminist Press, 1982); and Gloria Anzaldua, ed., *Making Face, Making Soul/Haciendo Caras: Creative and Critical Perspectives by Women of Color* (San Francisco: Aunt Lute Books, 1990).

12 Native Youth Sexual Health Network and Women's Earth Alliance, *Violence on the Land, Violence on Our Bodies: Building an Indigenous Response to Environmental Violence*, http://landbodydefense.org/uploads/files/VLVBReportToolkit2016.pdf.

13 Saidiya Hartman, *Lose Your Mother: A Journey along the Atlantic Slave Route* (New York: Farrar, Straus, Giroux, 2006).

14 Lee Maracle, *I Am Woman: A Native Perspective on Sociology and Feminism* (Vancouver: Press Gang, 1996), 9.

15 Clair Harris, "No God Waits on Incense," in *Making a Difference: Canadian Multicultural Literature*, ed. Smaro Kamboureli (Toronto: Oxford University Press, 1996), 143.

16 Dionne Brand, *No Language Is Neutral* (Toronto: McClelland & Stewart, 1990), 47.

9 Truth-Telling amidst Reconciliation Discourses: How Stories Reshape Our Relationships

JEFF GANOHALIDOH CORNTASSEL

Introduction

One cold, fall, rainy day in Victoria, British Columbia, I picked my daughter up early from school and started driving north on the highway with her to K'omoks First Nation, which was about a two and a half-hour drive. Kwakwaka'wakw and Stó:lō artist Hayalthkin'geme (Carey Newman) had invited us to a Witness Blanket ceremony at the K'omoks First Nation Bighouse and we were both looking forward to taking part in this important event. Several years earlier, in 2012, Carey envisioned the Witness Blanket as a national monument to recognize the atrocities of residential schools and to honour the survivors through the construction of a blanket made out of solid objects. Carey spent over two years creating the Witness Blanket (to be discussed in more detail in subsequent sections of this chapter), which was made out of approximately 887 donated objects woven together, such as moccasins, hockey skates, photographs, etc., as well as pieces of the residential schools themselves, from seventy-seven different Indigenous nations.[1] After a public unveiling of the Witness Blanket in 2014, it was shown all over Canada for the next four and a half years.

Today, however, it was time to hand over responsibility for care of the blanket to someone else. The Canadian Museum for Human Rights (CMHR) asked to host the Witness Blanket but Carey didn't want to merely sign a typical transfer of ownership contract. He wanted to develop both an oral and written process that gave the Witness Blanket agency as a living being. The result was a living document that recognized the Witness Blanket as having its own spirit along with all of the stories that come with it. Rather than provide ownership to the CMHR, the legal document was written from the perspective of the Witness Blanket and each party determined what was required to care for this living being while at the CMHR.[2] While in the K'omoks Bighouse, we were witnessing the document of "collective stewardship" coming to life around the fire.[3] It was a moment of reclaiming our stories and finding new ways to express our responsibilities and sacred relationships.

Drawing on this example of the Witness Blanket, this chapter critically examines reconciliation discourses within the Canadian context. Nuuchah-nulth scholar Johnny Mack poses an important question: "What would we as Nuu-chah-nulth do differently if we took our stories seriously?"[4] The Witness Blanket ceremony is the embodiment of taking our stories seriously by honouring protocols and the stories of survivors who contributed to the blanket through ceremony. This chapter examines what it means to take our stories seriously and to ask when and how Indigenous knowledge systems and living histories have agency within the state system. Answers to these questions provide a deeper understanding of how Indigenous self-determination and community resurgence are practised and asserted amidst discourses of reconciliation.

Witnessing and storytelling are important methodological frameworks for this chapter. Rather than being a bystander or observer, witnessing is grounded in action. During the Witness Blanket ceremony, my daughter and I were actively listening in order to remember the event and also to act on those remembrances to ensure that the relational responsibilities are upheld. Kwakwaka'wakw scholar Tłaliłila'ogwa (Sarah Hunt) discusses how acts of witnessing are important aspects of truth-telling within Indigenous contexts. According to Hunt, witnessing as a methodology "means sometimes creating new language, new stories, new avenues for validating those voices that are most at risk of being erased."[5] The ceremony was an example of a new story that was a way of giving the Witness Blanket agency and voice in collective knowledge sharing.

In order to challenge shape-shifting colonial erasures and calculated deprivations of relationships that maintain Indigenous community and individual health and well-being, truth-telling and witnessing work hand-in-hand to de-naturalize settler violence against Indigenous bodies and Indigenous relationships to their homelands and waterways. As Hunt points out, "Witnessing here is taking up a specific role in maintaining the integrity of Indigenous knowledge and community. It entails not just an obligation to recall but to action, given that violence continues to be normalized."[6]

Just as with witnessing, stories also shape who we are. They shape our relationships, our forms of governance, and even our legal traditions. Reclaiming our stories, as the Witness Blanket example points out, is about renewing our rebellious dignity as Indigenous peoples and nations and activating land-based resurgence. As Citizen Potawatomi Nation plant ecologist Robin Wall Kimmerer explains, "Our relationship with land cannot heal until we hear its stories."[7] In this sense, Indigenous bodies and Indigenous peoples' land and water are intrinsically interrelated in resurgence. According to Anishinaabe scholar and activist Leanne Simpson, "Resurgence must be concerned with the reattachment of our minds, bodies and spirits to the network of relationships and ethical practices and generates grounded normativity."[8]

This reattachment to "the network of relationships" occurs in everyday settings, where our relational bonds to land, culture, and community are renewed, reaffirmed, and regenerated. The ways we engage in our familial relationships within intimate spaces, such as our ceremonies and homes, mirrors the ways we manage and nurture our relationships with our plant nation and animal nation relatives, as well as with the natural world. However, there are colonial stories that sometimes distract our attention away from our relational responsibilities as Indigenous peoples. In the following section, I examine what it looks like to take stories seriously and four ways that the reconciliation discourse potentially decentres land and stories from our consciousness and actions.

Taking Our Stories Seriously

Building on Johnny Mack's question, what does taking our stories seriously look like? And what are our responsibilities when witnessing these stories being told? According to Cree/Saulteaux scholar Gina Starblanket and Anishinaabe scholar Heidi Kiiwetinepinesiik Stark, "We need to actively work against colonial narratives" by "ensuring we are creating space for relationships that are generative, that cultivate not just the continued *transmission* of indigenous knowledge but also ensure the *production* of Indigenous knowledge."[9] The creation of these new spaces for generative relationships is a key aspect of our relational responsibilities to place and the regeneration of Indigenous knowledges.

In order to demonstrate the significance of stories, I start by offering my self-location. I am a citizen of the Cherokee Nation and am living on the unceded lands and waters of Lekwungen and W̱SÁNEĆ nations. Despite generations of forced removal and dispossession from Cherokee homelands and waterways, connections and responsibilities to our homelands are unbroken. From our family history living in the Tsalagi homelands of Toqua, Tennessee, Lookout Mountain, Georgia, and Westville, Oklahoma, the Corntassel family's living historical legacy is to defend these places and honour our ancestral relationships. Like many Cherokee families, the consequences of forced removal and the Dawes Act (1901, 1906 amendments), which broke up collectively held land

and distributed plots of land to individual Cherokees (and other Indigenous nations across the United States), led to further forced migrations; today my family is dispersed from Tennessee to California, and all the way up to Alaska. How do we carry our community consciousness and stories with us even when we're not on our own territory? When visiting another Indigenous nation's territory, as Cherokees and Indigenous nations we carry the responsibilities of our communities, sense of place, and stories with us.

In order to demonstrate how stories shape us, I will share a Cherokee story "How Medicine Came to the People," which has been told many different ways. Common to all Cherokee stories is that the listener becomes an active participant in the story, as if it's happening directly to you. This version is told by Bob Thomas under the pseudonym of G.P. Horsefly:

> The way the Cherokees received help from the plants is another sacred story. I will just tell it briefly for you.... They say that the animals were getting put out with the Cherokees because, by that time, Cherokees had invented bows and arrows and they were killing off a lot of the game. In those days animals could talk just like human beings so each animal held a council to consider what to do. The bears had a council and they said, "The Cherokees are killing too many of us bears so we are going to have to do something to stop them." One of them said, "Why don't we make a bow and arrow like the Cherokees and fight them back?" Then another said, "How are we going to do that?" One bear spoke up and said, "I will sacrifice myself so you can make a bowstring out of my innards." So the bears made a bow, but when they tried to shoot the bow, they couldn't do it because they had such long claws. One bear cut off his claws and he could shoot the bow all right. The chief of the bears spoke up and said, "Wait a minute, we can't go around killing ourselves to get bowstrings or cutting off our claws. We will starve to death. We need our claws for digging." He said, "That's not going to work. Maybe we ought to get all the animals together to decide what to do." All the animals got together and they decided that the best thing to do was them to call disease, different illnesses, to the Indians. That would kind of thin them down a little bit. So the deer spoke up and said, "I will give him rheumatism." Then each animal spoke up and said what particular disease it would inflict on the Cherokees. Then the animals adjourned their joint council with that course of action in mind.
>
> Now the plants heard about what the animals had decided and since they were always friendly with the Cherokees, they decided that they would help the Cherokees out. The plants decided that for each disease the animals

brought to the Cherokees, there would be a plant that would offer itself to cure the disease. That's what the Cherokees had from the beginning. A doctor can go into the woods and it will come to him what plant to use. Sometimes there won't be any wind and you will see a plant move, and that will be the plant for you to use to cure that particular disease.[10]

This story is especially relevant amidst the COVID pandemic as it speaks to ways that we promote health and well-being through our actions. The story also gets at themes of relational responsibility, renewing relationships, and even consent. It is a story ultimately that centres upon the Cherokee word *tōhi:*,[11] which is about peacefulness or not being rushed; everything is flowing smoothly. Deviating from tōhi: means that you are rushing things and illness and aggravation often result. By taking so many deer, Cherokees were forgetting their sacred compact to honour the deer's lives by praying over them and offering tobacco. In their rush to take more, the once-harmonious relationship grounded in tōhi: was disrupted.

Additionally, the bears were trying to adapt to the "new" technology of bows and arrows, but in doing so were sacrificing too much, including their own lives. Instead of taking on the new threat as bears, they were changing themselves physically and ultimately compromising who they were. One can think of ways that we might respond to shape-shifting colonization that entails altering or compromising ourselves physically, mentally, spiritually, or emotionally to the point where we have given up parts of our identities to survive.

Another point to be drawn here is how forgetfulness is linked to a lack of respect for relationships. This story is told to remind Cherokees what can happen when they forget their priorities and how to practise and honour their relational responsibilities. While there are several interpretations for this story, it demonstrates how dynamic our stories are and how they have relevance in multiple contexts and places. These are the ways that stories shape us. I always think of our need for new stories as well. For example, what would the plant nations do if Cherokees selfishly took too many of their lives? There are serious implications to our governance, our tōhi:, and ultimately our relationships when we don't take our stories seriously.

What happens when you don't take stories seriously? In contrast to the Cherokee story, consider a story about reconciliation told by Reverend Mxolisi Mpambani during the South African Truth and Reconciliation Commission (1995–2002), which addressed the systematic violence of apartheid policies. Please note that I have expanded on the original version to highlight the colonial mindset even further:

There were two people, Peter and John. One day Peter steals John's bicycle. Then, after a period of some months, he goes up to John with outstretched hand and says, "Let's talk about reconciliation."

John says, "No, let's talk about my bicycle."

"Forget the bicycle for now," says Peter. "Let's talk about reconciliation."

"No," says John. "We cannot talk about reconciliation until you return my bicycle."

"Then let's talk about you renting the bicycle – I'd be willing to loan it to you for a small amount each month," Peter says.

"Why would I pay to rent a bicycle that is already mine?," says John.

"How about this: you could manage all of the rentals for this bicycle. I'll make you the manager and we can both benefit through reconciliation," says Peter.

"But you stole my bike. Why don't you return it?," says John.

Peter says, "We shouldn't let a misunderstanding like this ruin our friendship. Let's move forward. It's time to forgive and forget."[12]

This story encapsulates several critiques of reconciliation discourses that fail to address the central question of stolen land return and the superficiality of apologies when the same actions occur over and over again. The thief's success is premised on the forgetfulness of the survivor of the harm coupled with an unwillingness to return the stolen item. According to Unangax̂ scholar Eve Tuck and K. Wayne Yang, "Reconciliation is about rescuing settler normalcy, about rescuing a settler future."[13] What would meaningful reconciliation look like in Mpambani's story? As Gitksan scholar and activist Cindy Blackstock points out, "Reconciliation means not saying sorry twice."[14] She elaborates further: "Reconciliation is not just about saying sorry, it is about understanding the harm in a way that not only acknowledges the past but also leads to new awareness and commitment to avoid repeating the same mistakes in the future. Reconciliation requires not just saying the right thing but doing the right thing."[15]

Taken together, these stories expose important shortcomings of a reconciliation discourse when it promotes forgetfulness, relying on hasty solutions, and neglects relationships. They point to a compelling need to "restory the settler version of history."[16] It is important to provide further background to help better understand how the reconciliation discourse has evolved. The Truth and Reconciliation Commission (TRC) of Canada operated from 2008 to 2015 and was created to address the genocidal legacy of residential schools that forced the removal of over 150,000 Indigenous children (First Nations, Inuit, and Métis) from their families and homelands. The TRC was chaired by Judge Murray Sinclair along with two other commissioners, Marie Wilson and Chief Wilton Littlechild. The TRC only came about in response to the demands of residential school survivors as outlined in the Indian Residential School Settlement Agreement (IRSSA), which was ratified in May 2006. The IRSSA included the TRC, as well as the Common Experience Payment (CEP), the Independent Assessment Payment (IAP), Health and Healing Services for survivors and their families, and $20 million for the Commemoration Fund for both national and community commemorative projects. In the TRC Final Report, which was based on nearly 7,000 statements by survivors, and ninety-four Calls to Action, and published in 2015,[17] TRC commissioners urged Canadian officials and citizens to move from "apology to action" in order for meaningful reconciliation to occur.[18]

Unfortunately, since 2015 there has not been a comprehensive federal plan or policy to implement the ninety-four TRC Calls to Action. Shortly after the publication of the TRC Calls to Action in 2015, CBC News created a website entitled "Beyond 94" to monitor the progress of the recommendations being put into policy. Of the ninety-four recommendations, only ten have been completed as of 1 December 2019.[19] Sixty-seven per cent (sixty-three recommendations) have either not been started or are "in progress" with projects proposed.[20] Of these, the recommendation to "reduce the number of Aboriginal children in care" has seen no improvement since 2015, although it was a key aspect of the TRC's findings. In fact, according to government statistics, "More Indigenous children have been removed from their families and are in foster care today than were in residential schools at the height of that system."[21] These figures indicate a lack of meaningful action on some of the most critical aspects of the TRC recommendations, and Blackstock's notion of "not saying sorry twice" becomes a prescient warning. Sadly this is the result of not taking stories seriously and is not unique to Canada.

The more than forty-five truth commissions that have operated globally since the 1970s have sought truths as a way to repair disrupted or destroyed relationships. However, pursuing meaningful forms of truths and reconciliation often leads to intellectual and policy-driven cul-de-sacs for Indigenous nations and peoples. Such forms of reconciliation can serve as a "politics of distraction" that redirects community attention away from regenerating relationships with nationhood, homelands, and the natural world. When reconciliation processes serve a colonial function, they mirror statist and corporate agendas; maintaining the status quo and ultimately the territorial integrity of the state are prioritized. At least four reconciliation "dead ends" can divert the energies of

Indigenous peoples from resurgence and a reinvigoration of Indigenous nationhood towards a more colonial agenda:

1. Pursuit of reconciliation as economic and political certainty;
2. Pursuit of reconciliation as returning to a mythical previous condition;
3. Pursuit of reconciliation as a historical reboot;
4. And pursuit of reconciliation as risk management.

The pursuit of economic and political certainty is sought by federal and provincial authorities in order to secure Indigenous land and to promote corporate investment. If meaningful reconciliation is to take place, it must involve significant land return in order for Indigenous nations to engage in the relationships that keep them healthy. This is why, according to the late Secwepemc leader Art Manuel, Reconciliation Framework Agreements (RFA) are being employed in British Columbia to gain "access to the resources on Aboriginal title lands without waiting for treaties to be signed."[22] What do Indigenous peoples achieve through RFAs when giving the provincial governments economic certainty? Manuel found that "Indigenous peoples only get vague and limited benefits."[23] Uncertainty actually allows Indigenous nations to exercise greater self-determining authority. As Manuel states, "The existing uncertainty is, in fact, the biggest power we have for pushing the federal government to change the present extinguishment policy."[24]

Reconciliation connotes a return to a previous harmonious relationship. However, if that harmonious relationship never existed, reconciliation is based on a false premise. The state of Canada is founded on myths of terra nullius, Doctrine of Use, and Doctrine of Discovery, which necessitated the criminalization of Indigenous bodies to justify taking the land. According to Anishinaabe scholar Heidi Kiiwetinepinesiik Stark, "Casting Indigenous men and women as savage peoples in need of civilization and composing Indigenous lands as lawless spaces absent legal order, made it possible for the United States and Canada to shift and expand the boundaries of both settler law and the nation itself by judicially proclaiming their own criminal behaviors as lawful."[25]

When thinking of reconciliation as a historical reboot, "Forgive and forget" is a common refrain around gestures of reconciliation. According to the preamble to the Mandate for the TRC, "There is an emerging and compelling desire to put the events of the past behind us so that we can work towards a stronger and healthier future." This linear notion of time is often at odds with Indigenous knowledges and world views. According to a 2018 Angus Reid Survey of Canadians, 53 per cent of those surveyed believed that "Canada spends too much time apologizing for residential schools – it's time to move on."[26] Additionally, 53 per cent of those surveyed felt that Indigenous peoples should be "integrating more into broader Canadian society even if that means losing more of their culture and traditions."[27] These findings suggest that a majority of Canadians polled broadly identify with the notion of "moving on" from perceived historical events as well as placing Indigenous cultures and knowledges in the past.

Finally, reconciliation is often used as a tool to placate or co-opt Indigenous peoples into roles that take their energies away from land, cultural practices, and a community focus. Reconciliation as conflict management often focuses on deficit models of Indigenous peoples and attempts to bridge the economic gap between Indigenous and non-Indigenous people. However, closing the gap in wealth does nothing to close the gap between Indigenous and non-Indigenous world views. Unfortunately, a colonial compartmentalization of roles and responsibilities can detach Indigenous governance from land, water, and economies. According to the late Art Manuel, "All that talk about respect and reconciliation is self-serving rhetoric, because if the prime minister and the premiers actually respected indigenous peoples, they would recognize that they must first respect and affirm our indigenous rights to our lands before real reconciliation is even logically possible."[28]

So if we are to avoid the four intellectual and policy dead ends of reconciliation, it is important to focus on ways that stories and witnessing are taken seriously within Indigenous nations. In the following section, I examine Kwakwak'awakw and Sto:lo artist Carey Newman's process for taking stories seriously during the creation of the Witness Blanket.

The Witness Blanket

On 2 June 2018 I sat with Carey Newman in his kitchen to discuss the making of the Witness Blanket and the extensive process he went through. He started with his initial vision for the blanket, which was to honour his relationship to his father, who was a residential school survivor. At one point it struck Carey that he could weave a blanket together out of solid objects by collecting pieces of residential schools. With a clear vision in mind for making the blanket, Carey explained how difficult it was to earn the trust of survivors:

> And we had basically 15 months to make a blanket. And, you get out there, you hire a team out there, and you start asking people for these things. And you have to kind of build your credibility, you have to invest time and

effort in – in describing the concept, and making it accessible to people who can't envision it. When you can barely envision it yourself, that can be a challenging task. We figured out a bunch of different ways to communicate it, and I had such a great team of people travelling the country asking to sort of talk – talking about it, and asking for people to participate. And then you start getting things. And, of course, the first couple things that come through are pretty much what you expected. Like, brick, stone, some broken glass. And then – then all of a sudden you get a doorknob. And you start to think a little differently because that doorknob that I'm talking about came from the Blood Reserve, and it was from the boys} dormitory.... And I saw this doorknob, and it was just like, how many hands have turned this doorknob?... And that was like a big shift I guess in like my concept. The pieces from the buildings are witnesses themselves. They're a part of this history. And in my Kwagiulth teachings, our Big House is our ancestor. And the ridge board is the spine, and the – behind the dance curtain is the brain, and the heart is fire. And the door is the mouth. And so, if I take that concept and apply it to all buildings, these buildings, were the ancestors of the children who lived in them.[29]

This is when Carey began to think more deeply about the stories contained within the Witness Blanket and how to honour those living beings. He also had to reset his expectations when items were not coming in quickly enough for him to meet his goal of receiving 1,000 or more items. Each of these items had people and stories behind it. They were contributing things like photographs, merit badges, hockey skates, etc., so that these stories would not be forgotten.

Then Carey received an item that had a big impact on him:

Rosie was up in Carcross, in the Yukon, and she called – she was at this site collecting things, and listening to the stories of this man, and she came home, she was gone for a week, she came home, and first thing Friday morning, my doorbell rings, and it's eight o'clock in the morning, which is way earlier than anybody ever rings my doorbell. And I go down – I hop out of bed, go downstairs, and it's Rosie. She's standing in the door, and she has this shoebox. And she goes, "I'm sorry to wake you up, I know you've probably been sleeping, but, I had to bring you this. But before I give it to you, I have to tell you why I'm bringing it to you right now."

And then she proceeds to tell me about how she picked up this little child's shoe from the site of a burned down residential school in Carcross, and she put it in the shoebox, and she brought it back to her bed and breakfast, and was leaving the next day, so she went to bed. In the middle of the night, she woke up, having a nightmare, and like running and kicking in her sleep. And like, night terror kind of thing. She didn't think much of it then, she packed up and headed out the next day. And got home late that night. Threw down her bags, gave her husband a hug, and then went to bed. And in the middle of the night, he woke up with the same thing. And she's like, there's only one thing that it could be. It has to be the shoe. So, she brought it. Told me, "I just needed to make sure you know before you put it in your house, what happened to me, and what my experience with it was."

And so, I took it, and I brought it downstairs, and then later that night, before I went to bed, I took the shoe out of the box, and I held it, and I was so moved by the emotion that I could feel. And I'm not like a person who would consider myself a spiritual – I'm – what am I trying to say. I'm not normally the kind of person who is attuned with those things. I'm not a spiritual person in that way. But I held that shoe and I could feel something. And, so I started to do the only thing that I could think of to do, which was to talk. And I talked to the shoe like it was person. Like it was living. And I started to explain the work I was doing, and why I was doing it, and what it was about. And I just kind of sat there saying words out loud, and really moved by this whole – by this piece.

And I could by what I could sort of feel, sense from it. And I did that every night for the first week. And it was – it was important, because it taught me about the level of respect I was going to have to pay to the individual items.[30]

The story that Carey shared about the shoe expresses why it's so important to take stories seriously. The shoe had its own history and story that was being neglected. When Carey started speaking to the shoe and explaining what he was doing in the project, things changed. By treating the shoe as a living entity, the story was being honoured and respected. When Carey took the time to spend with the shoe, he was engaging in moments of tōhi: by moving at the pace of nature and not rushing to a conclusion or solution. As with residential school survivor experiences and accounts, the shoe didn't want to be neglected or forgotten.

The Witness Blanket as a whole is part of a collective process of jogging of our memories so that survivor stories and accounts will be remembered. There are stories with each part of the blanket that need to be heard and witnessed. In this sense, witnessing is an important way to give voice to these stories and draw on them to address the injustice and colonial legacies of residential school. Even though the dead-ends of reconciliation are still prevalent in the policy discourse, the Witness Blanket and these stories show us alternatives to shape-shifting colonization. The ceremony that my daughter and I witnessed, which treated the Witness Blanket as a living entity with its own decision-making agency, is an important component of our stories around governance and natural laws. These are the new stories being generated to new witnesses. How seriously will we take these new stories? The Witness Blanket ceremony was about generating new stories about community resurgence and nationhood.

Conclusion

I started this chapter with a story about a Witness Blanket ceremony. These new stories and understandings are about reclaiming Indigenous landscapes and fully expressing our self-determining authority. Stories are a critical dimension of resurgence and often take place in everyday contexts, within a family, ceremonial, or other intimate settings. Ultimately, focusing on everyday actions allows us to appreciate and engage in extended notions of kinship where our families and more-than-human relations can thrive together.

A Cherokee notion of leadership starts with a person having a vision or dream. That person begins to embody that vision by putting it into everyday practice. While implementing it, the person also has a responsibility to make that vision understandable to other people through his or her words and actions. After gaining this experience, the person offers some direction for people to mobilize around that vision. In short, this is leadership by example, which is common to most Indigenous nations. Key to this process is making the vision relatable to other people. This form of leadership by example is encompassed in the ways we honour and nurture our families and homelands every day. Stories are some of the ways that we make our experiences and actions relatable to others. They help us put our teachings in the forefront and move beyond performance and/or symbolic gestures to meaningful everyday practices of witnessing, storytelling, and truth-telling.

Remembering is a key part of being a witness for change and relational accountability. When people are out on the land and water, they begin to remember the sources of their strength, whether it is their relationship to water, plants, animals, or other aspects of the natural world. This work provides important insights into how we educate future generations about relationships for the perpetuation of our nationhood. The examples of witnessing and storytelling offer different but overlapping directions for sustainable self-determination and ways to enable the transmission and production of Indigenous knowledges for future generations. By restorying Indigenous landscapes, Indigenous nations are honouring and practising community resurgence so that future generations will remember.

NOTES

1 CBC News, "Witness Blanket Weaves Residential School Memories Together," 14 December 2015, https://www.cbc.ca/news/canada /manitoba/witness-blanket-cmhr-winnipeg-1.3363889.

2 Andrea Smith, "The Witness Blanket, and the Hard Lessons of Treaties," *Tyee*, 17 May 2019, https://thetyee.ca/Culture/2019/05/17 /Carey-Newman-Witness-Blanket-Hard-Lesson-Treaties/.

3 Marsha Lederman, "The Witness Blanket, an Installation of Residential School Artifacts, Makes Canadian Legal history," *Globe and Mail* 21 October 2019, https://www.theglobeandmail.com/arts/art-and-architecture /article-the-witness-blanket-an-installation-of-residential-school-artifacts/.

4 Johnny Mack, "Hoquotist: Reorienting through Storied Practice," in *Storied Communities: Narratives of Contact and Arrival in Constituting Political Community*, ed. Hester Lessard, Rebecca Johnson, and Jeremy Webber (Vancouver: UBC Press, 2011), 289.

5 Sarah Hunt, "Researching within Relations of Violence: Witnessing as Methodology," in *Indigenous Research: Theories, Practices, and Relationships*, ed. Deborah McGregor, Jean-Paul Restoule, and Rochelle Johnston (Toronto: Canadian Scholars' Press, 2018), 284.

6 Hunt, "Researching within Relations of Violence," 292.

7 Robin Wall Kimmerer, *Braiding Sweetgrass: Indigenous Wisdom, Scientific Knowledge and the Teachings of Plants* (Minneapolis, MN: Milkweed Editions, 2014), 9.

8 Leanne Betasamosake Simpson, *As We Have Always Done: Indigenous Freedom through Radical Resistance* (Minneapolis: University of Minnesota Press, 2017), 44.

9 Gina Starblanket and Heidi Stark, "Towards a Relational Paradigm: Four Points of Consideration," in *Resurgence and Reconciliation: Indigenous-Settler Relations and Earth Teachings*, ed. Michael Asch, John Borrows, and James Tully (Toronto: University of Toronto Press, 2018), 190–1 (authors' emphasis).

10 G.P. Horsefly, *A History of the True People: The Cherokee Indians* (Detroit: Oral History Publication, 1979), 9–10.

11 H.M. Altman and T.M. Belt, "Tōhi: The Cherokee Concept of Well-Being," in *Under the Rattlesnake: Cherokee Health and Resiliency*, ed. L.J. Lefler (Tuscaloosa: University of Alabama Press, 2009), 9–22.

12 The original version of this story is in Andrew Rigby, *Justice and Reconciliation: After the Violence* (Boulder, CO: Lynne Rienner Publishers, 2001), 142.

13 Eve Tuck and K. Wayne Yang, "Decolonization Is Not a Metaphor," *Decolonization: Indigeneity, Education and Society* 1, no. 1 (2012): 35.

14 Cindy Blackstock, "Reconciliation Means Not Saying Sorry Twice: Lessons from Child Welfare in Canada," in *From Truth to Reconciliation*, ed. Marlene

Brant Castellano, Linda Archibald, and Mike DeGagne (Ottawa: Aboriginal Healing Foundation, 2008), 163.

15 Blackstock, "Reconciliation Means Not Saying Sorry Twice," 174.

16 Jeff Corntassel, Chaw-win-is, and T'lakwadzi. 2009. "Indigenous Storytelling, Truth-telling, and Community Approaches to Reconciliation," *ESC: English Studies in Canada* 35, no. 1 (2009): 138.

17 For the TRC findings, see http://www.trc.ca/about-us/trc-findings.html.

18 CBC News, "Truth and Reconciliation Commission Urges Canada to Confront 'Cultural Genocide' of Residential Schools," 2 June 2015, https://www.cbc.ca/news/politics/truth-and-reconciliation-commission-urges-canada-to-confront-cultural-genocide-of-residential-schools-1.3096229.

19 CBC News, "Beyond 94," 19 March, 2018, https://newsinteractives.cbc.ca/longform-single/beyond-94.

20 CBC News, "Beyond 94."

21 Roy Stewart and Derek Simon, "By Fighting a Compensation Ruling, the Government Denies First Nations Children justice – Again," CBC News, 8 October 2019, https://www.cbc.ca/news/opinion/hrt-ruling-1.5312191.

22 Art Manuel, *The Reconciliation Manifesto: Recovering the Land Rebuilding the Economy* (Toronto: James Lorimer, 2017), 204.

23 Manuel, *Reconciliation Manifesto*, 206.

24 Manuel, *Reconciliation Manifesto*, 208.

25 Heidi Stark, "Criminal Empire: The Making of the Savage in a Lawless Land," *Theory and Event* 19, no. 4 (2016), https://muse.jhu.edu/article/633282.

26 Angus Reid Institute, "Truths of Reconciliation: Canadians Are Deeply Divided on How Best to Address Indigenous Issues," 6 June 2018, http://angusreid.org/wp-content/uploads/2018/06/2018.04.23_indigenous_fullreport.pdf, 3.

27 Angus Reid Institute. "Truths of Reconciliation," 3.

28 Manuel, *Reconciliation Manifesto*, p. 203.

29 Newman, "Witness Blanket Interview."

30 Newman, "Witness Blanket Interview."

10 Political Action in the Time of Reconciliation

COREY SNELGROVE AND MATTHEW WILDCAT

> While more traditional studies of how the environment influences actors are important, studying how actors influence the environment helps us to understand not only how the world works, but how to change it.[1]

In the last few years reconciliation has become a central concept within Canadian politics. Although deployed in multiple arenas to rethink Indigenous–non-Indigenous as well as Indigenous-state relations over the past three decades, reconciliation remained marginal even as the Truth and Reconciliation Commission (TRC) held hearings across the country. Yet the release of the TRC's *Calls to Action* in June 2015,[2] unlike any other document on Indigenous politics, has had a gravitational like pull on Canadian public consciousness and politics. Reconciliation became a dominant theme in the 2015 election that saw the Justin Trudeau Liberals defeat the reigning Conservative Party partly on the basis of a promise to implement the Calls to Action and embrace the "nation-to-nation relationship." Reconciliation has also been included as a goal in almost every cabinet mandate letter across the country, and in recent federal budgets reconciliation justifies a range of policies and associated funding.[3]

Still, reconciliation remains a highly contested political idea, normative orientation, and goal, eliciting a wide range of critical responses. In this chapter we have ignored perspectives on reconciliation that deny the violence of colonization and express hostility to or dismiss Indigenous self-determination. Instead, our interest is in two opposing perspectives on reconciliation – considered as ideal types – expressed by those who seek to further Indigenous self-determination. On the one hand is a perspective that involves an embrace of reconciliation, where the idea of reconciliation is a vehicle for positive change in the Indigenous–non-Indigenous and/or Indigenous–state relationship. While the degree of embrace fluctuates within this perspective, one predominant form takes the argument of contrasting definitions or conceptions of reconciliation. On the other hand is a constellation of critiques that normatively reject reconciliation as a political movement and language. The reductionist version of this critique is captured by the sentiment "Reconciliation equals assimilation." Here reconciliation is a political sleight of hand where the Canadian state uses a benevolent front to recognize Indigenous rights, title, and political authorities while quietly carrying out its intended goal of extinguishing Indigenous peoples as legal and political entities through incorporation under provincial and federal jurisdiction.

In the following we offer an alternative approach to the politics of reconciliation that sees reconciliation as a unique *moment of colonial reconfiguration*. This moment also signals openings that are strategically significant. This approach is based on two premises. First, reconciliation has not emerged through Canadian self-reflexivity, introspection, socio-historical learning, or progressive enlightenment but by generations of Indigenous peoples' sustained legal, political, and economic action that has *forced* a reckoning within Canadian society and responses by the state – motivated in part by Canada's self-image as a land of justice. Here Canada attempts to reconcile its self-image with the fact of colonization. We use the term *reconfiguration* to describe Canada's attempts to reorder itself to account for injustice against Indigenous peoples. But this attempt is short-circuited as federal and provincial sovereignty, and the economic imperatives of Canadian governments remain substantially unchanged. Resource extraction has not diminished in importance, and Canada maintains a white populace that remain invested in their claims to colonial sovereignty and racial superiority. Thus the moment of reconciliation is still a *colonial reconfiguration*.

Second, despite the colonial underpinnings, the attempt by the Canadian state at reconfiguration *signals openings* and opportunities that can be taken advantage of through strategic political action. Our approach in this chapter is less concerned with whether reconciliation is good or bad. Instead, we want to attend to the importance of *also* asking what opportunities exist in this conjuncture. In other words, we think of reconciliation as signalling an opening for strategic action rather than seeing the outcome of *colonial reconfiguration* as already predetermined (as either progress or regressive continuity).

The first section of the chapter offers a survey of responses to the question of reconciliation in order to draw out an overlooked element in these otherwise important interventions: reconciliation as a *moment of colonial reconfiguration*, which is also a moment of relative vulnerability for the Canadian state and this vulnerability *signals openings* for political action where Indigenous actors can make strategic gains.[4] The second section offers a brief history of reconciliation in order to defend our premise that this moment has emerged from generations of Indigenous resistance that has forced a response within Canadian society and by the state. The third section provides an example of how the current context was taken advantage of by the Maskwacîs Cree and their efforts to create a new education authority. Snelgrove was the main author on the initial two sections, the third section was authored by Wildcat, and both authors helped to shape each section.[5]

The Question of Reconciliation

Identified with the global project of transitional justice that emerged in the mid-1990s, scholars such as Glen Coulthard have shown how the deployment of reconciliation in non-transitional contexts is a way to "ideologically manufacture" a transition from a colonial past to a post-colonial present through apologies and other symbolic expressions of regret and guilt.[6] In this view, reconciliation is seen to suture a potential rupture, where Canada and Canadians' acknowledgement of the oppression of Indigenous peoples becomes a sign of progress, while Indigenous peoples' progress is similarly marked by the degree to which reconciliation is embraced.[7] Here reconciliation is condemned for its elision of colonization as a systematic, purposeful, and ongoing project, in light of which resentment (in contrast to reconciliation) can be seen as a rational response and indicator of critical consciousness.

For others, the current reconciliation project is really a misnomer. Here responses take the form of contrasting "false" and "true" visions of reconciliation, where present government-led policies and closely associated approaches are criticized from an alternative perspective on and definition of reconciliation. For example, reconciliation requires restitution rather than an apology;[8] land rather than closing the gap in program and service provisions;[9] or reconciliation based on Indigenous peoples' understandings of treaty rather than the doctrine of discovery and state interpretations of treaty.[10] A similar but distinct type of response contests less the definition of the concept than its order of appearance, thus introducing a temporal element into the question. Examples here include the notion of truth *before* reconciliation,[11] decolonization *before* reconciliation,[12] or the end of the termination policy and substantive recognition of Aboriginal rights and title *before* reconciliation.[13]

Another type of response attends to the potential subjects and objects of reconciliation and the ways in which this shapes the definition of reconciliation and its evaluation as a project of social justice, affirming some forms but not others. For example, reconciliation can be between or within Indigenous nations;[14] between Indigenous nations and the federal and/or provincial government(s); between Indigenous nations and Canadian citizens; between Indigenous nations and civil society organizations (such as religious institutions or unions); between Indigenous nations and corporations; between Indigenous nations and marginalized peoples (as opposed to white settlers; for example, that between the Khalsa Aid Canada and the Ahousaht Nation[15]); between Indigenous nations, non-Indigenous peoples, and the earth;[16] between Indigenous *individuals* and a variety of institutions and organizations; and/or between and across *generations* of Indigenous and non-Indigenous peoples.[17] Still others argue that reconciliation has been possible only for certain subjects and with respect to certain objects.[18] In other words, reconciliation is possible only for a select few and for select political projects. The critique here is often about how reconciliation is contingent and non-transformative, consequently ameliorating violence for some and/or displacing violence onto various others – an amelioration and/or displacement more often than not along the lines of race, sexuality, gender, and class.

More recently, though, some suggest that reconciliation is nothing new. In this view, reconciliation is but the latest iteration of Canada and Canadians' attempts to steal land and ignore Indigenous legal and governance orders with the end goal of eliminating Indigenous polities and transforming citizens of those polities into individual though culturally recognized members of Canada. Here reconciliation *equals* assimilation. This formulation is understandable, given the ways reconciliation has failed to produce transformative change.[19] However, inasmuch as the formula of reconciliation equals assimilation is a reasonable assessment of our present moment, offering a critical and decisive statement on the continuity of the colonial relation, it risks overlooking the challenges Canada faces over how it reproduces the colonial relation with Indigenous peoples – challenges signalled by the reconciliation project itself.

As we note in the introduction, instead of approaching the question of reconciliation from an overly discursive or normative standpoint, we foreground a history that illustrates how reconciliation is a moment of colonial reconfiguration that signals openings by attending to its historical emergence. This move towards colonial reconfiguration is in response to Indigenous-led political struggles' causing what Nancy Fraser refers to in a different context as a "legitimation deficit," which threatens to move into a "legitimation crisis" in its expression of and articulation with other political and economic crises affecting the Canadian settler colony.[20] These contradictions and crises, which have not been resolved, signal the challenge of reproducing the colonial relation. Our concern then is that both the discursive and moral critique of reconciliation over-look the conditions that gave rise to reconciliation as a *project* and con-tinue to remain in the present. These are openings that can be leveraged for immediate, long-term, and potentially transformative change.

But just as these openings are missed by an uncritical embrace of rec-onciliation that conceals the political struggles and the underlying crises that gave rise to the project, we argue that they might also be missed by a normative rejection of reconciliation. While we agree with approaches that highlight colonization and its effects as ongoing, systemic, purpose-ful, *and* differentially distributed, we want to highlight the contradictions of that system and its vulnerabilities. We believe a more accurate view of colonial power emerges by highlighting the openings that occur within this colonial reconfiguration. Rather than viewing colonial power as to-talizing and unmoving, our analysis focuses on how colonial power must be reproduced. The reproduction of colonial power is never guaranteed and must constantly respond to the efforts of Indigenous peoples to seek justice. Colonial power is constantly in need of new strategies to repro-duce itself, and the reconciliation project represents a vulnerability that signals openings within colonial power structures. It is in this moment of vulnerability that we should emphasize the power and potential of political action that works against colonial domination.

A History of Reconciliation: Struggle and Crisis

While a more thorough account of reconciliation's historical emergence would require a much longer discussion, the account here focuses more narrowly on the period from the 1970s to the present. This period is the basis for reconciliation in the present in that (1) it marks a period of a global and enduring economic downturn that sees an increase in the relative importance of financialization, extraction, and logistics[21], as well as (2) a shift in approach by the courts to the question of Aboriginal rights and a subsequent if reluctant and circumscribed shift from White Paper liberalism to a politics of recognition in light of Indigenous polit-ical resistance.[22]

Reconciliation emerged first as a (still-evolving) judicial concept through a series of Supreme Court of Canada (SCC) decisions in the early to mid-1990s on Aboriginal rights.[23] Yet the recognition of those rights in the contemporary era has its origins in the 1973 *Calder* decision and the 1980 Constitutional Express. The *Calder* decision recognized the possibility of Aboriginal title by abandoning, at least in part, racist interpretations of Indigenous political organizations as non-existent.[24] This caused a shift in the approach of the federal government away from the White Paper and towards the comprehensive land claims policy.[25] According to Michael Asch this era "marked the beginning of the journey towards reconciliation."[26] Since the Constitutional Express of 1980 ensured the recognition of Aboriginal rights in the repatriation of the Canadian Constitution, it too is a crucial moment in the emergence of reconciliation.

At around the same time as the emergence of the concept in the SCC, and with express attention to the limits of the courts, reconciliation became a political-social concept with the Royal Commission on Aboriginal Peoples (RCAP) that lasted from 1991 until the release of its final report in 1996. RCAP originated as a response to the Oka Crisis of 1990 and allied blockades across the country along with increased coverage of socio-economic disparities between Indigenous and non-Indigenous peoples. The 440 recommendations in that report are cited as "avenues of reconciliation," while historic treaty and treaty-making practices are invoked as models of reconciliation.[27] Chapter 10 of that 4,000-plus page report discussed the residential school system, and in 1998 the federal government issued a "Statement of Reconciliation" – the only direct government response to that report – which announced a $350 million fund and the establishment of the Aboriginal Healing Foundation.[28]

With precedents in the RCAP, reconciliation became a moral-social concept in the Truth and Reconciliation Commission (TRC). The TRC emerged as one part of the Indian Residential Schools Settlement Agreement (2006) – an alternative to the failed Alternative Dispute Resolution process that sought to address a class-action lawsuit led by residential school survivors and the subsequent financial liability of the federal government for the residential school system.[29] As Aimee Craft notes, the definition of reconciliation by the TRC – establishing and maintaining mutually respectful relationships – differs from that offered by the SCC – a procedural approach that appears to amount to a framework to justify infringement.[30] Moreover, while reconciliation at the SCC and RCAP tended to be directed towards federal and provincial governments, the TRC was unique in its attempt to connect directly with non-Indigenous individuals, civil society organizations, and corporations through public outreach and dissemination.[31] As chair of the TRC, Justice Murray Sinclair decided to target the Canadian public in light of his previous work for Manitoba's Aboriginal Justice Inquiry (1988–91), which failed to change society. Since the release of the inquiry's findings, incarceration rates for Indigenous peoples in the province doubled overall, while tripling (!) for Indigenous women, despite increased representation in policing and legal professions.[32] The confluence of the work of the TRC – which pointed to the responsibility of Canadian individuals for addressing colonization and its effects – and the Idle No More movement that emerged in December 2012 along with associated or adjacent movements against pipelines and fracking operations (such as in Elsipogtog in 2013), the removal of children into state "care" (especially the work of Cindy Blackstock and the First Nations Child and Family Caring Society), alongside other struggles paved the way for reconciliation to occupy its current spotlight.

An important aspect to this history is the way in which it registers the role of political action in making reconciliation a central point of contestation through persistent struggle at particular and increasingly vulnerable sites. This brief history shows how the development of the concept at the SCC and RCAP was in part a result of Indigenous-led political and legal struggles, including blockades that interrupted the circuit of capital, while the TRC was in part a response to the financial liability stemming from the federal government's responsibility for the Indian residential school system and initiated by the legal action of residential school survivors. As noted above, the choice to direct the TRC at least in part to non-Indigenous individuals and civil society organizations was also a strategic decision in light of recent history. More recently, the Idle No More movement as well as associated and adjacent actors were able to connect public discourse around the TRC to ongoing colonization – in the form of omnibus bills that sought environmental deregulation that would both erode treaty *rights* and violate the treaty *relationship* in order to facilitate economic development – while at the same time continuing the history of direct action, including blockades and occupations at sites of circulation and extraction.

This history of Indigenous struggle amidst increasingly fragile conditions of capital accumulation may also help explain why, while available as an idea/concept as early as 1990 and most obviously since the RCAP report in 1996, it was not until the election of the Trudeau Liberals that reconciliation became a guiding idea or governing rationale. This is because, as suggested by the 2013 Eyford Report, reconciliation appeared to offer an answer to the impasse between Indigenous peoples' resistance to the latest rounds of dispossession, which have caused greater uncertainty for extractive projects that are increasingly important for Canadian society and their government.[33] The Conservative government's general indifference to optics, not to mention their specific approach to the Idle No More movement, meant it was far too late to reform their image and heed this advice. By claiming to be the face of change, the Trudeau Liberals were able to return to government in part through an embrace of the idea of reconciliation.

As noted above, this alliance between the reconciliation project and resource extraction has led some to the conclusion that reconciliation equals assimilation with a corresponding demand to reject it. What we have tried to stress in this section is the role of political action and systemic contradictions in leading to this moment. Again the point of which is not to call for the embrace of reconciliation but to instead recall the *effects* of political action and the ways in which the state struggles to respond to such action, grasping at different solutions over the last near half-century. To us, this reaction discloses its own internal systemic contradictions and undermines its own claims to certainty.

As noted above, Coulthard argues that reconciliation works to "ideologically manufacture" a break from a colonial past through a claim that reconciliation marks the beginning of a postcolonial present. Canada has also effectively narrated the history of reconciliation as a story of its own moral progress, rather than emerging from a history of Indigenous struggle as shown in this section. That is, reconciliation becomes a story of Canadian progress that exists *above* rather than emerging as a *result* of Indigenous struggle. Another trick of reconciliation then may be the ways in which this narration projects Canadian morality and certainty over its past, present, and future, while also working to depoliticize non-state actors by downplaying their efficacy. Yet in critiquing the idea of reconciliation as moral progress, it is easy for a slippage to occur where our rejection of reconciliation also obscures the history of struggle that produced it. The irony of the normative rejection of reconciliation is that it seems to affirm Canada's own narration.

As we will argue in the next section and through the example of the Maskwacîs Education Schools Commission (MESC), the continuing uncertainty in the reproduction of the colonial relation causes a *colonial reconfiguration* that *signals openings* missed by a normative rejection of reconciliation. The education agreement between the Maskwacîs Cree and Government of Canada is an expression of Indigenous self-determination, represents a significant material gain for the community, and has the potential to usher in increasing self-determination in the future.

Maskwacîs Education Schools Commission

In May 2018 the Maskwacîs Education Schools Commission held a ceremonial signing of the Maskwacîs Education Agreement. Maskwacîs is composed of four First Nations in central Alberta – Montana, Louis Bull, Ermineskin, and Samson. Until 2018, these four nations each ran its own K–12 school system – eleven schools with around 2,300 students. Although formally separate, the different authorities have undertaken increasing degrees of collaboration since 2011 when they formed the Maskwacîs Education Steering Committee.[34] In 2015 the chief and councils of Maskwacîs passed a motion authorizing the Steering Committee to explore the possibility of merging the four systems into a single education authority. The steering committee was incorporated as the Maskwacîs Education Schools Commission (MESC) in 2016 and began researching the creation of the new school division. From 2016 to 2018, MESC undertook the research and consultation necessary to vet the idea of creating a unified education authority. The work included school needs assessments, seven leadership summits, twenty-five community meetings, community outreach through social media, mail outs and information packages, the creation of a Maskwacîs Declaration on Education, and a Maskwacîs Education Law. Finally, in addition to these community and organizational initiatives, MESC coordinated a team of educators, political leaders, and lawyers, almost exclusively from the community, to negotiate the Maskwacîs Education Agreement and Maskwacîs funding formula with the federal government.[35]

This work happened under the shadow of two widely condemned attempts at First Nation education reform by the federal government. First there was the failed First Nations Control of First Nations Education Act in 2014.[36] The second was the initiation of the Education Partnership program in late 2017 by the Trudeau government that had the amalgamation of existing school systems as a condition for creating new education agreements. Both initiatives were criticized as further examples of paternalistic government interventions that at best ignored First Nation treaty rights, or at worst sought to eliminate these treaty rights. The funding for the partnership program was justified as an expression of reconciliation in the federal budgets, which only seemed to confirm the idea that reconciliation equals assimilation.

At times this has led a small but vocal group to criticize the work of MESC as an initiative that was giving up the treaty right to education. If the interpretive frame of "reconciliation as assimilation" is applied, it is easy to view the actions of Maskwacîs as falling for a government trap. But when the context of reconciliation we previously described is applied to understand the actions of MESC, we can see how the Maskwacîs Cree were taking advantage of an opening made available as the state sought to reconfigure itself. Importantly, it was not the opening alone that created the opportunity but rather the strategic capacity the Maskwacîs Cree had built up over decades of community development around education – an example of how "turning away" from the state[37] was an opportunity to build strategic capacity necessary to take advantage of moments when the state found itself vulnerable.

In his study of the politics of recognition and Indigenous liberation, Coulthard argues that the politics of recognition will reproduce the same relationship of colonial domination between Indigenous peoples and Canada that was enacted under a policy of assimilation.[38] Coulthard's insight is to show how colonial domination continues to occur within state-Indigenous negotiations that recognize Aboriginal rights and title. The state maintains domination not simply through unequal power relations that allows the state to set the terms of negotiation; the uneven field of power also works on the subjectivities of Indigenous participants so that they come to identify with the aspirations of the state.[39] In response Coulthard calls for a *turning away* from seeking state recognition to find an emancipatory praxis grounded in one's own traditions, upholding one's own self-worth as the source of Indigenous liberation.[40] Within Coulthard's work it is clear that he imagines the turn away as describing/motivating grassroots movements and does not apply his insights to Indigenous institutional contexts. Here I would like to argue that the history of building education systems in Maskwacîs was the result of an internal focus on building the schools rather than an externally focused politics of looking towards the state as a source of change. In other words it is possible to *turn away* in Indigenous institutional contexts.

The underfunding of First Nations schools is well publicized. A major funding challenge for First Nation schools is that school budgets are determined by student enrolment. For status Indian children who attend school off-reserve, Indian Affairs sends tuition to the neighbouring provincial system instead of the First Nation. In most cases the majority of students on reserve attend schools off reserve. On the basis of this situation, an obvious strategy for First Nation schools to increase their budget was to recruit students who were attending provincial school systems. However, Miyo Wahkohtowin Education in Maskwacîs (one of the four former school systems) did not deploy this strategy. Rather, their priority was focusing on the students who were already attending their schools and working to ensure they were able to provide the best possible education for those students. While this strategy did not provide short-term gains in student recruitment, over the long term it meant that Miyo Wahkohtowin retention rates gradually increased, eventually becoming a school of first choice for parents and students, not only in Maskwacîs but in the region.

The best evidence is that in 2016, and for the first time, the neighbouring provincial school system sent tuition payments *to* Miyo Wahkohtowin Education for the twenty students who were travelling from the neighbouring town of Wetaskiwin to attend Miyo Wahkohtowin schools. Other indications include increasing graduation rates. In 2003 eight students became the first class of high school graduates, while in 2017 that number rose to fifty-eight.[41] Furthermore, while 32 per cent of children went to school on-reserve in 1990, today 70 per cent of children go to school on-reserve.[42] Finally, the schools are innovation leaders in multiple arenas. Two studies by Shauna Bruno demonstrate how educators in Maskwacîs implement unique solutions to student conflict and alternative education. The results demonstrated an increase in student achievement, attendance, and safety, and a decrease in punitive intervention hearings. Further, educators devised local forms of data collection in order to assess performance, make adjustments, and alter and revise their strategies in light of the data.[43]

The internally driven focus of the schools helps to improve education outcomes, but it also created a cohort of education leaders who developed a high degree of what Marshall Ganz calls "strategic capacity."[44] Ganz defines strategic capacity as a confluence of three factors – a group's access to the right information, the ability to have open inter-group dialogue that contributes to ongoing learning, and the motivation of a group to achieve their goals.[45] In the work of MESC, the strategic capacity of the education leadership combined with young people in the community who were skilled at communications, graphic design, governance, and law, as well as political leaders from all four nations who offered their support and articulated a political philosophy that added momentum to the work of the commission. The work of articulating a new political philosophy involved drawing from traditional and spiritual knowledge, and reinscribing a shared political identity instead of emphasizing division between the nations. As well, the leadership insisted and ensured that merging the school systems and negotiating the Maskwacîs Education Agreement was an exercise of inherent political authority and not the result of an agenda driven by the federal government. As a former chief of Montana stated, "We are not giving up our treaty right to education. What we are doing is figuring out how we pursue the treaty right to education from our interpretation."[46]

The result is that Maskwacîs was able to generate the strategic capacity necessary to take advantage of the federal government's attempt to reconfigure how it operates in the realm of First Nation education. By the time the Harper government initiated their reforms of First Nations education mentioned above, it was clear the state of education on reserves was a national disgrace *and* a liability.[47] Yet the federal government was unwilling to relinquish control over how this reform would take place. The Maskwacîs negotiation team was able to overcome this situation because the existing strategic capacity meant that it was easy to satisfy many of the stipulations required by the federal government, and MESC could push back on those they disagreed with – sometimes without effect, but overwhelmingly with effect. To give one example, as part of MESC's activities, an education law was developed to govern the schools. Inclusion of this law in the Maskwacîs Education agreement was originally rejected by federal negotiators. The response to the rejection, as MESC legal counsel Koren Lightning describes it, was "That's OK, we're going to create it anyways."[48] Through the course of negotiations, the federal position changed and the law was eventually included in the Maskwacîs Education agreement.

The Maskwacîs Education agreement provides Maskwacîs the autonomy to deliver curriculum based on local priorities, recognizes Cree as an official language of instruction, and includes budget enhancements for Cree language and culture. Proposal-driven funding that creates burdensome reporting requirements for First Nations is also eliminated and replaced with 100 per cent core funding. The overall operating funds will increase by 17 per cent, and the new school authority will have full budgetary discretion to allocate resources to community priorities. MESC will also orient all of its yearly reporting and data collection to the priorities of the community, and these will be the same reports provided to the federal government. Finally, the agreement recognizes the Maskwacîs Education Law and Maskwacîs Board Governance structure developed independently by the community as the governing structure of the schools. For good measure, a definition of the Cree principles *iyiniw mamtohnehicikan* (Cree knowledge), *wahkohtowin* (kinship), *nehiyawewin* (Cree language), and *nehiyaw pimatisowin* (Cree way of life) are acknowledged in the agreement as the foundational principles of the new school system.[49]

As noted above, the Maskwacîs Education Agreement is an expression of treaty and self-determination that affirms local control over education while ensuring greater funding to build on past successes. The history of education in Maskwacîs did not emerge from a history of the successful lobbying of the federal government for increased education dollars, nor is the agreement the result of finally gaining the upper hand of principled debate that First Nation schools should be funded at the same rates as provincial schools. Rather, the Maskwacîs Education agreement was the result of a history of turning away from the federal government, focusing instead on internal measures that promoted student success and strategic capacity, which enabled political intervention when an opportunity emerged. Not only does a predetermined application of the "reconciliation equals assimilation" frame risk mischaracterizing the work of Maskwacîs and the political lessons involved, but it also would overlook other openings the era of reconciliation signals – openings created from Indigenous resistance.

Conclusion

This chapter has argued for the importance of thinking about the historical emergence of reconciliation as a *moment* of colonial reconfiguration that signals openings by foregrounding the role of political struggle and state vulnerability. The purpose of foregrounding reconciliation as emerging from political struggle rather than Canada's progressive enlightenment was also aimed at remembering the efficacy of Indigenous political action. Along the way we also suggested that a trick of reconciliation is in the ways in which it downplays and depoliticizes non-state actors through a historical narration that replaces the actual history of political struggle with a story of progressive enlightenment. One motivating concern was that a normative rejection of reconciliation tends to miss the opening that reconciliation signals and the efficacy of political action.

Turning to the example of the Maskwacîs Cree and the establishment of the Maskwacîs Education Authority illustrates one way in which political action at opportune times can be an expression of Indigenous self-determination that is able to deliver immediate and long-term gains. While we agree that reforms in service delivery – such as the Maskwacîs Education Authority – do not equal decolonization, and that keeping our eyes on such transformative visions remain crucial, given the violence that is foundational to and constitutive of colonial capitalism, we are also wary of dismissing such immediate gains and caution against drawing strict dichotomies between the return of land versus improvement in services, or reform versus transformative change. While these dichotomies highlight the gap between the ideal (decolonization) and the real (ongoing settler colonization in an age of reconciliation), they risk overlooking how to get to the former from the latter.

In sum, the past forty-five years of political recognition for Indigenous peoples have not fundamentally transformed the colonial relationship, but it has shown how new tactics are required to guard against the systemic contradictions of the state and capital and to maintain colonial domination. Here we agree with the methodological sensibilities of Ganz, who asks us to focus not simply on how the structure determines actors, but on how actors can organize to alter the structure through strategic capacity and action. As Ganz states, "The greater an organization's strategic capacity, the more informed, creative, and responsive its strategic choices can be and the better able it is to take advantage of moments of unique opportunity to reconfigure itself for effective action."[50] We think characterizing the colonial relationship as uniformly oriented towards assimilation versus one that must constantly reconfigure itself in order to maintain colonial domination is an important distinction. It is within these reconfigurations that vulnerabilities are created that can be taken advantage of. In this we hope to bring attention to a different perspective on reconciliation that asks us to view it not as progress or regressive continuity – a perspective that seems limited to the register of morality – but as a window created by Indigenous resistance that opens possibilities for political action.

NOTES

1 Marshall Ganz, *Why David Sometimes Wins: Leadership, Organization, and Strategy in the California Farm Worker Movement* (Don Mills, ON: Oxford University Press, 2009), 20.

2 https://www2.gov.bc.ca/assets/gov/british-columbians-our-governments /indigenous-people/aboriginal-peoples-documents/calls_to_action _english2.pdf.

3 While reconciliation was mentioned in relation to the forthcoming activities of the TRC in the 2006 budget, it was not until the 2016 budget that it came to express a governing rationale:

> To support our shared economic interests and to advance the process of recon-ciliation, this Government proposes an unprecedented level of investment to support Indigenous communities and the aspirations of Indigenous peoples. The proposed investments, including in on reserve education and infrastruc-ture, begin to address some of the root causes of poverty, promote opportunity and inclusive growth, and help to lay the foundation for growth in Indigenous communities. This will benefit the broader Canadian economy. Budget 2016 proposes to invest $8.4 billion over five years, beginning in 2016–17, to improve the socio-economic conditions of Indigenous peoples and their communities and bring about transformational change. This represents a significant increase over the investments that would have been made under the Kelowna Accord. The unprecedented scale of this investment underscores the Government's intent to renew the relationship between Canada and Indigenous peoples. The proposed investments in education, infrastructure, training and other programs will directly contribute to a better quality of life for Indigenous peoples and a stronger, more unified, and prosperous Canada. (Budget 2016, 134)

In the 2018 budget "reconciliation" had its own chapter.

4 One notable exception in the literature on reconciliation is the late Art Ma-nuel's *The Reconciliation Manifesto* (Toronto: Lorimer Publishing, 2017).

5 This chapter emerges from a lecture delivered by Wildcat for the Edmonton Public Library and the Faculty of Native Studies in August 2017.

This sparked an ongoing conversation between Snelgrove and Wildcat that helped to further the ideas contained here.

6 Other essays that attend to the movement of reconciliation from transitional to non-transitional contexts and potential problems that follow include Bashir Bashir and Will Kymlicka, "Introduction," in *The Politics of Reconciliation in Multicultural Societies*, ed. Bashir and Kymlicka (Don Mills, ON: Oxford University Press, 2008), 1–25; as well as Courtney Jung, "Canada and the Legacy of the Indian Residential Schools: Transitional Justice for Indigenous Peoples in a Nontransitional Society," in *Identities in Transition: Challenges for Transitional Justice in Divided Societies*, ed. Arthur Paige (New York: Cambridge University Press, 2010), 217–50; and Courtney Jung, "Walls and Bridges: Competing Agendas in Transitional Justice," in *From Recognition to Reconciliation: Essays on the Constitutional Entrenchment of Aboriginal and Treaty Rights*, ed. Patrick Macklem and Douglas Sanderson (Toronto: University of Toronto Press, 2016), 357–88. Jung attends to competing agendas in the application of transitional justice to the Canadian context: the government invoked transitional justice to mark a "wall" between past and present, whereas Indigenous peoples used transitional justice as a "bridge" between past and present.

7 Glen Coulthard, *Red Skin, White Masks: Rejecting the Colonial Politics of Recognition* (Minneapolis: University of Minnesota Press, 2014), esp. chap. 4; see also Robert Meister, *After Evil: A Politics of Human Rights* (New York: Columbia University Press, 2011).

8 See, for instance Taiaiake Alfred, "Restitution Is the Real Pathway to Justice for Indigenous Peoples," in *Response, Responsibility, and Renewal: Canada's Truth and Reconciliation Journey*, ed. Gregory Younging, Jonathan Dewar, and Mike DeGagné (Ottawa: Aboriginal Healing Foundation, 2019), 171–91. Leanne Simpson, "Land & Reconciliation: Having the Right Conversations," *Electric City Magazine*, 5 March 2016, http://www.electriccitymagazine.ca/2016/01/land-reconciliation/.

9 Manuel, *Reconciliation Manifesto*.

10 Sheryl Lightfoot, *Global Indigenous Politics: A Subtle Revolution* (New York: Routledge, 2016). See also Craft, "Neither Infringement Nor Justification: The SCC's Mistaken Approach to Reconciliation," in *Renewing Relationships: Indigenous Peoples and Canada*, ed. Brenda Gunn and Karen Drake (Saskatchewan: University of Saskatchewan Native Law Centre, 2019), 59–82.

11 Patricia Barkaskas and Sarah Hunt, "Truth before Reconcliation: Reframing /Resisting/Refusing Reconciliation" (Vancouver: Simon Fraser University, 2017), https://www.youtube.com/watch?v=mB_7odACIpI&ab_channel=InstitutefortheHumanities.

12 Nelson Maldonando-Torres, "Reconciliation as a Contested Future: Decolonization as Project or beyond the Paradigm of War," in *Reconciliation, Nations and Churches in Latin America*, ed. Iain S. Maclean (Boca Raton, FL: CRC, 2006), 225–45.

13 Manuel, *Reconciliation Manifesto*.

14 See such a call in Zebedee Nungak, *Wrestling with Colonialism on Steroids: Quebec Inuit Fight for Their Homeland* (Montreal: Véhicule, 2017), 116–18; as well as that of Maria Campbell to the TRC in 2014, quoted in Craft, "Neither Infringement Nor Justification," 81.

15 Emilee Gilpin, "Two Communities Take ReconciliACTION into Their Own Hands," *National Observer*, 30 October 2018, https://www.nationalobserver.com/2018/10/30/news/two-communities-take-reconciliaction-their-own-hands.

16 John Borrows, "Earth-Bound: Indigenous Resurgence and Environmental Reconciliation," in *Resurgence and Reconciliation: Indigenous-Settler Relations and Earth Teachings*, ed. Michael Asch, John Borrows, and James Tully (Toronto: University of Toronto Press, 2019), 49–82; James Tully, "Reconciliation Here on Earth," in *Resurgence and Reconciliation*, 83–132.

17 Truth and Reconciliation Commission, *Honouring the Truth, Reconciling for the Future: Summary of the Final Report of the Truth and Reconciliation Commission of Canada* (Ottawa: Truth and Reconciliation Commission of Canada, 2015), 16. Also available online at https://truthcommissions.humanities.mcmaster.ca/wp-content/uploads/2021/03/TRC_Summary-of-the-Final-Report-of-the-Truth-and-Reconciliation-Commission-of-Canada.pdf.

18 See Sarah Hunt, "Violence, Law, and the Everyday Politics of Recognition: Commentary on *Red Skin, White Masks*" (presentation at the Native American and Indigenous Studies Association, Washington, DC, 6 June 2015), https://www.academia.edu/12834803/Violence_Law_and_the_Everyday_Politics_of_Recognition_commentary_on_Red_Skin_White_Masks_; and Hunt, "Embodying Self-Determination: Resisting Violence beyond the Gender Binary" (presentation at the Social Justice Institute, University of British Columbia, Vancouver, 2015); Manuel, *Reconciliation Manifesto*; Frank Wilderson, *Red, White & Black: Cinema and the Structure of U.S. Antagonisms* (Durham, NC: Duke University Press, 2010).

19 This is evident in incarceration and child apprehension rates, police violence, gender violence, lack of clean water, safe housing, and other funding shortages on and off reserves, the continued push for pipelines, the failure to return land, the acquittal of both Gerald Stanley and Raymond Cormier in the deaths of Colton Boushie and Tina Fontaine, among too many other indicators.

20 Nancy Fraser, "Legitimation Crisis? On the Political Contradictions of Financialized Capitalism," *Critical Historical Studies* 2, no. 2 (2019): 181.

21 See, for instance, Robert Brenner, *The Economics of Global Turbulence: The Advanced Capitalist Economies from Long Boom to Long Downturn, 1945–2005* (New York: Verso, 2006); Joshua Clover, *Riot. Strike. Riot: The New Era of Uprisings* (New York: Verso, 2016); Wolfgang Streeck, *Buying Time: The Delayed Crisis of Democratic Capitalism* (New York: Verso, 2017); and Norbert Trenkle, "Labour in the Era of Fictitious Capital," *Krisis*, 3 August 2015, http://www .krisis.org/2015/labour-in-the-era-of-fictitious-capital/.

22 Michael Asch, "Calder and the Representation of Indigenous Society in Canadian Jurisprudence," in *Let Right Be Done: Aboriginal Title, the Calder Case, and the Future of Indigenous Rights*, ed. Hamar Foster, Heather Raven, and Jeremy Webber (Vancouver: UBC Press, 2007), 101–10; Coulthard, *Red Skin, White Masks*; and Gérard V. La Forest, "Reminiscences of Aboriginal Rights at the Time of the Calder Case and Its Aftermath," in Foster, Raven, and Webber, *Let Right Be Done*, 54–60.

23 See Kent McNeil, 2003. "Reconciliation and the Supreme Court: The Opposing Views of Chief Justices Lamer and McLachlin," *Indigenous Law Journal* 2, no. 1 (2003): 1–26; and Craft, "Neither Infringement Nor Justification," for a discussion of the court's definitions of the concept. See also Hannah Wylie, "Towards a Genealogy of Reconciliation in Canada," *Journal of Canadian Studies* 51, no. 3 (2017): 601–35, for a contextualization of reconciliation that links it to the Quebec question.

24 Edward Allen, "Reflections on the 40th Anniversary of the *Calder* Decision," *Northern Public Affairs* 2, no. 1 (2013): 18.

25 As Prime Minister Pierre Elliott Trudeau famously remarked at the time, "Perhaps you have more legal rights than we thought you had when we did the White Paper" (cited in Allen, "Reflections on the 40th Anniversary," 19). For a fascinating first-hand account of this moment, see La Forest's reflections in "Reminiscences of Aboriginal Rights." La Forest was serving in the Department of Justice at the time and crafted the draft position that recommended the acceptance of Aboriginal title (57).

26 Asch, "Calder and the Representation of Indigenous Society," 114. This change in perspective should also be understood in the context of the Second World War in terms of a condemnation of the racial thinking that led to the Holocaust and the contributions of Indigenous veterans, the civil rights struggle that was taking place across North America, and the global struggle for decolonization. Scholars examining US racial formations, such as Charisse Burden-Stelly, "Cold War Culturalism and African Diaspora Theory: Some Theoretical Sketches," *Souls: A Critical Journal of Black Politics, Culture, and Society* 19, no. 2 (2017): 213–37; and Jodi Melamed, *Represent and Destroy: Rationalizing Violence in the New Racial Capitalism* (Minneapolis: University of Minnesota Press, 2011) have also attended to the importance of the Cold War in the reconfiguration of racial orders. While suggestions

of a similar concern can be found in Coulthard's account of the Dene Nation's struggle for self-determination (*Red Skin, White Masks*), we have yet to come across sustained analyses in the Canadian context, though it is plausible that there would have been at least an indirect influence though the United States.

27 Royal Commission on Aboriginal Peoples, *Looking Forward, Looking Back: Report of the Royal Commission on Aboriginal Peoples* (1996), 1:12, 122, 658.

28 Well short of the $1.5–2 billion annual increase in spending recommended by RCAP, however.

29 For a fascinating genealogy of transitional justice, see Paige Arthur, "How 'Transitions' Reshaped Human Rights: A Conceptual History of Transitional Justice," *Human Rights Quarterly* 31, no. 2 (2009): 321–67.

30 Craft, "Neither Infringement Nor Justification," 60–1.

31 See the Final Report's discussion of its mandate (Truth and Reconciliation Commission, *Honouring the Truth, Reconciling for the Future: Summary of the Final Report of the Truth and Reconciliation Commission of Canada* (2015), 27; as well as the discussion of this aspect of the TRC in Nancy Macdonald and Meagan Campbell, "Lost and Broken: The Inquiry into Missing and Murdered Indigenous Women Is Crumbling amid Defections, Bureaucratic Chaos and Personal Conflict. Inside the Meltdown – and the Desperate Bid to Turn Things Around," *Maclean's*, 13 September 2017, https://www .macleans.ca/lost-and-broken/.

32 Thanks to Heidi Stark for drawing our attention to this.

33 Douglas Eyford, *Forging Partnerships, Building Relationships: Aboriginal Canadians and Energy Development* (2013), 4, https://caid.ca /AboCanEneDevRep2013.pdf. I'm (Snelgrove) deeply indebted to the work of Russ Diabo and Shiri Pasternak for pointing me to this report. See "Harper v. First Nations: The Assimilation Agenda," *Ricochet*, 21 October 2014, https://ricochet.media/en/125/harper-first-nations-assimilation -agenda.

34 Maskwacîs Education Schools Commission, *Report to the Community 2018: Kiskinwahamaw Awasisak Nehiyaw Pimatisiwin (Teaching Children the Cree Ways)*, 2018, 12, https://www.Maskwacised.ca/download/communityreport2018.

35 I (Wildcat) was involved with work of the Maskwacîs Education Schools Commission as a senior advisor on governance and communications, although I am also intimately familiar with the longer history of locally control education in Maskwacîs. My father was director of education and later superintendent of the Ermineskin Cree Nation school system, Miyo Wahkohtowin Education – the largest of the four school systems. Between 1989 and 1996 the four Nations of Maskwacîs assumed control of their school systems.

36 For analysis of act, see Judith Rae, "The Federal Control of First Nations Education Act," OKT Law, 2014, http://www.oktlaw.com/federal-control -first-nations-education-act/.

37 Coulthard, *Red Skin, White Masks*.

38 Coulthard, *Red Skin, White Masks*.

39 Glen Coulthard, "Subjects of Empire: Indigenous Peoples and the 'Politics of Recognition' in Canada," *Contemporary Political Theory* 6 (2007): 452.

40 Coulthard, "Subjects of Empire," 453–5.

41 Maskwacîs Education Schools Commission, *Report to the Community 2018: Kiskinwahamaw Awasisak Nehiyaw Pimatisiwin (Teaching Children the Cree Ways)*, 2018, 13, https://www.Maskwacised.ca/download/communityreport2018.

42 Brian Wildcat, "Best Practices in Education Workshop," Saskatoon, SK, 2018.

43 Shauna Bruno, "Miyo Wahkohtowin Education Restorative Practices," Indspire series, Nurturing Capacity: Building Community Success, 2016, https://indspire.ca/nurturing-capacities/miyo-wahkohtowin-education -ehpewapahk-alternate-school/; and Bruno, "Miyo Wahkohtowin Education Ehpewapahk Alternate School," Indspire series, Nurturing Capacity: Building Community Success, 2016. Report in the possession of Wildcat.

44 Marshall Ganz, "Resources and Resourcefulness: Strategic Capacity in the Unionization of California Agriculture, 1959–1966," *American Journal of Sociology* 105, no. 4 (2000): 1003–62.

45 Ganz, "Resources and Resourcefulness," 1003–7; Ganz, *Why David Sometimes Wins*, 10–21.

46 MESC, *Report to the Community 2018*, 4.

47 See Judith Rae, "The Federal Control of First Nations Education Act," OKT Law, 2014, http://www.oktlaw.com/federal-control-first-nations-education -act/.

48 Koren Lightning, personal communication with Matthew Wildcat, 2017.

49 MESC, *Report to the Community 2018*, 18–21, 24.

50 Ganz, *Why David Sometimes Wins*, 8.

PART FOUR

Reconciling Lands, Bodies, and Gender

11 Body Land, Water, and Resurgence in Oaxaca

ISABEL ALTAMIRANO-JIMÉNEZ

Introduction

This chapter explores the nexus between resource extraction, Indigenous bodies, and the ways in which Indigenous people, specifically Indigenous women, respond. Focusing on the anti-mining struggle of the Zapotec community of Calpulalpan in Oaxaca, Mexico, I argue that Indigenous embodied experiences of resource extraction demand that we consider them simultaneously within the broader structures of colonial capitalism and the Indigenous place-based practices of resurgence. By focusing on this experience, I am interested in highlighting how Indigenous women challenged and imagined the Zapotec resurgence of communal practices in transformational ways.

I begin by mapping a body land framework that, on the one hand, historicizes dispossession and gender relations, and on the other, centres place-specific embodied experiences as prefigurative of collective Indigenous resurgence. I focus on relationality to explore how communalism prefigures practices that re-member body, community, and territory. Then I examine how Capulalpan's place-based resurgence practices have been shaped by Indigenous women. Finally, I offer some concluding remarks on Indigenous women and resurgence.

Body Land, Relationality, and Indigenous Resurgence

Resource extraction has long been a site of contestation over place, identity, feelings, and experiences.[1] It operates through material and immaterial processes in which experiential meanings and life forms are transformed into commodities.[2] However, the term *resource* conceals the fact that natural resources are constituted in place.

Indigenous stories of how people relate to place and the non-human world encourage us to envision alternative ways of being in the world. As an analytical tool, body land is useful to explore the mutually constitutive relationships between Indigenous embodied experiences and place. This unified concept not only centres the ontological relationship between different bodies but also the conscious actions that uphold and maintain such relationships.

These relationships exist at the epistemological level and in the everyday practices through which people embody their relationality. Relationality is not metaphorical; it does not exist just because we claim it is there, but rather because we practise it in present, active, and engaged ways. Reciprocal relationships come into existence through the active responsibility to act them out. Relationality can be understood as an action-oriented way of seeing the world, organizing Indigenous polities and producing and enacting knowledge. Relationships among human beings and between humans and the non-human world shape ceremonial cycles, economic practices, laws, and ways of being with one another and carrying the land in our bodies. For example, Indigenous peasants' experiences of climate change do not necessarily correspond with how scientific studies are conducted but rather with the changes they observe through their activities in co-producing ecosystems with other non-human beings.

In the book of Mayan laws, the *Popol Vuh*, for example, human beings are not above nature. Rather they are part of a whole and their responsibility is to protect it. Similarly, Indigenous peoples conceptions of community are made of the interdependent relationships among human bodies, spirits, non-human beings, and supranatural forces. From a Zapotec point of view, territory cannot be divided into surface and subsurface, land and water, or different silos of resources. Water and forest are considered sacred forms of life on the land. The subsoil represents the roots or the seeds that make possible the existence of mountains, water, plants, and so on. The surface and subsurface together constitute the spiritual, symbolic, and material life of Indigenous communities.[3] Indigenous stories reveal the corporeal knowledge that people have developed through the interactions with their territory. Such stories teach how disrespecting the land, water, spirits, and other beings is intimately implicated in one's experience of well-being, illness, and even death. Interactions among human beings, the environment, animals, spirits, land, water, and natural forces evoke actions and inactions that shape people's behaviour, governance systems, and gender roles. Thus territory is not only the geographical space on which bodies are located but also the network of relationships constituted by different beings and people.

While relationality connects the strands of materiality, corporeality, kinship, affect, and land and body,[4] I propose to work with the concept of body-land. It can help us centre not only how these relationships play out in distinctive yet interconnected processes but also the transformative capacities of different bodies coming together. I understand body-land as the ontological relationships between people and territory, which combine with collective histories and experiences to shape Indigenous peoples' present-day social practices.[5] However, these relationships are not given or fixed, they are established, maintained, transformed, and honoured through the active and conscious practices of making relatives, of landing relationships in place. I call these body-landing practices. These relationships can change and be reclaimed in ways that are transformational.

Like colonialism, capitalism maintains categories and hierarchies between life non-life, human non-human, men and women, and other forms of life, fragmentating relationships and reorganizing gender relations. Colonialism and capitalism have produced dynamics to erode the relationships that constitute communal life. Against the anti-relationality impulses of colonialism and capitalism, Indigenous peoples in Oaxaca have insisted in surviving as communities. Communal ways of doing and living or "communality," the term used in Oaxaca[6] has been key to Indigenous resurgence since the late 1970s. Communality is considered central to Indigenous survival and the process of building a transformative political project based on Indigenous laws. Mixe thinker Floriberto Díaz wrote that self-determination, interdependence, reciprocity, and people's attitudes towards common life and the environment they inhabit is what constitute Indigenous communities in Oaxaca. Through the reproduction of these principles, community members express their sense of being in the world and belonging to a community. Being part of a community involves the responsibility to be with one another in good relations.[7]

Zapotec thinker Jaime Martínez Luna, on the other hand, explains that communality comes from self-determined individuals who are willing to live in community. It is through people's actions and practices that a sense of us and of being a community has been maintained up to the present, despite colonial and nation-state efforts to assimilate Indigenous peoples. Martínez Luna observes that communality is an experience, a practice, an attitude, an ethos that has four interrelated elements: territory, governance, work, and fiestas (community celebrations). To Martínez Luna, territory is the physical space where life is organized and joy, ceremony, relationships, food production and consumption, work, authority, learning, creation, and reflection occur. Governance is based on an ethos of service and reciprocity and on Indigenous laws and institutions, which shape how people organize, manage themselves, and solve conflicts. This governance finds expression in the Indigenous cargo system or the set of communal services and obligations performed by community members. Communal services are both a responsibility and a possibility. Work performed by community members aims at improving and maintaining collective life. As a possibility, the services performed are oriented to the reproduction of communal social relations and creation of a better future. Lastly, fiestas are about the joy of being with one another and non-human beings. Fiestas mediate between the past and the social relations in the present.[8]

Although this concept is crucial to understanding Indigenous struggles to defend territory in Oaxaca, there are limitations in the way communality has been theorized. First, while the idea of territory as a physical space is central to the specific place where communality is practised, this understanding undermines the networks of relationships between the human and non-human worlds. Through these relationships, both human and non-human commune with each other, constituting our territories. Emphasizing only the physical dimension of territory has the effect of reducing territory to a geographic place. Second, discussions of communality have tended to represent an essentialized notion of community, which has been challenged by Indigenous women. Colonial and state policies and legislations have produced gendered and racialized categories of belonging and exclusion, which have been naturalized in Indigenous communities. For example, Indigenous women's land rights in Oaxaca vary. In some communities, they can be landholders, and in others, they can hold land only when they become widows or inherit it from parents. Although in some communities, women may hold land or perform communal work, family responsibilities and community practices often prevent them from doing so. Moreover, since cargos or posts (governance positions) are considered a service to the community, the services provided to the community are not paid. This means that for someone (usually a man) to perform these public duties, he too relies on the support of women to maintain the family household. Thus, while men are the public face of cargos, these positions are in fact a family responsibility, in which women's work and actions remains largely invisible.

Communality emphasizes symmetry and balance relationships among different bodies. However, Aymara feminist and activist Julieta Paredes reminds us that such emphasis can conceal unequal division of work, in which one part of the complement ends up performing work that is perceived to be of less value within the community.[9] Similarly, Aymara feminist Audra Cumes argues that it is important to analyse the reality of Indigenous peoples as human communities that are historically and politically constituted.[10] While we can acknowledge that gender relationships were different before, colonial and state intrusion and policies have naturalized hierarchical gender relations. Thus, efforts asserting self-determination and resurgence should not be limited to revitalizing practices in abstract but should also include efforts to critically think, feel, and experience what actions have made us survive as peoples. We have a history, memory, and desires, and we need to have a dialogue about them that includes everyone. By challenging essentialized notions of community, Indigenous feminists and activists insist on assessing such practices, actions, and efforts. Thus, while supporting their communities' laws and communal ethos, Indigenous women and gender non-conforming individuals not only challenge how communality was practised, embodied, and enacted in the past but also today and in the future.

Indigenous Resurgence in Oaxaca

Oaxaca, specifically the Northern Highlands, has a common history of land defence that has evolved into a resurgent politics. Capulalpan de Méndez is a Zapotec town governed by Indigenous laws and, like other communities in the region, it is characterized by the strength of its communal governance practices. The region is covered with pine and pine-oak forests, which are communally owned and sustainably managed because of this community's struggle to regain control over these areas in the 1980s. This town is considered emblematic of Indigenous communities successfully managing their own communal forest. However, Calpulalpan is no stranger to the extraction of natural resources, which started with mining in the 1870s with the discovery of gold and silver. Mining was then represented as the economic activity that was supposed to finally bring "progress" to Oaxaca, especially the Highlands. By the early 1900s, the Natividad mine had become the richest operation in Oaxaca, employing Zapotecs and other Indigenous peoples from different communities. For over a century, generations of men and women worked at the Natividad mine, socializing as unionized miners while fulfilling their community obligations as Zapotecs.[11]

Despite Capulalpan's communal land title, in 1954 the community learned that the federal government had granted a timber concession to a paper mill company (FAPATUX) without its consent.[12] Over two decades, through intensive and devastating practices, the mill company exploited both the forest and Indigenous labour. Calpulalpan's resentment with the government reverberated throughout the region. This community joined twelve other Zapotec and Chinantec communities to create the Organization for the Defence of Natural Resources in the Juarez Highlands (ODNRJH) in the early 1980s. The purpose was to reclaim their communal forests and revitalize their governance systems and forms of solidarity within and among Indigenous communities.[13] The political process unfolding in Oaxaca, and specifically the Northern Highlands, was characterized as Indigenous re-emergence or resurgence in which Indigenous communities consciously acted upon their Indigenous laws and authority.[14] Against colonial and capitalist imperatives that separate land and body, life and non-life, and human and non-human, Indigenous communal practices centred relationships and coming together.

In early 1982, when the timber concession was about to expire, a woman from Calpulalpan learned that the government was planning to renew and extend the permit. She quickly mobilized other women and together they decided to act on their responsibility to protect their community's resources. Although women's participation in the cargo system and the communal assembly is often limited, the women felt the need to act and defend their territories. They literally used their bodies to prevent trucks from getting in and out of the community. A Calpulalpan resident noted, "Women's response was practically stronger than men. It was women who decided to block the roads, it was women who used their bodies to stop the trucks."[15] As part of their strategies, Calpulalpan residents collectively refused to work at the paper mill.[16] The movement of women's bodies coming together, the quietness of their bodies blocking the road or what Foster calls "still-activism"[17] was crucial to stop the circulation of timber extracted from their territory. Capulalpan prevented the expansion of the concession and created a communal forestry that emphasized local use value over profit and the close connection between community and forests. In doing so, community members transformed social control and domination into a social change force.

Women not only participated in the movement for the defence of communal forests but were also instrumental in building the communal project. Women challenged male authorities' sense of responsibility and insisted on revitalizing the communal ethos.[18] While initially not everyone supported women's vision of building a communal alternative for the benefit of both the community and the environment,[19] eventually the community came together. Through their participation, Indigenous women created new practices for community leaders to act upon their authority and responsibility. Capulalpan became a model of sustainable, community-driven forestry recognized nationally and internationally for the strength and vitality of its communal governance institutions. This community was among the Early Action Areas and Communities to receive payment for ecosystem services from the federal government.[20]

Calpulalpan also created other economic projects including a toyshop and an ecotourism company. In 2005 the town was granted the "magic town" designation granted by the Mexican government, a title that highlights the historical, cultural, and aesthetic qualities of small towns. In the view of the mayor, "These [economic] projects have been central to preventing migration of our people and keeping our community together."[21]

While celebrated for its sustainable, communal forestry, in 2000 Capulalpan learned that the Ministry of Economics had granted a concession to a Canadian mining company, Continuum Resources, over 62,000 hectares of their lands. At first the company's representatives attempted to garner community support for an open pit mine by promising jobs. Calpulalpan refused to allow the company on its lands. Then the company attempted to bribe community authorities, but those attempts also failed because the communal governance system prevents individual landholders and authorities from making decisions about resources without the consent of the communal assembly. Despite the community's refusal to grant permission, the company initiated exploration activities in 2005, expanding them in 2007.

Calpulalpan's mayor was critical of the company, announcing that thirteen water springs had been contaminated by the company's illegal practices.[22] Like the forest, water is of significant importance to Indigenous communities. Water is a life-giving entity, permeating all organic entities and organisms. Water circulates and connects territories, bodies, and beings. To community members, "[a] community without water has no life on which future generations can depend."[23] This community is not alone in its struggle against Canadian mining, which has left a violent, contaminated legacy in different regions. On October 2018 the neighbouring Zapotec of San Jose del Progreso reported a stream of white liquid in one of their water tributaries and insisted the source of water contamination was a tailing dam of another Canadian company, Fortuna Silver Mines.[24] Mining has had devastating effects on water availability and quality in different regions in Latin America.[25] Water as a life force provides a useful focus to think about the environmental violence that is committed against different bodies: human, land, water, non-human, and community. The struggle against mining cannot be separated from the struggle to defend Indigenous life. Unlike other anti-mining movements, in Capulalpan there are no leaders, no visible spokesperson, but rather a communal organization that reflects how the community senses and thinks, privileging history, ways of being in the world, and embodied experiences. The struggle to defend Indigenous life is a fight to defend life lived in community, is survival.

Once again, women were instrumental in mobilizing to protect their territory. While the assembly of communal landholders was considering its strategies, women blockaded the community's road. Women and their families also organized a blockade of the Oaxaca–Mexico City highway interrupting the circulation of goods through a central artery of the country. Men's opposition to mining has often been framed in relation to the process of granting concessions, explorations, and consent over land. Women are concerned with the social reproduction of their families and communities.

From this perspective, the social reproduction of Indigenous communities cannot be separated from the defence of bodies of water, human bodies, bodies of land, and non-human bodies. In refusing mining, memories, feelings, and thoughts have been central to bring people together in the present. Community members still remember the legacy of exploitation, death, and water contamination left by past mining.[26] Women still remember the stress of losing loved ones at the mine and the workload they had to assume after their deaths. These memories and felt experiences stand at odds with the industry's official registers, which emphasize jobs and economic rationality. The feelings and memories of situated bodies evoke an embodied consciousness and collective history that reveal the violence of resource extraction.

The mining company was found to be in serious violation of waste-disposal procedures and was ordered to suspend activities. The mayor of Calpulalpan noted, "In the new phase of mineral extraction, it is not only land that is at risk but also biodiversity, water, and our sacred places."[27] In other words, it is Indigenous life that is at risk. In 2011 the community learned that another mining company, Minera Teocuitla, was planning an exploration project. Once again the community mobilized to reject it. Collective memory, feelings, and experiences were crucial for the community to articulate a communal response. The communal assembly confirmed it would not consent to the project and noted, "The community of Capulalpan, exercising our rights as an Indigenous and peasant municipality, refuses permission to the companies Natividad, Minera Teocuitla, Continuum Resources, Arco Exploration, or companies using any other name to carry out exploration or exploitation of minerals in our lands."[28]

The community initiated legal action to permanently stop mining on their territory. While Indigenous communities have no control over mining concessions, I would argue that the inalienability of Indigenous communal land rights in the Mexican Constitution and the strength of communal practices and governance institutions have provided a legal recourse to temporarily stop mining in this community. This time the mining company was found guilty of violating the law when it started to operate without even requesting a land-use change on areas considered forestry land.[29]

To Capulalpan, refusing extraction it is not only about rejecting mining but also a communal act for building an alternative for future generations. At different regional encounters, Indigenous community members have noted the need for communities to revitalize their governance systems and institutions and remember embodied experiences. In the view of Calpulalpan's authority, their success in interrupting mining relies on the practice of remembering and producing communal knowledge. Indigenous organizations often note that mining companies foster and capitalize on community divisions and lack of Indigenous women's land rights in order to gain access to Indigenous lands.

In 2013 the elders and children from Calpulalpan painted the *Mural of Memory and Life*. A note explains that such a mural reminds future generations that Calpulalpan builds a political project that is anchored in the past yet projected into the future. Through everyday communal practices, the anti-mining struggle in Calpulalpan is grounded on the collective will to self-determine other forms of being in the world that re-members embodied experiences and the relationships that constitute territory.

Indigenous Women and Resurgence

As the anti-mining Indigenous struggle expands and communities embark on the revitalization of their communal institutions and laws, Indigenous women have claimed that the defence of territory cannot be separated from the defence of their bodies and aspirations. They have insisted on the need to consider gendered exclusion, violence, heavy workloads, and lack of representation within their communities. For example, despite having had a role in the struggles to defend their forests and against mining, women's participation continues to be seen as secondary. Often they are represented as taking specific actions without looking into their own motivations to resist capitalism and patriarchy.

By employing a body-land analytic, I have centred Indigenous women's embodied experiences of resource extraction as prefigurative of communal practices of resurgence in Calpulalpan, Oaxaca. In doing so, I provided the context for a more complex story, one that illuminates the violence of resource extraction and the ways in which domination and exploitation can be transformed into social change. I showed how despite their invisible work, women have been central to enacting communality and acting relationally. Through their actions, Zapotec women critically challenge essentialized notions of community. Although the political potential of communality is key in fighting resource extraction and the revitalization of relationships and forms of everyday mutual cooperation, the desires of individual bodies are not separated from those of the community of bodies. Transforming relationships to maintain communality may seem like a paradox. However, it expresses an aspiration to change in order to remain together in community in liberating ways.

Similar to the Zapatista women's movement in Chiapas and the Revolutionary Law of Women 1993, Zapotec women conceive of their bodies as a territory with a history, memory, and personal knowledge. When communities of bodies revitalize that knowledge, history, and memory, the struggle for body-land becomes a struggle for Indigenous life. After all, body-land highlights the fact that struggles for territorial defence is a struggle for a place where the bodies of Indigenous women, two-spirit, and transgender individuals can live a dignified, full life.[30]

Building spaces for a dignified Indigenous life involves making love, friendship, and kinship relationships that is inclusive of multiple bodies. The autonomy of individual bodies is central to relationality. The struggle to protect communal life is also a struggle to defend individual freedom and dignity. This involves centring to the embodied experiences of Indigenous women, two-spirit, and trans individuals within communities, whether sexual, urban, geographic, or political. If colonialism and capitalism produce Indigenous territories and bodies as extractible, Indigenous communal practices must function as a reservoir of collective knowledge that builds alternative visions for communities, bodies, and territories.

NOTES

1 Melina Ey, Meg Sherval, and Paul Hodge. 2017, "Value, Identity and Place: Unearthing the Emotional Geographies of the Extractive Sector," *Australian Geographer* 48, no. 2 (2017): 153–68.

2 See Isabel Altamirano-Jiménez, *Indigenous Encounters with Neo-liberalism: Place, Women and the Environment* (Vancouver: UBC Press, 2013); Macarena Gómez-Barris, *The Extractive Zone: Social Ecologies and Decolonial Perspectives* (Durham, NC: Duke University Press, 2017).

3 Salvador Aquino Centeno, "La lucha por el control del territorio en Capulalpam. Diferentes maneras acerca de la comprensión del subsuelo, el oro, la plata, la ley y el capital," Comisariado de Bienes Comunales de Capulalpam, Oaxaca, México. Presented at III Jornadas Mesoamericanas, October 2011.

4 See Melanie Yazzie and Cutcha Risling Baldy, "Introduction: Indigenous Peoples and the Politics of Water," *Decolonization: Indigeneity, Education,*

and Society 7, no. 1 (2017): 1–18; Kim Tallbear and Angela Willey, "Critical Relationality: Queer, Indigenous, and Multispecies Belonging beyond Settler Sex and Nature," *Imaginations: Journal of Cross Cultural Image Studies* 10, no. 1 (2019), https://journals.library.ualberta.ca/imaginations/index.php/imaginations/article/view/29422; Mishuana Goeman, "Ongoing Storms and Struggles: Gendered Violence and Resource Exploitation," in *Critically Sovereign: Indigenous Gender, Sexuality, and Feminist Studies*, ed. Joanne Barker (Durham, NC: Duke University Press, 2017), 99–126.

5 Isabel Altamirano-Jiménez, "Possessing Land, Wind and Water in the Isthmus of Tehuantepec, Oaxaca," *Australian Feminist Studies* (2021): 321–35. https://doi.org/10.1080/08164649.2021.1919989.

6 See Floriberto Diaz, *Comunalidad, energía viva del pensamiento Mixe* (Mexico City: UNAM, 2007); and Jaime Martínez Luna, "The Fourth Principle," in *New World of Indigenous Resistance: Noam Chomsky and Voices from North, South and Central America*, ed. Lois Meyer and Benjamin Maldonado Alvarado (San Francisco: City Lights Books, 2010), 85–110.

7 Floribert Díaz, *Comunalidad, energía viva del pensamiento Mixe*.

8 Jaime Martínez Luna, "The Fourth Principle" in *New World of Indigenous Resistance: Noam Chomsky and Voices from North, South and Central America*, ed. Lois Meyer and Benjamin Maldonado Alvarado (City Lights Books: San Francisco, 2010), 85–110.

9 Julieta Paredes, *Hilando Fino, desde el feminismo comunitario* (La Paz: Comunidad Mujeres Creando Comunidad, 2011), 48.

10 Audra Cumes, "Patriarcado, dominación colonial y epistemologías mayas" (2019). https://img.macba.cat/public/uploads/20190611/Patriarcado_dominacinin_colonial_y_epistemologn_as_mayas.4.pdf.

11 Patrick McNamara, *Sons of the Sierra: Juárez, Díaz and Ixtlán, Oaxaca 1855–1920* (Durham, NC: University of North Carolina Press, 2007).

12 David Barton Bray and Leticia Merino, 2004. La experiencia de las comunidades forestales en México. Mexico City: SEMARNAP, Instituto Nacional de Ecología, Ford Foundation; and Anna Lee Mraz Bartra, "Los haceres de la sociedad en torno al medio ambiente. Capulálpam de Méndez, Sierra Juárez, Oaxaca, México," *Sociedad y Ambiente* 1, no. 3 (2013): 78–88.

13 Isabel Altamirano-Jiménez, "De Eso Que Llaman Movimiento Indio en México, 1970–1994" (senior thesis of Social Anthropology, Mexico City, National School of Anthropology and History, 1998); David Bray, "Toward 'Post-REDD+ Landscapes': Mexico's Community Forest Enterprises Provide a Proven Pathway to Reduce Emissions from Deforestation and Forest Degradation," *InfoBrief* 30 (November 2010), http://www.cifor.org/publications/pdf_files/infobrief/3272-infobrief.pdf.

14 Altamirano-Jiménez, "De Eso Que Llaman Movimiento Indio en México," 69.

15 Anna Lee Mraz Bartra, "Los haceres de la sociedad en torno al medio ambiente. Capulálpam de Méndez, Sierra Juárez, Oaxaca, México." *Sociedad y Ambiente* 1, no. 3 (2013): 78–88.

16 Catherine Tucker, "Aiming for Sustainable Community Forest Management: The Experience of Two Communities in Mexico and Honduras," in *Working Forest in the Neotropic: Conservation through Sustainable Forestry?*, ed. D.J. Zarin, J.R.R. Alavalpati, F.E. Putz, and M. Schmink (New York: Columbia University Press, 2004), 187.

17 Susan Leigh Foster, "Choreographies of Protest," *Theatre Journal* 55, no. 3 (2003): 412.

18 Edgar Javier Lugo Lopez, "La transformación del espacio en Calpulalpan de Mendez, Oaxaca. Una mirada historica (MA thesis, CIESA Golfo, 2016), 162.

19 Lugo Lopez, "La transformación del espacio," 163.

20 Tucker, "Aiming for Sustainable Community Forest Management," 189.

21 Anayeli García Martínez, "Mujeres de Capulálpam: la defensa del territorio frente a la explotación minera," *La Jornada*, 8 November 2015. https://www.proceso.com.mx/reportajes/2015/11/8/mujeres-de-capulalpam-la-defensa-del-territorio-frente-la-explotacion-minera-154714.html.

22 *La Jornanda*, "Minera acaba con manatiales," 28 October 2007. https://www.ocmal.org/3968/.

23 Aquino Centeno, "La lucha por el control del territorio en Capulalpam," 14.

24 Servicios para una Educación Alternativa A.C. EDUCA, *Land Defenders from San Jose del Progreso, Oaxaca, Mexico*, 24 October 2018. https://www.youtube.com/watch?v=zRF6x0WTrOs.

25 See Susana Sawyer Suzana and Edmund T. Gomez, *The Politics of Resource Extraction: Indigenous Peoples, Multinational Corporations and the State* (London: Palgrave Macmillan, 2012); Kalawatie Deoanandan and Michael Dougherty, *Mining in Latin America: Critical Approaches in the New Extraction* (New York: Routledge, 2016).

26 Elia Méndez García, *De relámpagos y recuerdos. Minería y tradición serrana por la lucha por lo común* (Guadalajara: Universidad de Guadalajara-CIESAS Jorge Alonso, 2017), 15.

27 Raymundo Cruz Miguel, "Calpulalpan: un volcán latente contra las mineras," *Desinformémonos*, 1 October 2011, https://desinformemonos.org/calpulalpan-un-volcan-latente-contra-las-mineras/.

28 David Bacon, *The Right to Stay Home: How US Policy Drives Mexican Migration* (Boston: Beacon, 2013).

29 NVI Noticias, 2016

30 Lorena Cabnal, *Feminismos diversos: el feminismo comunitario* (Madrid: ACSUR-Las Segovias, 2010), 23.

12 To Respect Indigenous Territorial Protocol: Hosting the Olympic Games on Indigenous Lands in Settler Colonial Canada

CHRISTINE O'BONSAWIN

The consolidation of action item 91 within the Truth and Reconciliation Commission of Canada's (TRC) calls to action has been celebrated within Indigenous sports circles as it outwardly advocates for the protection of Indigenous rights in the planning of the Olympic Games and other major games. Call to action 91 appeals to "officials and host countries of international sporting events such as the Olympics, Pan Am, and Commonwealth games to ensure that Indigenous peoples' territorial protocols are respected, and local Indigenous communities are engaged in all aspects of planning and participating in such events."[1] Through call to action 91, Indigenous participation in international sporting events has formally become enveloped within Canada's reconciliation fold. Taken at nominal value, this action item is seemingly straightforward: territorial protocols are to be respected and Indigenous communities are to be engaged in the planning and hosting of major games. However, a more in-depth reading of this call to action reveals that its basis rests in a long history of legal and political exploitation of Indigenous nations within the structure of international sporting events hosted in settler colonial Canada and elsewhere. As such, call to action 91 is not so much about advancing an action item within Canada's reconciliation project as it is about affirming Indigenous laws and legal traditions within international sporting spaces, controlled by settler states and sovereign global subjects with vested interests in accessing and exploiting Indigenous lands. Whether this is a worthwhile endeavour is the question explored in this chapter.

The model developed and implemented for the Vancouver 2010 Olympic and Paralympic Winter Games is heralded as the most advanced model for Indigenous participation in major games programming to date.[2] It can certainly be argued that significant strides forward were made in the planning and hosting of these Games, evidenced by a seeming adherence to territorial protocols as well as extensive Indigenous participation in the bid, planning, hosting, and legacy stages of these Olympic Games. However, even this most advanced model failed to eradicate the profound power disparity between Indigenous nations and Olympic and state organizers.[3] As the Vancouver example exposes, there exist three discernible obstacles when Indigenous nations engage the state and powerful global sovereign subjects, such as the International Olympic Committee (IOC), with an expectation that Indigenous laws will be respected and affirmed in such spaces. First, and most obvious, the Olympic movement is built on xenophobic principles and heteronormative patriarchy. The creation of even the most advanced Indigenous participation programs does not easily eradicate such deficiencies within the movement. Second, the arrival of a powerful sovereign global subject on Indigenous lands allows the state to manipulate and exploit further its already imbalanced legal and political relationships with Indigenous nations, leading to potentially violent confrontations. Finally, there is a hidden assumption that respect for territorial protocols will mean the same thing to settler populations as it does to Indigenous nations who have lived by these long-standing traditions since time immemorial. As the Vancouver example demonstrates, when territorial protocols are performed in the form of land acknowledgments, they become performative and thus Olympic spectacles. At this point in the Olympic schedule, territorial protocols have most likely been broken, and the Olympic process has already facilitated further the dispossession of Indigenous lands.

Colonizing Frameworks of the Olympic Movement

For over a century, the Olympic movement has moved freely around the globe with little to no regard for the rights of marginalized and oppressed peoples. In the latter part of the twentieth century and beyond, we have witnessed (and many have experienced first-hand) the far-reaching colonial powers of the Olympic movement. Through the authority of the Olympic Charter, and accompanying organizational measures, the movement continues to rationalize its imperial desire to encroach upon all geographic, political, ethnic, and religious regions of the world. Although the Games have evolved in size in scope over the years, and into the malignant cyclops it is today, its colonizing and nationalistic missions have remained consistent. As Olympic studies scholar Jules Boykoff reasons, "Engaging the history of the Olympics provides an exceptionally useful foundation for comprehending larger cultural, social and political processes of the last 120 years – and in particular, for understanding class, privilege, indigenous repression, activist strategy, and capitalist power."[4]

The political history of the Olympic Games exposes how the movement serves as an instrument of repression for oppressed and marginalized groups and peoples across the globe.

At its inception, Pierre de Coubertin (the individual most often credited with reviving the Olympics) remained unwavering in his position that the Games be hosted in different locations around the world and on a four-year schedule. He believed the future prosperity of the Olympics depended on its global prominence. In establishing a sporting institution that was global in scope, Coubertin sought to disseminate messages of civilization and progress to all regions of the world. As such, the Olympic Games were premised on three founding logics: amateurism privileged the middle and upper classes through its exclusion of the lower orders; heteronormative forms of masculinity were celebrated through male athletic competition and further reinforced through the exclusion of women; and the superiority of the white race was to be preserved.[5] As expressed in the 1908 writings of Coubertin, the Olympics were to be the cornerstone of progress for the civilized world and a "means of bringing to perfection the strong and hopeful youth of our white race, thus again helping towards the perfection of all human society."[6] Through these writings and other works produced by Coubertin in the first two decades of the movement, we see the origins of an Olympic philosophy, which has come to be known as Olympism.

It should be understood that Olympism was and remains an instituted philosophy – a formulated and planned venture by Coubertin and early members of the International Olympic Committee (IOC) who were entirely white, male, and bourgeois, who sought to use the ill-defined concept of Olympism to elevate the Olympic Games above all other sporting competitions. Early proponents of Olympism avowed that the movement was to espouse virtues of peace, brotherhood, and humanity, and that Olympic-like or global athletic competitions that incorporated political, religious, or racial propaganda were to be renounced. As Olympic historian Kevin Wamsley asserts, however, "In many respects, the two [Olympism and the Olympic Games] are incongruous ... during the twentieth century, the nebulous concept of Olympism became the structural apologetic for the Olympic Games."[7] Although Olympism spoke in truisms of peace, brotherhood, and humanity, the reality is that the Olympic movement was founded upon xenophobic principles and a politicized schema contoured by a group of individuals who privileged the superiority of the white race and the rise of the nation state. For over a century, this edifice has remained mostly in place.

In its present form, the Olympic Games is a spectacle of the many, and they are a political spectacle par excellence. At its centre is a social relationship between people that, in the case of the Olympic Games, is mediated by images controlled by the IOC.[8] The Olympic Games become a highly mediated commodity spectacle used by the IOC to rule over social life. In *The Society of the Spectacle*, Guy Debord famously wrote, "The spectacle corresponds to the historical moment at which the commodity completes its colonization of social life."[9] The endgame is dispossession and capital accumulation, to which the Olympic spectacle is inextricably linked.

The Olympic Games is a spectacle of celebration, packaged through exquisite aesthetics, proposing hypothetical benefits, including economic gains, social benefits, sporting prowess, and public entertainment. It is intended that members of the public become diverted from reality. While very few individuals benefit economically, the public is inevitably left to pay the substantial price tag and over-expenditures. Boykoff has developed an innovative theory, coined "celebration capitalism," to expose how the Olympic Games has become a massive prearranged economy whereby the public pays and the private profits. Through celebration capitalism, a celebratory space is created. Those involved in anti-Olympic behaviour are ejected, leading to Olympic-induced gentrification, forced removal, displacement, class polarization, repression, and dispossession.[10]

Under celebration capitalism, the Olympic Games thus become an alibi for state opportunism and political economic exception. Olympic host countries essentially become "states of exception," whereby nation-states draw from the global sovereign subject power of the IOC to assert national sovereignty and legal and political jurisdiction. As Boykoff contends, "the state of exception is like a gateway drug on the road to a full-blown–if legalized–addiction to a repressive technique of government, an addiction that is quietly interlaced into the political fabric of everyday life."[11] Through the Olympic state of exception, governments are authorized to put forward repressive laws and policies, ultimately suffocating citizenry rights and exposing the most vulnerable to political and legal repression.

By the close of the twentieth century, amid a global bribery scandal, the IOC proactively engendered an image of the Olympic movement as mindful of vulnerable groups, environmentalism, and sustainable development. In 1999 the United Nations ratified *Agenda 21 for Sustainable Development*, offering a detailed global action plan and stated commitment to environmentalism and sustainability. This United Nations document stresses the important role Indigenous nations serve in matters of environmentalism and sustainability.[12] Following the lead of the United Nations, the IOC adopted its own agenda on sustainability in 1999. Formally titled the *Olympic Movement's Agenda 21*, the Olympic action plan was published seven years later (with the support of Shell International) and is an embarrassingly lesser document.[13] In the Olympic plan, Indigenous peoples are mentioned on very few occasions and only in the context of being vulnerable groups that require strengthening. The IOC's stated commitments to Indigenous peoples were unmistakably divorced from its promises to its two other major groups (women and young people) and steeped in paternalistic language. This Olympic action plan sought to "pay adequate attention" to Indigenous communities who "often suffer social exclusion." It was believed the Olympic movement could "contribute to the use of [Indigenous] traditional knowledge in matters of environmental management."[14] In the end, *Agenda 21* mostly served the economic aspirations of the Olympic movement. In the first decade following the implementation of *Agenda 21*, partnership arrangements were established between organizing committees and Indigenous peoples in three of the six Olympic Games, with the Vancouver model considered by many to be the most advanced.[15]

The 2010 Olympic Games and Indigenous Land Defence

An important distinction with Vancouver's organizing model was that Indigenous partners were secured early in the process, which can be attributed to two factors. First, the introduction of *Agenda 21* provided a clear indication that the IOC was eager to establish relationships with Indigenous peoples, which it would do through local organizing committees. Second, Vancouver officials understood they could not ignore critical domestic matters related to legal and political processes underway in the province to remedy historical failures to negotiate treaties with Indigenous nations.[16] Establishing Indigenous partnerships early in the process was critical to Vancouver's successful bid.

The Olympic Winter Games were awarded to Vancouver in July 2003. The bid corporation immediately transitioned into an organizing committee, formalizing protocol agreements with local Indigenous nations on whose territories the Games were to be hosted, including xʷməθkʷəy̓əm (Musqueam), səl̓ilwətaʔɬ (Tsleil Waututh), Sḵwx̱wú7mesh (Squamish), and Lílwat7úl (Lílwat) nations.[17] The 2004 Four Host First Nations Protocol Agreement cemented the relationship between the host nations and the organizing committee, detailing obligations on all sides. Shortly after, two legacy agreements were negotiated and implemented. The Shared Legacy Agreement was signed between the federal and provincial governments, Olympic organizers, and the Sḵwx̱wú7mesh and Lílwat7úl nations, and the Olympic Legacy Agreement was signed between these same public-private partners and the xʷməθkʷəy̓əm and səlilwətaʔł nations. The intent of the legacy agreements was to ensure these host nations were appropriately compensated and recognized. Accordingly, the four host First Nations received "special benefits," including financial transfers, economic development and employment opportunities, and fee simple land transfers.[18]

The Indigenous participation model produced for these Olympic Games was indeed the most advanced to date, and helped establish tangible benefits for some Indigenous nations and individuals. However, what cannot be ignored is that the arrival of the Olympic movement on these unceded territories also allowed the state to exploit further an already imbalanced legal and political relationship with Indigenous nations, resulting in community divisions and violent confrontations in the lead-up to the Games. In fact, the negative consequences that resulted from these Olympic Games were felt within Indigenous communities throughout British Columbia (and further).[19] As Jules Boykoff reasons, the Olympic Games routinely help facilitate a security boon (particularly in the post-9/11 era) that often translates into a repressive state for those who express anti-Olympic dissent.[20] As demonstrated in the examples below, in the lead-up to these Olympic Games, Canada's state security and legal systems swiftly suppressed anyone expressing anti-Olympic dissonance, including Indigenous nations and peoples.

By the close of the twentieth century, land claims negotiations were deteriorating throughout the province. For politicians and industry leaders, a successful Vancouver bid held a potential to remedy matters of uncertainty concerning land claims and offer a renewed sense of legal and political certainty throughout British Columbia. In anticipation of a successful bid, the province had prepared its Spirit of 2010 Strategic Plan, unveiled only weeks after Vancouver was awarded the Games. The Plan sought to rectify the economic uncertainty caused by the faltering treaty process by strengthening the construction, oil and gas, and tourism and resort industries, promising to maximize opportunities associated with hosting the 2010 Olympic Games.[21] Building partnerships with First Nations became central to the Spirit of 2010 platform. As explained in the British Columbia Resort Strategy and Action Plan, resort expansion was contingent on such partnerships because "Court rulings indicating the need for increased consultation and accommodation for First Nations cause uncertainty for investors who are unclear on their obligations on how to proceed."[22] Indigenous nations throughout the province certainly had cause for concern.

The Secwepemc people of Skelkwek'welt have always opposed the development and expansion of Sun Peaks Resort on their territory. In fact,

Secwepemc opposition to resort development in the early 1990s led to the creation of the Skwelkwet'welt Protection Centre in 2000. As Vancouver officials moved the Olympic bid forward in the early 2000s, Secwepemc land defenders recognized that a successful bid would have devastating effects on their and other Indigenous territories. In June 2002, one year before Vancouver was awarded the Games, elders, land users, and youth of Skelkwek'welt and Sutikalh submitted a forty-six-page complaint to the IOC president. The official grievance detailed the catastrophic threats the Olympics posed to ecosystems within their unceded territories and further described how the Olympic Games would more broadly infringe on the human and legal rights of Indigenous peoples throughout Canada.[23] In 2004 the provincial government approved development plans to expand the Sun Peaks Resort, which was (not surprisingly) supported by the British Columbia Resort Strategy and Action Plan. In September 2004 land defenders who had mobilized at the Skwelkwet'welt Protection Centre were handed an injunction by members of the Royal Canadian Mounted Police (RCMP). Secwepemc leader and spokesperson George Manuel Jr. was immediately arrested. Tensions escalated once again in April 2006 when the Canadian Master's Alpine Championships were held at Sun Peaks Resort and following the announcement that the national Austrian ski team planned to train on unceded Secwepemc territories in preparation for the 2010 Olympic Games.[24] In September 2007 Manuel Jr. issued a press release that reaffirmed Secwepemc reasons for opposing the Austrian ski team's presence at Sun Peaks Resort and, more generally, towards the hosting of the 2010 Olympic Games. In this letter he openly criticized the divide-and-rule strategy used by settler governments, public misconceptions concerning elected and traditional governments, and renounced third party (i.e., Sun Peaks Resort and 2010 Olympic organizers) alienation of Indigenous territories.[25]

In another troubling example, Pacheedaht (Nuu-chah-nulth) hereditary leader, elder, mother, grandmother, and great-grandmother Tseybayoti (Harriet Nahanee), was arrested in May 2006 for her role in trying to save ecologically sensitive wetlands at Eagleridge Bluffs in the lead-up to the Games. Tseybayoti (and others) were not opposing construction upgrades to this treacherous stretch of highway, but rather, the decision to construct an additional 2.4 kilometre stretch of roadway through ecologically sensitive wetlands when sustainable alternatives were available. She understood that as a steward of the territories, she had a cultural obligation to defend the lands, water, non-human relations, and future generations from such violence. Tseybayoti also understood that she possessed legal rights, entrenched in Indigenous and Western legal systems. Upon her arrest and at her sentencing, she held firmly onto a copy of the Royal Proclamation of 1763. Supreme Court of British Columbia Justice Brenda Brown saw this as an act of defiance and sentenced the seventy-one-year-old great-grandmother, who was not well at the time, to two weeks in a provincial jail for criminal contempt of court. Tseybayoti served this sentence at the Surrey Pretrial Services Centre, a male-dominated facility notorious for overcrowding and frigid temperatures. While detained in this provincial jail, she contracted pneumonia and was eventually hospitalized. Tseybayoti died on 24 February 2007, at St. Paul's Hospital; doctors cited pneumonia and complications as the cause of death. On the evening before Tseybayoti's death, strangers and loved ones held a vigil outside her hospital room, as some prayed, drummed, and sang the "Women's Warrior Song."[26] This act was meaningful in that it was a form of public condemnation for the harsh punitive treatment of a hereditary leader and elder who was carrying out her sacred duties and asserting her Indigenous rights. Tseybayoti's life work has since inspired a new generation of Indigenous land defenders, now better positioned to defend their rights and assert Indigenous laws and practices, thereby standing up against the powerful interests of settler states, industry, and sovereign global subjects, such as the Olympic movement.

As this historical background and these examples illustrate, even the most advanced models for Indigenous participation failed to eradicate the profound legal and political power disparities between Indigenous nations and the state. In fact the arrival of the Olympic Games on these unceded territories established a state of exception whereby Indigenous rights were further repressed in the lead-up to these Olympic Games.[27] The public persona that organizers sought to demonstrate was one of respect for the territorial protocols of Indigenous nations, which was contained mostly within the opening and closing ceremonies. However, within the medium of the Olympic ceremonies, territorial protocols were presented in the form of land acknowledgments and were thus reduced to mostly performative spectacles that largely served colonizing and nationalistic objectives.

Territorial Protocols as Olympic Spectacle

There are two clear examples where Coast Salish territorial protocols were observed during the planning and hosting of the Vancouver Games, including the closing ceremony of the Turin 2006 Olympic and Paralympic Winter Games and the opening ceremony of the Vancouver 2010 Olympic and Paralympic Winter Games. The Handover Ceremony in the closing ceremony of the 2006 Winter Olympics marked the transfer of the Games from Turin, Italy, to Vancouver. This eight-minute interlude, which Vancouver organizers were responsible for coordinating, began with a Coast Salish *Uts'am* (witness) ceremony. For this ceremony, leaders and representatives from the host nations invited visitors to xʷməθkʷəy̓əm, səl̓ilwətaʔɬ, Sḵwx̱wú7mesh, and Lílwat7úl territories for the occasion of the 2010 Games. The approximately 33,000 spectators in attendance in Turin were called to bear witness. In Coast Salish cultures, being called to bear witness is a sacred honour. The responsibility of the those bearing witness is to listen and watch the work taking place so that they can carry these messages to their home communities. If there is a question or concern over what took place, witnesses are responsible for recalling the messages and events so that they can be verified at a later date.[28] Through this practice, witnesses are usually gifted in some form, symbolizing the exchange and the responsibility of witnesses to remember and possibly recall the events at a later date. At the closing ceremony of the 2006 Turin Games, all in attendance were gifted a medallion created by Sḵwx̱wú7mesh artist Jody Broomfield.[29]

The second example is the opening ceremony for the 2010 Games. For it, the four host First Nations were invited to provide a welcome to their territories. There is a general principle in Coast Salish cultures that visitors should wait until they are welcomed before entering another's territory; however, there is a modification in some Coast Salish cultures' protocol. Historically, ocean-going canoes were the most common form of transport among coastal people, so wooden "welcome figures" or "welcome poles" sat on the outskirts of many villages. As explained in the opening ceremony media guide, "Many of these welcome poles had hinged arms, and if the expected visitors were welcome, the arms would be raised in a gesture of greeting, if not, the figure's arms would remain down, by its sides."[30] On the occasion of the 2010 opening ceremony, the arms of all four welcome poles raised, indicating that visitors were welcome to the host nations' territories. The physical welcome was followed by official greetings from leaders and representatives of these nations.[31]

Some may view adherence to these territorial protocols as positive strides forward. In many respects, this is true, as these four Indigenous nations tactically used the most global stage imaginable to assert their sovereign authority and to invigorate their legal traditions. However, as these examples demonstrate, two obvious tensions arise when observing territorial protocols within the Olympic structure. First are obvious ontological and epistemological differences. In both examples, host nations engaged in time-honoured protocols that carried important meanings, grounded in the histories, traditions, cultures, spiritualities, and laws of the respective Indigenous nations. Nonetheless, their importance became lost on viewing publics, as settlers, outsiders, and global spectators had no frame of reference to receive such messages, much less respect their sacredness.[32] Within such spaces, the act became largely performative because the receiving audiences had already most likely accepted that the acknowledged lands were settler state property.

A second tension arises when territorial protocols assume a performative aspect that, in turn, becomes Olympic spectacles. The performance of territorial protocols within Olympic ceremonies have the potential to serve broader colonizing and nationalistic objectives of settler states. For example, in the 2006 Handover Ceremony in Turin, Canada's history was told using symbolic narrative. Following the *Uts' am*, the Indigenous representatives left centre stage, giving way to the children who played on the symbolically open (read: empty) terrain. The children gave way to teens as an urban landscape developed; the teens then gave way to adults who began to transform the landscape into a modern city.[33] The narrative presented in this short interlude was distressingly similar to that presented in the 2002 Salt Lake City Games opening ceremony. Upon reflecting on the 2002 performance, Suzan Shown Harjo (Cheyenne and Hodulgee Muscogee) appropriately reasoned that "after the Indians had their moment in the spotlight, they danced their way back into history, making way for miners, cowboys and settlers of all races to do-se-do together."[34] The message sent and likely received by millions worldwide following both Olympic ceremonies was that the histories of these settler colonial states could be represented metaphorically, as each had seemingly metamorphosed from primitive to civilized nation. Further, the land acknowledgment observed in the 2010 opening ceremony demonstrates how the Olympic medium sustains colonizing and nationalistic objectives of settler states. In this case, a land acknowledgment was observed *after* the official dignitaries (including the IOC president, Jacques Rogue and the governor general of Canada, Michaëlle Jean) were introduced, members of the RCMP escorted the Canadian flag into the stadium, members of the Canadian Forces Honour Guard raised the flag, and Canada's national anthem was performed.[35] This strict adherence to Olympic protocol ultimately privileged the authority of the colonial settler state and, in the process, relegate the long-standing protocols and laws of Indigenous nations to a secondary and thus performative position within the Olympic framework.

Conclusion

The consolidation of action item 91 in the TRC calls to action provides an opportunity to ask critical questions about whether there exists an opportunity to affirm Indigenous legal traditions within international sporting spaces. The Indigenous participation model produced for the

Vancouver Games was indeed the most advanced in Olympic history; however, even it failed to uphold longstanding laws, legal traditions, and Indigenous rights. There is a long history of legal and political exploitation of Indigenous peoples (and other marginalized groups) in the hosting frameworks of international sporting events. They continue to be controlled by settler state governments and sovereign global subjects that remain deeply invested in accessing and exploiting Indigenous lands. As it stands, the framework for respecting Indigenous peoples' territorial protocols within international sporting events, such as the Olympic Games, remains largely affixed to disingenuous Indigenous participation models. Respecting Indigenous territorial protocols in the planning and organizing of international sporting events requires that we begin by accepting Indigenous territorial protocol as law. As Heidi Kiiwetinepinesiik Stark affirms, Indigenous laws persist, adapt, and give shape to our engagement with other nations; they fortify the legitimacy of the settler colonial state while ensuring the enduring sovereignty of Indigenous nations.[36] Disregard for such principles requires the full and expansive re-evaluation of whether it is possible in the future to host international sporting events, such as the Olympic Games, in settler colonial Canada.

NOTES

1 Truth and Reconciliation Commission, *Truth and Reconciliation Commission of Canada: Calls to Action* (2015), 10. https://ehprnh2mwo3.exactdn.com /wp-content/uploads/2021/01/Calls_to_Action_English2.pdf.

2 "Aboriginal Involvement in Games Makes History," CBC News, 14 February 2010, https://www.cbc.ca/news/canada/british-columbia/aboriginal -involvement-in-games-makes-history-1.945693.

3 Olympic organizers include state partners (municipal, provincial, and federal governments), industry and corporations, and the IOC.

4 Jules Boykoff, *Power Games: A Political History of the Olympics* (London: Verso, 2016), 1.

5 David Young, *The Modern Olympic: A Struggle for Revival* (Baltimore, MD: Johns Hopkins University Press, 2002).

6 Pierre de Coubertin, "Why I Revived the Olympic Games," *Fortnightly Review* 86, no. 499 (July 1908): 115.

7 Kevin B. Wamsley, "Laying Olympism to Rest," in *Post-Olympism? Questioning Sport in the Twenty-First Century*, ed. John Bale and Mette Krogh Christensen (Oxford: Berg, 2004), 231.

8 Guy Debord, *The Society of the Spectacle*, trans. Donald Nicholson-Smith (New York: Zone Books, 1995), 28.

9 Debord, *Society of the Spectacle*, 28.

10 Jules Boykoff, *Celebration Capitalism and the Olympic Games* (London: Routledge, 2014).

11 Boykoff draws from Judith Butler, *Precarious Life: The Power of Mourning and Violence* (London: Verso, 2004), in Boykoff, *Celebration Capitalism*, 10.

12 United Nations Conference on Environment & Development, *United Nations Sustainable Development: Agenda 21* (Rio de Janeiro: United Nations, 1992), https://sustainabledevelopment.un.org/content/documents /Agenda21.pdf.

13 The UN's *Agenda 21* is a 351-page document, which mentions Indigenous peoples 160 times throughout the plan. Conversely, the IOC's *Agenda 21* is a 50-page document and mentions Indigenous peoples on three occasions. See International Olympic Committee, *Olympic Movement's Agenda 21* (1999). https://stillmed.olympic.org/media/Document%20Library /OlympicOrg/Documents/Olympism-in-Action/Environment/Olympic -Movement-s-Agenda-21.pdf.

14 International Olympic Committee, *The Olympic Movement's Agenda 21*, 42, 42, 45.

15 From 2000 to 2010, the Olympic summer schedule included Sydney (2000), Athens (2004), and Beijing (2008), and the winter schedule included Salt Lake City (2002), Turin (2006), and Vancouver (2010). For the 2000 Sydney Olympic Games, a National Indigenous Advisory Committee, representing Aboriginal and Torres Strait Islanders' interests, was struck to advise the Sydney organizing committee. In 2002 organizers for the Salt Lake City Olympic Winter Games partnered with Utah's five tribal Indian nations, including the Ute, Navajo, Paiute, Goshute, and Shoshone.

16 John Price and Nicholas Xemŧoltw Claxton, "Whose Land Is it? Rethinking Sovereignty in British Columbia," *BC Studies* 204 (2020): 115–38; Hamar Foster, "'We Want a Strong Promise': The Opposition to Indian Treaties in British Columbia, 1850–1990," *Native Studies Review* 18, no. 1 (2009): 113–37; Hamar Foster and Alan Grove, "'Trespassers on the Soil': United States v. Tom and a New Perspective on the Short History of Treaty Making in Nineteenth-Century British Columbia," *BC Studies* no. 138/9 (2003): 51–84; and Taiaiake Alfred, "Deconstructing the British Columbia Treaty Process," *Balayi: Culture, Law and Colonialism* 3 (2001): 37–65.

17 The four host First Nations fell within the organization structure of the broader Aboriginal Participation and Collaboration Program, comprising five branches, including Participation and Collaboration, Sport and Youth, Economic Development, Cultural Involvement, and Awareness and Education.

18 Robin Sidsworth, "Aboriginal Participation in the Vancouver/Whistler 2010 Olympic Winter Games: Consultation, Reconciliation, and the New Relationship" (MA thesis, University of British Columbia, 2010).

19 For example, numerous Indigenous nations opposed the arrival of the Olympic flame in their communities and territories in the weeks prior to the 2010 Olympic Games. See Christine O'Bonsawin, "Igniting a Resistance Movement: Understanding Indigenous Opposition to the 2010 Olympic Torch Relay," in *Critical Dialogues on the Olympic and Paralympic Games*, ed. Janice Forsyth and Michael Heine (London: International Centre for Olympic Studies, 2012), 99–104.

20 Boykoff, *Celebration Capitalism*, 5.

21 British Columbia, *British Columbia Resort Strategy and Action Plan* (Victoria: British Columbia, 2004).

22 *British Columbia Resort Strategy and Action Plan*, 15.

23 Sutikahl and Skwelkwek'welt, "Official Complaint by the Elders, Land Users and Native Youth of Sutikahl and Skwelkwek'welt to the International Olympic Committee (June 2002), http://www.firstnations.de/media/06-4-1-ioc.pdf.

24 First Nations, "'Hell No to Yellow Snow': Secwepemc Protest Sun Peaks Use of Recycled Sewage Wastes to Make Snow on Their Sacred Mountains," press release, 8 April 2006. http://www.firstnations.eu/media/06-3-2-nym .pdf.

25 Arthur Manuel, "Sun Peaks: Indian Land for Sale," 30 September 2007, Indigenous Network on Economies and Trade, http://www.firstnations.de /media/01-1-indian-land.pdf.

26 Zoe Blunt, "First Nations Activist Dies after Release from Jail: In Memory of Harriet Nahanee, Age 71," *Dominion: News from the Grassroots*, 29 March 2007, 44; and Dianne Meili, "Harriet Nahanee: Activist Still Inspires Years after Her Death," *Windspeaker* 3, no. 1 (April 2012): 22. https://data2 .archives.ca/e/e449/e011200907.pdf.

27 Christine O'Bonsawin, "Showdown at Eagleridge Bluffs: The 2010 Vancouver Olympic Winter Games, the Olympic Sustainability Smokescreen, and the Protection of Indigenous Rights," in *Intersections and Intersectionalities in Olympic and Paralympic Sport*, ed. Janice Forsyth, Christine O'Bonsawin, and Michael Heine (London: International Centre for Olympic Studies, 2014): 82–8.

28 Sarah Noël Morales, "*SNUW'UYULH*: Fostering an Understanding of the HUL'QUMI'NUM Legal Tradition" (PhD diss., University of Victoria, 2014), 2–14; and Rachel Thompson, "Uts'am: Bearing Witness: A Traditional Coast Salish Ceremony," *Women and Environments International Magazine* 56/7 (2002): 27–30.

29 Vancouver Olympic Organizing Committee for the 2010 Olympic and Paralympic Winter Games, "Torino Closing Ceremony: Vancouver 2010 Segment Colour Commentary Information," 26 February 2006.

30 Vancouver Organizing Committee for the Olympic and Paralympic Winter Games, *Opening Ceremony of the XXI Olympic Winter Games: Media Guide*, 12 February 2010, 35.

31 CTV, "Complete Vancouver 2010 Opening Ceremony: Vancouver 2010 Winter Olympics," *Olympic Programming*, 26 February 2010), https://www.youtube.com/watch?v=MxZpUueDAvc.

32 Irwin Oostindle, "Place-Based Redress and the Spectacle of Reconciliation" (MA thesis, Simon Fraser University, 2020); and Christine O'Bonsawin, "A Coast Salish Olympic Welcome: The 2010 Vancouver Opening Ceremony and the Politics of Indigenous Representation," in *Rethinking Matters Olympic: Investigations into the Socio-Cultural Study of the Modern Olympic Movement*, ed. Robert K. Barney, Janice Forsyth, and Michael Heine (London: International Centre for Olympic Studies): 255–64.

33 Vancouver Olympic Organizing Committee, "Torino Closing Ceremony."

34 Suzan Shown Harjo, "Indians in the Opening Ceremony: Postcard from the Past," *Indian Country Today*, 16 February 2002.

35 CTV, "Complete Vancouver 2010 Opening Ceremony."

36 Heidi Kiiwetinepinesiik Stark, "Stories as Law: A Method to Live By," in *Sources and Methods in Indigenous Studies*, ed. Chris Andersen and Jean M. O'Brien (London: Routledge, 2016): 249–56.

13 "Descendants of the Original Lords of the Soil": Indignation, Disobedience, and Women Who Jig on Sundays[1]

DANIEL VOTH

In what follows, I engage Métis discussions of being the "descendants of the original lords of the soil" across moments in time to outline a gender-centric Métis self-conception of the *we* that make up the nation and the nation's relationships with land and territory. The Métis are a people composed of communities on both sides of the Canada-US border, a people of the northwest plains with kinship ties to the Dakota, Nehiyaw (Cree), Dene, and Saulteaux (Anishinaabe/Ojibway) nations. While much has been written about Métis history and legal activism, comparatively little research on Métis nationalist self-conceptions has linked the gender-informed traditions of the nation to models and modes of Métis governance. I argue that an empirically grounded reimagining of Métis nationalist roots centres Métis and other Indigenous women at the heart of the *we* of the nation by establishing a link between Indigenous women and claims to land and territory. This gendered self-conception of the nation and territory can be operationalized in the nation's practices of governance. To this end, this article contributes two new interrelated governance frameworks informed by my reimagining of Métis nationalist roots: indignant governance and indignant disobedience.

Several reasons motivate my use of the term *indignant* as the key conceptual building block of this work. In what will be illustrated in more detail below, in the nineteenth century, at a key juncture of Métis organizing against the imposition of Euro-Canadian power structures, Métis gathered in what were referred to in the local paper as "indignation meetings." These meetings were designed to push back against outsider claims to Métis territory, and in so doing, the Métis articulated the nature and logic of their own relationships to the land using the language of "original lords of the soil." The term *indignation* connects directly to foundational Métis discussions of colonialism, gender, and the land.[2] In addition, the indefensible exclusion of women from the spaces of power in national governance has long been criticized by Indigenous women and activists across nationalist struggles. The indignation meetings and Indigenous women's disempowerment in governance structures form the key interventions that give rise to indignant governance and indignant disobedience. In both cases, indignation is an appropriate emotional response to being treated unfairly, and Métis people and Indigenous women more broadly, in the nineteenth century and today, have a great deal to feel indignant about. Linking practices of governance to a feeling of indignation legitimizes those emotions while also transforming them into action.

Following a brief overview of the contours of the Métis nation, my argument unfolds in three sections. The reduction of Métis identity to historical mixed marriages is not something that only settlers do. Other Indigenous peoples do it as well. To this point, the first section uses a recent court filing to show how the leadership of the Treaty One nations deploys a male-centric and patriarchal orientation to Indigenous relationships to land in the twenty-first century using racial mixing narratives that unwittingly advance Indian Act sexist logics. The section then contrasts this patriarchal logic with a gendered analysis of Métis claims in the nineteenth century of being the descendants of the lords of the soil.

The second section provides a deeper exploration of the historical account in section 1 through the literature linking Métis women to land and territory. The third section uses the analysis developed in the previous two sections to build a new gender-centric Métis governance theory in the form of my two governance frameworks. Indignant governance seeks to turn symbolic nationalist self-expressions, like being descendants of the original lords of the soil, into action-oriented nationalist symbols that enact gender-empowered governance, and in so doing, the concept aims to activate the political potential of indignation. Indignant disobedience takes up the concerns of feminist scholars, arguing that framing women as nationalist symbols has not stopped the oppression of women within nationalist movements, Indigenous or otherwise. I place the literature on feminist and Indigenous women's engagements with nationalism and governance in conversation with the story of an indignantly disobedient Métis woman who was told by her priest that she was not allowed to dance on Sundays. I argue that in this story we can find key lessons for transforming the indignation felt by Indigenous women into a model of Métis governance that guards against patriarchal disempowerment of Indigenous women within the governance of the Métis nation. Across all three sections I aim to give form and direction to the gendered self-conceptions outlined in the first section to offer a new way forward for Métis governance that at once pushes back against the imposition of male-centric conceptions of the *we* of the nation while also recentring relationships with the Indigenous women that settler colonialism has tried to disempower.

Who Are the Métis?

The Métis Nation are a people from the northwest plains with territories and inter-Indigenous relationships that stretch down the Red River Valley in the province of Manitoba to the Ontario edge of Lake Superior and then west and north to what is now Edmonton in the province of Alberta. In addition, the contemporary Métis National Council has a political presence in British Columbia and the Northwest Territories. In the nineteenth century, prior to the full-scale settlement of the West, the Métis were an economically diverse people grounded by a connection to the bison (or buffalo, as it was discussed in Indigenous contexts) hunting economy, associated canoe brigades, and pemmican trade. They engaged in military conflict and treaty making with the Dakota and Lakota to gain and maintain access to the herds. They were part of kinship alliances with other Indigenous peoples and challenged the economic and political monopolies of the Hudson's Bay Company. Perhaps most famous for their military resistances against the expanding Canadian state, their military strength forced the Canadian and British governments to negotiate Métis entry into Canadian Confederation in 1869–70. Canada put down a second military conflict with the Métis in 1885.[3] After the 1885 hanging of a prominent Métis resistance leader, the Métis were socially, economically, and politically marginalized by the entrenching Canadian state. The Métis formed political organizations over the next century that allowed them to organize and agitate through protest, while also seeking the entrenchment of their rights in the Constitution Act of 1982 and eventually taking up the tactics of other Indigenous peoples by suing the Canadian government for hunting rights and land theft in the late twentieth and early twenty-first centuries.[4]

Métis Rights to Land through the Eyes of Treaty One Peoples

At the conclusion of the *Manitoba Métis Federation v. Canada and Manitoba* court case, decided by the Supreme Court of Canada on 8 March 2013, the Métis celebrated a hard-fought victory. The Court found that the Crown did not disburse lands to the Métis in the nineteenth century in a fashion consistent with the promises and gravity of the task. This long-in-coming victory, taking over forty-five years to move from its roots in community organizing to reach the Supreme Court, was punctuated by a triumphant Manitoba Métis Federation president, David Chartrand, marching down the steps inside the Supreme Court of Canada building. The moment had all the ingredients of what Indigenous nationalists love: a male Indigenous political leader surrounded by many other male Indigenous leaders, arms in the air, shouting slogans of victory inside an institution that had been violently imposed on a defiant Native people. It's the kind of image someone might cast in bronze in 150 years. Chartrand's exuberant march down those stairs in 2013 was a vindication that all of the human, emotional, and material resources devoted to the case were worth it. Yet at the same time, focusing on the case and the man marching down the stairs elides the complexities of what happened during the hearings. Instead, paying attention to some of the less well known elements of Métis and First Nations politics that played out during the case illuminates some troubling ways other Indigenous peoples masculinize Métis relationships with land and territory.

One of the lesser-known elements of the case was that the Treaty One First Nations collectively intervened to challenge a Métis right to land. Scholars such as O'Toole[5] and Teillet and Madden[6] have examined in detail the logic, the legal nuances, and the Court's decision in the case; elsewhere I have studied the legal politics and strategic choices deployed by Treaty One nations in their intervention on the Métis relationship to land in southern Manitoba.[7] What follows picks up where these scholars left off and moves away from the established body of literature on the legal elements of the case. What is needed is a closer examination of the way the arguments advanced by First Nations peoples in the case decentre and misconstrue Métis conceptions of the nation away from gender-centric kinship and toward patriarchal logics.

Treaty One peoples intervened collectively in the case to challenge any right, title, or access to land that the Métis might secure from winning the case.[8] The weight of Treaty One peoples' argument rests on their characterization of Métis people's rights to land within the constellation of Indigenous peoples in what is now called southern Manitoba. Treaty One peoples argued that "any alleged Métis title [to *any* lands in Manitoba] could only flow from the *subservient* rights that the Métis would have as the aboriginal people descended from the antecedents of the Treaty One First nations, therefore, any declarations with respect to any Métis right to land in Treaty One territory must be limited by the proviso that such rights if granted by declaration are *inferior* to the pre-existing and unfulfilled existing right to land of the Treaty One First Nations that remain protected by the section 35(1) of the *Constitution Act, 1982*.[9]

While I have outlined elsewhere the strategic, racialized, and historically inaccurate logics at play in this formulation of Métis relationships to land, there is an additional problem that I missed in my 2018 work. The position staked out by Treaty One peoples has a troubling patriarchal understanding of Métis relationships to land.

The logic chain of Treaty One's position is that *because* the Métis are not full-blooded relations of the signatories to Treaty No. 1, they cannot have rights and relationships to the land that are equal to those of full-blooded signatories. While this has the trappings of a troubling racialized position, it *also* has gendered implications for Métis kinship relationships. While Métis people have both European and Indigenous heritage, this is also true for other Indigenous peoples, including the signatories to Treaty No. 1. However, for the most part, Métis families did not possess kinship links to the peoples who would sign Treaty No. 1 through First Nations *men*; instead, their links were through First Nations *women*. In the above statement, Treaty One peoples set up a position that disproportionately disrupts Indigenous women's ability to pass along relationships and responsibilities to the land. To be clear, in the nineteenth century there likely were Métis families with linear kin relationships to First Nations fathers. But as Sylvia Van Kirk points out, "An important reason for the strength of the attachment between white traders and Indian women lies in the fact that for many decades no white women were present in the Indian Country.... [N]o white women made their appearance in the Canadian West until the early nineteenth century."[10] When European women did arrive, they ensconced themselves at the top of a racial and social hierarchy and had little to do with First Nations men. By framing the Métis as possessing only fractioned rights to a First Nations whole right, Treaty One peoples are saying that Indigenous women were never capable *in their own right* of passing along relationships and responsibilities with the land. As a result, Indigenous women are disproportionately disempowered in the rendering of Treaty One's understanding of Métis relationships with the land.

This disempowerment mirrors much of the long history of Indian rights discourse and Indian Act gender discrimination.[11] After more than 140 years of Indian Act discrimination, perhaps it is not surprising that Treaty One's position would also reflect that past of gender discrimination. Without being explicit, Treaty One nations are perpetuating the history of gendered violence while also setting up the character of *true* and *full* Indigenous relationships with land as patrilineal. Recall that prior to 1985, the act of First Nations men with Indian Act status marrying non-status (and/or non-Indigenous) women would bring those women into the settler legal fold of the First Nation, and First Nations women with Indian Act status marrying non-status men would lose their status and lose the right to live in their community (even after a divorce).[12] In that same vein, Treaty One's submission in the twenty-first century implies that when Indigenous women married non-First Nation men, they somehow lost the ability to pass on their relationships with the land, making Métis relationships to land "subservient" and "inferior" to the rights of their male-descended First Nations family members. These Indigenous women were not able, on their own, to pass along relationships with land to their Indigenous children.

Interestingly, the Métis staked out their claim to land in the nineteenth century by using terms that, at first glance, appear to be in alignment with Treaty One's framing in the twenty-first. However, where Treaty One's logics discriminate against Indigenous women and are patently sexist, Métis people's nineteenth-century discussions of their relationship to their lands and territories were animated by a logic that centres Indigenous women as the link between community, land, and territory. Importantly, the discussion of the nineteenth-century land debates that follow are not guided by settler-state power relations or colonially imposed laws. Instead, Indigenous peoples are talking with each other in a context where Indigenous nations are the dominant power brokers in the region. One of the earliest instances of the phrase "lords of the soil" appeared in connection with Métis relationships with land and territory in the aftermath of the 1816 Battle of Seven Oaks. I pick up the trail there to outline the use of this particular phrase.

In the aftermath of the Métis winning the 1816 battle against non-Indigenous fur trade interests, an 1817 pamphlet attributed to John Halkett sought to defend the British traders and the program of settlement responsible for sparking hostilities.[13] Halkett included a footnote describing the Métis position on their relationship with the land as relayed by a Mr. M'Gillivray.

The note indicates that the Métis are "'a daring and numerous race, sprung from the intercourse of the Canadian Voyageurs with Indian women, and who consider themselves as the possessors of the country, and lords of the soil.' – It was some time ago rumoured that a formal petition had been presented to Government in behalf of these illegitimate Bois-Brulés as 'lords of the soil'! – If they have become so, it doubtless must be by right of *conquest*, as even Mr. M'Gillivray will scarcely contend that they hold the lands by right of *inheritance*."[14] Halkett had begun to formulate a phrase that will appear again several decades later.

Clearly, British men were baffled by and dismissive of any Métis claim to a relationship with the land that would trump British claims. It is unsurprising and uninteresting that a politicized defence of the battle includes a section dismissing the Métis claim. But three additional points are worth drawing out of this footnote. First, the note refers to a petition, which indicates the Métis were organizing politically on the land question even before the battle. Second, the "lords of the soil" claim is oriented toward possessing an Indigenous relationship to the land. Third, it is never made clear why a claim by virtue of being related to other Indigenous peoples on the plains is inconceivable.

Similar phrasing, along with debates about Métis relationships with the land, emerged again during a series of land meetings that came to a head in the 1860s and played out on the pages of the *Nor'Wester* newspaper in the Red River Settlement. On 14 March 1860, the *Nor'Wester* printed a report from a meeting of "Halfbreeds," as the Métis were described in English, at the Royal Hotel.[15] The meeting was called by leaders in the community and was chaired by Pascal Berland. The purpose of the meeting was to advance a Métis claim to the land in light of statements made by other Indigenous leaders and a Hudson's Bay Company (HBC) desire to settle title to the land. The leaders of this gathering argued that because the Saulteaux people were not originally from the region, the only nation that could have treated with the HBC (and then potentially disposed of the land) was the Cree. The paper reported Berland to have said, "Now ... I think there is a third party that can urge a claim – namely those natives who are partly the descendants of the first owners of the soil." Berland continued, "I maintain that Senna [a well-known and respected Cree chief], who had the best, if not the only, right to dispose of these lands, did never dispose of them; and if *he* did not, it matters little who else did. Well, seeing that no satisfactory arrangement has yet been made for the lands, I think it not unlikely that the 'Halfbreeds' of the country – representatives of the Crees and other tribes – might put in a good claim."[16]

On this point, the gathering was addressed by Urbin Delorme, William Dease, Pierre Falcon, William Hallet, George Flett, John Bourke, and William McGilles. The paper reported the consensus arrived at to be:

1st. That the Cree chief, Senna, who has the best claim to this country, never disposed of it to the Earl of Selkirk or the Hudson's Bay Company.
2nd. That the Hudson's Bay Company do not, as is alleged, pay £8 stg per annum to each of the five chiefs mentioned in Mr M'Dermot's letter.
3rd. That the paltry presents given to some or all of these chiefs for many years after 1816, were not given in the way of payment for lands; but merely to keep them friendly towards the Company. The friendship of these chiefs was important, not only because their hostility might have been dangerous, but because they could, by using their influence with their people, bring a large quantity of furs to the [HBC].

4th. That presents similar to those given after the years 1816, were given for 30 or 40 years before that date, for the purpose of "keeping in" with the Indians; and given not only to the chiefs of this district, but to every influential Indian throughout the country.

5th. That as no proper arrangement has been made with the native tribes regarding their lands, the "Halfbreeds" who are now on the soil, and who, besides being natives, are the immediate representatives of these tribes, ought to use every legitimate means to urge their claims to consideration in any arrangement which the Imperial Government may see fit to make.[17]

These items articulate several key inward- and outward-looking orientations to other Indigenous nations in the Red River area and surrounding region. First, the gifting obligations and economies associated with north-west plains diplomacy do not a land surrender make. Second, the Saulteaux are known to be recent arrivals to the area. Third, and most importantly, the Métis are describing themselves in complex terms of indigeneity. The logic and arguments at play in this meeting did not disappear in the weeks and months that followed. On 14 June 1860, the paper ran another story detailing that old Andre Trotier, an elder in the Métis community and a witness to HBC and Saulteaux/Cree treaty making, emphatically stated that the Saulteaux and the other "chiefs did not in any sense *sell* the land ... but rented it" to non-Indigenous interests for the purposes of settlement.[18]

On 15 June 1861, another article was printed from two additional meetings held on this land question. The title of this article was "Indignation Meetings." The HBC was reported to have sent letters to residents living along the Assiniboine River demanding that those Métis residents pay the HBC for their lands or risk having that land sold against their will, "in which case all improvements would be forfeited." In response, the Métis struck a committee consisting of Pascal Breland and Urban Delorome, "among other influential men in that district," at which "they declared they would not pay one cent." The article stated that "the principal reasons urged against compliance with the late claims are, that the Company have no right to the land themselves, never having purchased it, and that the Halfbreeds have a very palpable right, being the descendants of the original lords of the soil.".[19]

There are two reasons why these articulations are important. First, across several debates with differing animating facts, the Métis have maintained a logical consistency to their claims to the land. Second, while these nineteenth-century statements and declarations appear to conform to Treaty One's twenty-first-century intervention in the *MMF* case, the statements operate on a different set of logics than those used by Treaty One. The nineteenth-century statements are anchored to a sense of being *Indigenous*. Indigeneity is not talked about as a subset of a pure indigeneity with a correlating portion of rights from those pure peoples. Rather, it is exclusively talked about in the language of a relationship to land by virtue of being a Native people. Consider the fifth point from the 14 March 186, article quoted above. The first phrase affirms a general suspicion that no agreement had ever been made with either Lord Selkirk or the HBC. The gathering adjourned with the intention of waiting until elders in the community who were wintering outside of Red River returned in the spring to corroborate that suspicion. The second part is a collective declaration of being Indigenous. Note the use of the phrase "besides being natives." This is important because of its position in the logic chain. Independent of their relationships with other Indigenous peoples, the Métis are themselves native to the land in question. To deepen this declaration, they also identify themselves as "immediate representatives of these tribes." This is not necessarily an act of usurpation or a statement of possessing partial rights. All the attendees at the meetings would have had relatives in other Indigenous nations. They would have been part of a network of Indigenous peoples bound together by political alliances, economic activities, and – importantly – kinship. Indeed, recall that in the petition noted by John Halkett, the question of inheritance and relationships with other Indigenous peoples was close at hand. Where Treaty One peoples in the twenty-first century saw rights that were diluted through Indigenous women marrying out and thus magically ending their ability to pass on relationships with the land, Métis people in the nineteenth century were asserting a connection to the land as one of a number of interrelated Native peoples *of* that land. Treaty One peoples advanced a patriarchal rights regime in the Supreme Court, while Métis people articulated Indigeneity and kinship in their nineteenth-century political gatherings.

It is also worth noting that the Métis advanced their nineteenth-century arguments in a context that was fundamentally an Indigenous social, political, and economic space. These debates emerged before section 91(24) of the British North America Act 1867, which established federal jurisdiction for Indigenous peoples and their lands; or the Manitoba Act 1870, which brought the Red River region into Confederation; or the Indian Act 1876, which created a legal regime for Indians and their lands; or the Indian residential and industrial school system, which sought to destroy Indigenous peoples by assimilating Indigenous children. All of these violent impositions of Euro-American law and society that helped dig the racialized and sexist chasms between Indigenous peoples did not yet exist in western Canada. When read in context, it simply does not make sense to interpret the land and indignation debates as informed and animated by a regime of racialized and patriarchal logics that had not been operationalized or even introduced in the North West.

A number of scholars have narrated and noted these land question and indignation debates, framing them variously as the conditions that would help spark the Resistance in 1870, led by Louis Riel and other men,[20] or as demonstrations of a long-standing understanding of Métis land rights using the logics that would inform Aboriginal law and the law of derivative Indian title.[21] However, what is missing is an appreciation of what these debates mean for gendered relationships of kinship and Métis governance. If one examines the statements made by Métis people in a kinship context rather than a patriarchal one, kinship takes on a highly gender-centric formulation. As noted above, the Métis people invoking "the original lords of the soil" are not, in general, talking about Native men. They are talking about Native *women*. Recall Van Kirk's quote above pointing out that these mixed marriages featured European men and First Nations women.[22] Even Treaty One peoples' submission to the court is founded on this relationship. These Métis leaders are clearly invoking a relationship to the land as an Indigenous people; however, that relationship to the land is anchored to Indigenous women. Absent the violent and racist Canadian regime that would assert itself in Red River and beyond over the century and a half after 1870, these Métis men seem to be making reference to their mothers, aunts, grandmothers, and great-grandmothers in whose care and under whose tutelage they were reared.

In light of these meaning-rich indignation meetings, there is an opportunity to reconceptualize Métis orientations to the *we* of the nation with significant effect. If the *we* is about foundational relationships between Indigenous women and the land, then one is also compelled to think about how the nation governs itself in the face of those relationships. Indignant governance is a commitment to shape the way we make decisions (about Métis people and communities and about relationships with non-Métis peoples) that reflects the connections between the land and kinship with Métis and other Indigenous women. Formulated this way, indignant governance is not just a nationalist symbol by which women connect the people to the land. Rather, it also demands that gender-centric principles be operationalized in the messiness and practices of interactions among people, peoples, and our other-than-human relations. Métis people are right to feel indignant about their treatment by both other Indigenous peoples and settlers. Indignant governance takes that feeling and transforms it into a generative model of action.

If we reflect on the great narratives that still dominate Métis politics and Métis nationalism, we can see many of the so-called great men of Native history. Cuthbert Grant, William Hallett, William Dease, Louis Riel Jr. and Sr., James McKay, Charles Nolin, Gabriel Dumont all come to mind. One is hard-pressed to name or even point to Indigenous women in this conception of the nation. If one thinks about the larger-than-life bronze statue of Louis Riel Jr. on the grounds of the Manitoba Legislative Assembly and the holiday named after him in February in the province, one begins to see how highly male-dominated framings of Métis nationhood contribute not only to Treaty One nations' submission to the Court but also to the moulding of Métis nationalism more generally. In light of the indignation and land meetings, my concern is that the inappropriate patriarchal logic advanced by Treaty One peoples in the Supreme Court is accompanied by an equally inappropriate masculinization of Métis relationships to land and nationhood. Both have symbolically and functionally disempowered Métis women within the governance structures and relationships with the land of the Métis Nation. What remains unclear about indignant governance is how this model can be operationalized while ensuring women's empowerment within the model. The subsequent two sections take on these questions directly.

Deepening the Interconnectedness between Land and Métis Women

While a number of Indigenous scholars have examined the interconnections between women, land, and Indigenous governance structures,[23] less is known about these relationships for the Métis nation.[24] As Nathalie Kermoal has argued in her study of Métis women's land-based knowledge, "Rather than reinforce colonial conceptions of gender, in which men's activities on the land somehow become more essential than women's, we need to understand how Aboriginal women perceived their connection to the land and to their cultural heritage."[25] The recounting of the land question and indignation meetings above tries to place the gendered conception of land and political power at the centre of our line of sight. In particular, the logic behind the land question and indignation meetings bears a striking resemblance to what scholars have identified in analyses of Métis kinship patterns. Brenda Macdougall has studied other instances in which it appears Indigenous women formed a key link to Métis relationships with their territories. She describes a balancing act between incoming outsider men and Indigenous insider women bringing those outsider men into Indigenous territories through trade relationships (specifically Sakitawak): "Outsider male employees of various fur trade companies entered the region to work and, in the process, helped lay a foundation for the emergence of the Métis. In subsequent generations, this connection between land and economy was further entrenched as people maintained their employment in the trade *while living in the homeland opened to them by their maternal connection to the land.*"[26] Macdougall found that the opportunities made available to outsider men came in part from being able to live in the territories of Indigenous women.

Macdougall further refines this analysis, expanding her framework empirically and geographically. She critiques the approach to studying Métis people and family networks using analyses that privilege racial origins rather than self and familial affirmations of identity. Importantly for the purposes here, Macdougall argues that scholars have inappropriately tried to understand Métis people and families through non-Indigenous categories of analysis. In honing the point, Macdougall states,

> Scholars of Canadian Metis history have been inordinately preoccupied with how to classify the Metis – were they more white or more Indian, more French or more British? Even Louis Riel, the archetype of nineteenth-century Metis political leadership, has had the authenticity of his Metis identity questioned. Some have reflected that Riel is best characterized as French Canadian because he had only one Dene grandparent and three French Canadian grandparents, which would make him only one eighth Indian. In this rendering, Riel's life course and his personal and political decisions are all meaningless. Instead, his identity is evaluated at the moment of conception rather than within his own historical cultural context.[27]

Macdougall engages the same tension identified in the land debates discussed above, namely, the desire, even by other Indigenous peoples, to place Métis within a non-contextual framework instead of the social, economic, and political context out of which the Métis emerge as a people.[28]

To this point, after shifting to an analysis that emphasizes family, Macdougall is able to identify the way Métis and other Indigenous peoples and families like James Ross, Mary Musgrove Mathews Bosomworth, the Morin family, the Trottier family, and the Laframboise family assert Indigenous connections to the land, with the connecting thread being kinship with Indigenous women.[29] As Macdougall powerfully phrases it, "What Mary [Bosomworth] shared in common with ... [other people, peoples, and families in her study] was an assertion of her rights to a physical landscape as defined and supported by her connection to her maternal relatives. In short, her rights flowed from her membership in the family and, through that membership, a claim to being part of the land itself.".[30] Macdougall concludes that "across the North American continent, Métis forged amongst themselves communities defined by their maternal ancestors and then continued to redefine themselves via ongoing female familial connections to land. *Métis identity, therefore, is based on the historical interconnections to land and women.*"[31]

The final quote from Macdougall is strikingly similar to what appears to be at play in the land question and indignation meetings. If one takes seriously the lessons from Diane Payment[32] that the historical record suffers from a clear male bias in who gets recorded and how those records are read, then we must read the land and indignation debates with a sharper eye to gender dynamics.[33] If one privileges family and kinship over masculine parentage, the statements made above by, admittedly, Métis men take on a complex and rich form that is more consistent with the political context out of which those statements emerge. The Métis relationship to the land is linked to being the descendants of the original lords of the soil. What has been missed is that the "lords" the Métis are talking about are Indigenous women. The analysis here demands the question: How might the relationship among Métis women, other Indigenous women, and the land be operationalized in Métis governance structures?

Métis Women, Nationhood, and Power beyond the Symbolic

Rather than framing the issue as maternally grounded "rights to a landscape," as Macdougall does, it may be more productive to construct the issue in the language of nationalist symbols that demand substantial action. My concern with using the language of rights is that it tends to funnel contemporary Métis struggles into courts that are in turn tasked with interpreting a justiciable right. Part of the problem with Treaty One peoples' position in the Supreme Court is that they tried to deploy an Indigenous context-specific discourse in an explicitly non-Indigenous juridical arena. To realize the full potential of what Macdougall and others are offering in their analyses, Métis people ought to align their governance principles in accordance with Métis goals and aspirations rather than with settler courts, judges, legislatures, constitutions, and rights.

The land debates and indignation meetings position Indigenous women as the anchors to the land within Métis nationalism. If that were to be where it ended, this formulation would have predominantly symbolic properties. Many feminist scholars of nationalism have identified a tendency of nationalist movements to relegate the women of the nation to symbolic positions. As McClintock has argued, "All nations depend on powerful constructions of gender," and "all too often in male nationalisms, *gender* difference between women and men serves to symbolically define the limits of *national* difference and power between *men.* Excluded from direct action as national citizens, women are subsumed symbolically into the national body politic as its boundary and metaphoric limit.... Women are typically construed as the symbolic bearers of the nation, but are denied any direct relation to national agency."[34] Gender symbolism has been examined and identified by a range of thoughtful scholarship.[35] Nor is this exclusively a view animated by second-wave feminist analysis. As Lina Sunseri[36] has pointed out, Indigenous women are also wrapped up as symbols in Indigenous nationalism.

One important lesson from these feminist critiques of nationalism is that the symbolism of women as the progenitors, mothers, and life-givers of the nation is found to be a feature of many nationalist movements, but rarely, if ever, is it accompanied by *actual* political empowerment for women. Indeed, nationalist movements often frame the emancipation of women from colonial or counter-nationalist forces as a lesser priority than the higher-order concerns of confronting the opponents of the nationalist movement. However, Joanne Sharp has wondered, "Is it possible for a change in leadership, however revolutionary, to facilitate emancipation for all if gender problems are not addressed before and during the revolution?"[37] Sharp's critical insight into the relationship between the active structure and outcome of nationalist movements is instructive. First, it is not enough to simply *say* that Métis and other Indigenous women are the anchors to the land. This must manifest in actual political power. Second, it is not appropriate to simply *say* that the settler-colonial disempowerment of Métis women will be addressed after victory has been achieved on other fronts.

Nationalism and the symbolic role created for women of the nation seem to also demand something from women that is fundamentally dangerous: obedience for the purposes of national unity. Joane Nagel has traced the "pressure felt by women and nationalists to remain in supportive, symbolic, often suppressed and traditional roles. Faced with these constraints, sometimes women attempt to enact nationalism through traditional roles assigned to them by nationalists – by supporting their husbands, raising their (the nation's) children and serving as symbols of national honour.... A nationalist movement that encourages women's participation in the name of national liberation often balks at feminist demands for gender equality."[38] What should concern Métis people about the demand for obedience is that it has frequently manifested through intimate family relations. Kinship structures that have been attacked by Christian notions of the organic family seem particularly susceptible to this type of familial "hierarchy within unity."[39] Indeed, as

Payment's[40] foundational study of Métis life in Batoche, Saskatchewan, finds, the church in Métis life was structurally patriarchal, with women being asked to suffer indignities like unfaithful husbands and physical and sexual abuse in the name of God and family unity. This unity becomes a fundamentally oppressive orientation to the nation, as the place of women is continuously seen as the protectors of familial tradition, standing in silent obedience as the higher-order political, economic, and military affairs of the nation are conducted by men. Of key importance, women become expected to be deeply conservative rather than radical and/or disruptive.

The tension of obedient unity as a gendered imperative has been noted by Indigenous scholars. Perhaps most vividly and powerfully, Dawn Martin-Hill has argued that Indigenous nationalism is plagued by the relegation of women of the nation to the background of the great moments of Indigenous politics in the name of tradition. The silent, obedient figure that this relegation creates is called "She No Speaks" in Martin-Hill's analysis:

> The emergence of an Indigenous "traditional" woman who is silent and obedient to male authority contributes to the image of a voiceless woman whom I call She No Speaks. The stereotype of She No Speaks is a construction born from the tapestry of our colonial landscape. Her image emerged from our darkest era, similar to the infamous "end of the trail" warrior – defeated, hunched over, head down and with no future.
>
> Who is She No Speaks? She is the woman who never questions male authority. She never reveals her experiences of being abused by the man who is up there on that stage, telling the world about the sacredness of women and the land. While New Age woman – the middle-class white woman who seeks out Indigenous spirituality – flocks to soak up the traditional man's teachings, She No Speaks serves him coffee. She is the woman who knows about sexual abuse, since it has happened to her from her earliest memories. She is quiet, she prays, she obeys, she raises the children, she stays home, she never questions or challenges domination – she is subservient.[41]

Martin-Hill's use of the term *subservient* in this work is prescient. The term is regularly used to frame women's social position and legal rights and appears as *the* central framing of Treaty One peoples' submission to the Court noted above. Her analysis points to the structure of Indigenous nationalist movements that have entrenched the power of Indigenous men, a power that remains subservient to that of white men yet is still a power *over* Indigenous women. Thus, as one tries to make sense of the Métis land question and indignation meetings, great care must be taken not to approach the gender-centric kinship structures at play with an intention to create a deeply conservative, voiceless, powerless place within the Métis nation for women and others in Métis families who experience no shortage of disempowerment.[42]

If we return to the context of the land question and the indignation meetings, there is an opportunity to formulate concepts of governance that re-empower Métis women and that push back against patriarchal forms of Métis nationalism. I argue that indignant governance needs to be backed up by *indignant disobedience*. For indignant governance to avoid the weaknesses identified by feminist critiques of nationalism, first, the symbolism of land, indigeneity, and identity grounded by Métis and other Indigenous women cannot be perfunctory. The symbolism must be accompanied by substantive political power. Second, the construction of this animated symbolism must include a core commitment to an indignant disobedience toward both Indigenous and settler structures of power and authority. Third, indignant disobedience is necessary to guard against a hyperconservative nationalist movement. I will engage each point in turn.

But why *indignation* within these frameworks? First, I am reimagining the historical roots of Métis nationhood in a way that centres Métis self-expressions of the relationship among land, territory, and Indigenous women. As noted above, much of the evidence for this reimagining comes from a series of *indignation* meetings in which Métis people articulated their relationships to territory. As such, indignation helps home in on the links between the historical roots of this reimagining and the meanings, principles, and ethics those roots communicate. Second, during the indignation meetings, the Métis articulated their claims in a context where Métis relationships to the land were under threat and where other people and peoples in positions of power did not show respect for the Métis or their relationships with the land. This context gives rise to an indignant emotional response. Emotional indignation was appropriate in the nineteenth century, and it remains appropriate today. In the context of the rampant gendered colonial violence in which the Métis find themselves, Métis people, particularly Métis women, may find that their expressions of indignation can be productive and transformative. As emerging scholarship explores the transformative potential of Indigenous peoples' rage,[43] an action-oriented indignation rooted in the traditions and self-expressions of Métis people may be a powerful tool in Métis de-colonial politics and resurgence. The key, it seems, is to ensure that indignation is active, action-oriented, and operationalizable in the governance of the nation.

While several scholars have interrogated the central and traditionally equal role that women fulfil in Indigenous communities, it is important to note that filling an important, equal role is not the same as possessing substantive political power and authority in a community. As Kim Anderson points out, quoting Lee Maracle,

> The work-without-authority dynamic is typical of the interplay between Aboriginal female community work and the Aboriginal men who hold political or decision-making power. [Maracle] points to the emptiness of the frequently quoted expression "Women are the backbone of the nation." In our current political climate, this expression doesn't ring true: "We have become the builders without power – and we have built every organization on this continent. We have gone out and waged every single struggle. We have gone out and we have petitioned, we have demonstrated, we have done everything! But we don't have the authority and framework for directing action."[44]

Anderson and Maracle insist that connecting Métis relationships with the land through Métis women must actually *mean* something in the operation of Métis modes of governance. It is not enough for such a premise to inform governance. It must also *enact* governance.

It may be helpful to illustrate this point by returning to the context from which it emerged and imagining a governance model different from the one used to bring Canada to Red River. In 1869–70, a few years after the land debates and indignation meetings, an assembly styled the Convention of 40 was elected to lay out the Red River people's demands for allowing Canada to expand into the Red River area. This convention was controlled by a majority of Métis people. One way the delegates considered protecting themselves against the large-scale arrival of settlers was by controlling who could vote; they intended to delay the franchise to all new non-Métis arrivals so Métis could control the local legislative assembly. Alfred Scott, one representative whom Lawrence Barkwell[45] identifies as a non-Indigenous member of the convention, offered this on the franchise: "Is it the intention of the Convention to allow women to vote? No doubt many such will come in and be householders [laughter]," to which the chairman responded, "All these resolutions will have to be submitted to a good deal of filing."[46] It is not clear from the proceedings if Scott was making a joke, nor is it apparent who or how many people laughed or if other delegates thought this was a good idea. As Sherry Farrel Racette[47] and Émilie Pigeon and Carolyn Podruchny[48] make clear, one could also argue that Métis women were not voting because they were occupied with the running of Métis life in hunting brigade camps and in the community. However, the significance of this moment is not in discovering who laughed or why. Rather, the value can be found in asking what an *indignant* understanding of the *we* of the nation demands.

If Métis and other Indigenous women are the anchors to the land, then an indignant understanding of the *we* demands that this connection be not only thought about and acknowledged but also operationalized. Providing Métis women the vote is simply not good enough. One must also give Indigenous women real political power and authority in the new self-determining structures of the nation. The Métis-controlled legislature that emerged out of these and other negotiations included a lower chamber *and* an upper chamber styled the Legislative Council. One possible operationalization of Métis indignation could be to fashion an upper chamber composed entirely of Métis and other Indigenous women. This chamber would need to possess tools such as veto power, independent law-making power, the ability to oversee land use, and the capacity to remove a sitting premier. This structure of governance would then convert the symbolism of an indignant understanding of the *we* of the nation into operationalized *indignant governance*.

I suggest an upper chamber not because it is the best or even most appropriate way of operationalizing indignant governance but because it fits the context out of which the discussion of protecting Métis people in the face of settler expansion emerged. If one were reluctant to explore an Indigenous women's chamber in the legislature, one could also a build an indignant form of governance in other ways. However, as Anderson points out, "Other political activists have organized at the provincial level to establish women's councils as one way to gain political recognition. Yet Michéle Audette, president of the Quebec Native Women's Association, cautions that councils and secretariats are of little use unless they are given real political power. She advocates having authority that is clearly delineated in writing, having power that is officially recognized and having seats at the table when decisions are being made. For governance to be indignant in the sense discussed in this work, it must come with actual power in the intra- and inter-Indigenous affairs of the Métis Nation and in situations where settler affairs abut those of Indigenous nations.

In order to avoid the pressures that such a framework would place on Métis women to conform to a still masculinist vision of the past and future of the Métis people in the name of national unity, it also requires an operationalized appreciation that Métis women's power includes an expectation of disobedience. The colonial, racial, and misogynistic pressures that have normalized a state of brutality against Métis and other Indigenous women require constant and unyielding defiance. In order to build a Métis nationalism that explicitly defies structures of gendered violence, a culture of disobedience needs to be nurtured such that the expectations of a patriarchal national unity are not mobilized against Métis and other Indigenous women.

There is a cultural grounding to such a notion. As I was being taught to jig by Métis women in my twenties, having grown up only with square dancing, two stepping, and the cheautise, I was told the story about the Woman Who Jigged on Sundays several times. The woman in the story had been instructed by the priest of the community that she was not to jig on Sundays. Sundays were to be reserved for prayer and working on one's relationship with the Almighty. To enforce his edict, the priest would come around to the house and peer into a rectangular, shoulder-height window to check on the Woman. There he would see her standing completely still. Satisfied, he would mutter to himself, "Good, she is obedient," and then move on to the next house. What he did not see was that the Woman's upper body was completely stationary while her feet were flying to the tune of "The Red River Jig."

Now, the story was told to me because I was too bouncy in my jigging. My teachers were trying to convey to me that my jigging technique was wrong. However, the story also conveys a thread of indignant disobedience. The Woman Who Jigged on Sundays consciously disobeyed the priest's orders. The priest sought to deploy the patriarchal power he accrued as a man in the Catholic Church by imposing his expectation for behaviour on the Woman. This power places an arsenal of religious, social, political, and economic weapons at the priest's disposal to punish those who disobey his edicts. In the face of patriarchal power, the Woman Who Jigged on Sundays showed herself to be indignantly disobedient. I always imagine that she smiled coyly as the priest passed her window but relished being disobedient toward the patriarchal force deployed against her. In order to guard against nationalism's tendency to demand women conform in the name of national unity, as well as the pressures of a colonial state that is violently male, as outlined by Leanne Betasamosake Simpson,[49] Métis nationalism must constantly encourage, celebrate, and protect indignant disobedience against a patriarchal misogynistic backlash.

Finally, one feature left uninterrogated in this indignant framework is its understanding of gender. Further research is needed on the links between the two indignant frameworks developed here and a broader conception of gender diversity. Gender in this article has been framed to be exclusively about women within a framework of patriarchal nationalism. Scholars, artists, writers, and activists have all pointed out that this is an insufficient understanding of the gender diversity in

Indigenous worlds.[50] Future research needs to confront the challenge created by gender-nonconforming persons and queer kin being silenced by nineteenth-century records, recordkeepers, priests, traders, HBC officials, and politicians. While one can derive Métis women out of the land and indignation meetings, doing so for people for whom gender is not grounded in being a cis man or woman is substantially more challenging. However, this challenge needs to be confronted directly to think through the absenting of gender diversity from Indigenous nations and Métis forms of governance. If women need to be thought about and their power and authority operationalized at all levels within nationalist movements, then the same ought to be true of gender diversity beyond binaries.

Future research must also be attuned to the complicated role the Catholic and Protestant churches play in Métis communities. It is possible that heteronormative doctrines on the organic family have been imported into the daily life of the community. Exploring this question further is important. In order for Métis nationalism to be inclusive of gender-nonconforming, queer, two-spirit, gay, lesbian, bisexual family members and kin, there is a need for nationalism to respect and empower all our relations within our communities. It is possible that indignant governance, when coupled with indignant disobedience, can also guard against the conservatism that befalls many nationalist movements with demands that women be the gatekeepers of an immutable past and that limits be placed on the possibilities for gender diversity, all while creating re-empowered, dynamic leaders of an antipatriarchal nation. Such an ambitious project would need to be worked out through a distinct research design.[51]

Conclusion

An indignant understanding of the *we* of the nation is not about prescriptions for what ails Métis people. Instead, it is about possibilities for a decolonized future informed by a reimagining of Métis nationalism anchored to the land by Métis and other Indigenous women. Similarly, indignant governance and disobedience are not about building a reconciliation framework tied to a quaint and distant past that grants a sliver of one's former self to facilitate grinning and bearing life in the present. Rather, they are about reclaiming and reinvigorating the nation in the best tradition of Indigenous resurgence, the tradition where women and other marginalized voices are heard and empowered as much as the men marching down the steps in the Supreme Court of Canada building.

When Treaty One peoples set out their view of Métis relationships to land, they deployed a patriarchal logic that mirrored the violence done to Indigenous women over the last 150 years. I have argued that through petitions in the early 1800s, the land question, and the indignation meetings, Métis people located their relationships to land using kinship and connections to Indigenous women. Taking these self-expressions seriously allows one to operationalize the interconnections among land, women, and relatives to build a new set of models of Métis national governance.

If we return to the image of MMF president David Chartrand marching down the stairs in the Supreme Court of Canada building, it becomes clearer that casting Native men of the nation in bronze would not fit the reconceptualization of the nation discussed here. In articulating an alternative to a men-in-bronze idea, one could draw on a different kind of nationhood, a very particular form of *indig*nation.

NOTES

1 This work was made possible with funds from a Canada Social Sciences and Humanities Research Council Insight Development Grant and was originally published in *NAIS: Journal of the Native American and Indigenous Studies Association* 7, no. 2 (Fall 2019): 87–113.

2 While it is not clear if Métis themselves titled the meetings as "indignation meetings," at the time the use of the title would likely have been readily recognizable. The content of these debates shaped subsequent discussions during the 1869–70 Resistance. See Gerhard Ens, "Prologue to the Red River Resistance: Pre-liminal Politics and the Triumph of Riel," *Journal of the Canadian Historical Association* 5, no. 1 (1994): 111–23.

3 The historical literature on this era is well developed. See J.M. Bumsted, *Trials and Tribulations: The Red River Settlement and the Emergence of Manitoba 1811–1870* (Winnipeg, MB: Great Plains Publications, 2003); Gerhard Ens, *Homeland to Hinterland* (Toronto: University of Toronto Press, 1996); Gerald Friesen, *The Canadian Prairies: A History*, student ed. (Toronto: University of Toronto Press, 1987); W.L. Morton, *Manitoba: The Birth of a Province*, Vol. 1 (Altona, MB: D.W. Friesen, 1965).

4 The twentieth-century historical literature is less developed than the nineteenth. See Christopher Adams, Ian Peach, and Gregg Dahl, *Métis in Canada: History, Identity, Law and Politics* (Edmonton: University of Alberta Press, 2013): Gerhard Ens and Joe Sawchuk, *From New Peoples to New Nations: Aspects of Métis History and Identity from the Eighteenth to the Twenty-First Centuries* (Toronto: University of Toronto Press, 2016); Joe Sawchuk, "Negotiating

an Identity: Metis Political Organizations, the Canadian Government, and Competing Concepts of Aboriginality," *American Indian Quarterly* 25, no. 1 (2001): 73–92.

5 Darren O'Toole, "The Red River Jig around the Convention of 'Indian' Title: The Métis and Half-Breed Dos a Dos," *Manitoba History* 69 (Summer 2012): 17–29.

6 Jean Teillet and Jason Madden, "*Manitoba Métis Federation v. Canada (Attorney General)*: Understanding the Supreme Court of Canada's Decision" (2013), http://www.pstlaw.ca/resources/PST-LLP-MMF-Case-Summary -Nov-2013-v02.pdf.

7 Daniel Voth, "The Choices We Make and the World They Create: Métis Conflicts with Treaty One Peoples in *MMF v Canada*," *University of Toronto Law Journal* 68, no. 3 (2018): 358–404.

8 They were led by Chief Glen Hudson of Peguis First Nation on his, his people's, and all of Treaty One peoples' behalf. The actual case itself is not the object of analysis here, nor is it the intention of this article to offer a comment on the state of Métis law.

9 Rath, Khan, and Whyte 2011, 5, as cited in Voth, "Choices We Make," appendix A, emphasis added. Rath, Khan, and Whyte's factum is only available in "Choices We Make," appendix A. It is with the permission of Treaty One peoples' legal counsel that this factum was reproduced in that article's appendix.

10 Sylvia Van Kirk, Many Tender Ties: Women in Fur-Trade Society in Western Canada, 1670–1870 (Winnipeg, MB: Watson & Dwyer Publishing, 1980), 33–4.

11 For a detailed examination of these policies and their attending violence, see Bonita Lawrence, "Gender, Race, and the Regulation of Native Identity in Canada and the United States: An Overview," *Hypatia* 18, no. 2 (2003): 3–31; and Pamela D. Palmater, *Beyond Blood: Rethinking Indigenous Identity* (Saskatoon, SK: Purich Publishing, 2011).

12 Note that after 1985 the Canadian Parliament passed Bill C-31, which amended the Indian Act's "marrying out" provision (in addition to making other changes), replacing it with a two-generation cut-off for passing on Indian status when one parent is not a status Indian. This provision has been widely criticized for continuing the program of ending Indian status. See Palmater, *Beyond Blood*, 102–10; and Chelsea Vowel, *Indigenous Writes: A Guide to First Nations, Métis & Inuit Issues in Canada* (Winnipeg, MB: High-Water, 2016), 30–8.

13 John Halkett was the brother-in-law of the Earl of Selkirk and a shareholder in the Hudson's Bay Company. See Bruce Peel, Ernest Boyce, and Norman Merrill Distad, *Peel's Bibliography of the Canadian Prairies to 1953*, 3rd ed. (Toronto: University of Toronto Press, 2003), 13, 776. For a more detailed history of the Battle of Seven Oaks, see Ens and Sawchuk, *From New Peoples*

to New Nations; and Gerald Friesen, *The Canadian Prairies: A History*, student ed. (Toronto: University of Toronto Press, 1987).

14 John Halkett, *Statement Respecting the Earl of Selkirk's Settlement upon the Red River in North America; Its Destruction in 1815 and 1816; and the Massacre of Governor Semple and His Party* (London: John Murray, 1817), 35, emphasis in the original.

15 See *Nor'Wester*, "A Crown Colony for Red River!," 28 February 1860; and "Native Title to Indian Lands," 14 February 1860.

16 *Nor'Wester*, "The Land Question: The Council, and the Press," 14 March 1860, 2, col. 5.

17 *Nor'Wester*, "The Land Question."

18 *Nor'Wester*, "The Land Question," 14 June 1860, 3, col. 4.

19 *Nor'Wester*, "Indignation Meetings," 15 June 1861, 2, col. 5.

20 Gerhard Ens, "Prologue to the Red River Resistance: Pre-liminal Politics and the Triumph of Riel," *Journal of the Canadian Historical Association* 5, no. 1 (1994): 111–23.

21 Darren O'Toole, "Metis Claims to 'Indian' Title in Manitoba," *Canadian Journal of Native Studies* 28, no. 2 (2008): 241–87; O'Toole, "Red River Jig."

22 Métis people having mixed heritage is not factually inaccurate. As Métis scholar Chris Andersen has argued, "My point in emphasising this is, of course, not to suggest that 'Métis' are not of mixed Indigenous and non-Indigenous ancestry, but merely to question why, given all that Indigenous people are, it remains such a remarkable feature of the category." Chris Andersen, "Mixed Ancestry or Metis?," in *Indigenous Identity and Resistance: Researching the Diversity of Knowledge*, edited by Brendan Hokowhitu et al. (Dunedin: Otago University Press, 2010), 23–36.

23 Kim Anderson, *A Recognition of Being: Reconstructing Native Womanhood*, Women's Issues Publishing Program (Toronto: Second Story, 2000), 57; Maria Campbell, *Halfbreed* (Toronto: McClelland and Stewart, 1973); Dory Nason, "We Hold Our Hands Up: On Indigenous Women's Love and Resistance," in *The Winter We Danced*, edited by Kino-nda-niimi Collective (Winnipeg, MB: Arbeiter Ring Publishing, 2014), 186–90; Tiya Miles, "'Circular Reasoning': Recentering Cherokee Women in the Antiremoval Campaigns," *American Quarterly* 61, no. 2 (2009): 221–43; Rebecca Tsosie, "Native Women and Leadership: An Ethics of Culture and Relationship," in *Indigenous Women and Feminism: Politics, Activism, Culture*, edited by Cheryl Suzack, Shari Huhndorf, Jeanne Perreault, and Jean Barman (Vancouver: University of British Columbia Press, 2010), 34; Audra Simpson, "The State Is a Man: Theresa Spence, Loretta Saunders and the Gender of Settler Sovereignty," *Theory and Event* 19, no. 4 (2016): 4, https://www.muse.jhu.edu/article/633280.

24 See Sharon Blady, "Les Metisses: Towards a Feminist History of Red River," in *Issues in the North*, edited by Jill Oakes and Rick Riewe (Winnipeg, MB:

Canadian Circumpolar Institute, 1997), 2:179–86; Diane Payment, "'La Vie en Rose'? Métis Women at Batoche 1870–1920," in *Women of the First Nations: Power, Wisdom, and Strength*, edited by Christine Miller and Patricia Churchryk (Winnipeg: University of Manitoba Press, 1996), 19–36; Sherry Farrel Racette, "Nimble Fingers and Strong Backs: First Nations and Métis Women in Fur Trade and Rural Economies," in *Indigenous Women and Work: From Labour to Activism*, edited by Carol Williams (Urbana: University of Illinois Press, 2012), 148–62; and the texts cited below.

25 Nathalie Kermoal, "Métis Women's Environmental Knowledge and the Recognition of Métis Rights," in *Living on the Land: Indigenous Women's Understanding of Place*, edited by Nathalie Kermoal and Isabel Altamirano-Jiménez (Edmonton, AB: Athabasca University Press, 2016), 115.

26 Brenda Macdougall, *One of the Family: Métis Culture in Nineteenth-Century Northwestern Saskatchewan* (Vancouver: University of British Columbia Press, 2010) , 88, emphasis added.

27 Brenda Macdougall, "The Myth of Metis Cultural Ambivalence," in *Contours of a People: Metis Family, Mobility, and History*, edited by Nicole St-Onge, Carolyn Podruchny, and Brenda Macdougall (Norman: University of Oklahoma Press, 2012), 429.

28 If one continues to focus on the social and political context lived by Métis people, one can see that institutions like the hunting brigades and land settlement are influenced by kinship with key women. As Macdougall and St-Onge have pointed out, "Just like what we discovered in the Trottier brigade, tracing the genealogies of specific families associated with identifiable brigades reveals a pattern of sisters – more importantly, related women, sisters or otherwise – marrying brigade members and linking otherwise unconnected males into a kinship system predicated upon interfamilial structures. In the case of the Trottier brigade, three Laframboise sisters stand out as having connected unrelated men to one another in a hunting brigade." Brenda Macdougall and Nicole St-Onge, "Rooted in Mobility: Métis Buffalo-Hunting Brigades," *Manitoba History* 71 (Winter 2013): 237–9.

29 Macdougall, "Myth of Metis Cultural Ambivalence," 435.

30 Macdougall, "Myth of Metis Cultural Ambivalence," 446.

31 Macdougall, "Myth of Metis Cultural Ambivalence," 449; emphasis added.

32 Payment, "'La Vie en Rose'?," 19.

33 Payment makes a compelling case that one of the issues that researchers need to confront in their engagement with these questions of women's voices in history is that "the racism, bigotry, and sexism of the Victorian era persuaded many Métis to declare 'on n'est pas des sauvages' or to deny their grandmothers' origins and to assert their French-Canadian 'male' heritage" (Payment, "'La Vie en Rose'?, 20). As a result, we must be aware of the power dynamics that affect the safety for women to talk openly about

who they are and their connections to the land. As Payment argues, these expressions are often mediated through the overt patriarchy of the church.

34 Anne McClintock, "Family Feuds: Gender, Nationalism and the Family," *Feminist Review* 44 (Summer 1993): 61, 62, emphasis in the original.

35 Cynthia H. Enloe, *Bananas, Beaches and Bases: Making Feminist Sense of International Politics*, updated (Berkeley: University of California Press, 2000); Patricia Hill Collins, "It's All in the Family: Intersections of Gender, Race and Nation," *Hypathia* 13, no. 3 (1998): 63; Joane Nagel, "Masculinity and Nationalism: Gender and Sexuality in the Making of Nations," *Ethnic and Racial Studies* 21, no. 2 (1998): 252–3; Joanne Sharp, "Gendering Nationhood: A Feminist Engagement with National Identity," in *Bodyspace*, edited by Nancy Duncan (New York: Routledge, 1996), 97–108.

36 Lina Sunseri, "Moving beyond the Feminism versus Nationalism Dichotomy: An Anti-Colonial Feminist Perspective on Aboriginal Liberation Struggles," *Canadian Women Studies* 20, no. 2 (2000): 146.

37 Sharp, "Gendering Nationhood," 103.

38 Nagel, "Masculinity and Nationalism," 253.

39 Anne McClintock, "Family Feuds: Gender, Nationalism and the Family," *Feminist Review* 44 (Summer 1993): 64.

40 Payment, "'La Vie en Rose'?," 25.

41 Dawn Martin-Hill, "She No Speaks: And Other Colonial Constructs of the 'Traditional Woman,'" in *Strong Women Strong Stories: Native Vision and Community Survival*, edited by Kim Anderson and Bonita Lawrence (Toronto: Sumach, 2003), 108.

42 For an examination of revisiting histories to look for gendered perspectives, see Blady, "Les Metisses." Blady shows how scholars can return to their earlier work to interrogate the erasure of gender in the Métis histories they write. When thinking about Métis in the fur trade, Blady looks at Hudson's Bay Company governor George Simpson's "reference to Company men's Amerindian wives as 'petticoat politicians.' The term 'petticoat politicians' is a concept based on gender. Simpson saw these women as interlopers into the Company world and chose to objectify them based on their apparent influence and autonomy. By reducing these individual women to a meddlesome lot he stripped them of identity and agency. He also labelled these women based on their gender and ethnicity and their actions which infringed on class boundaries. These remarks are indicators of the degree of gender-based subordination present in the Victorian period and in Simpson's personal and corporate philosophy" (181–2).

43 See Glen S. Coulthard, *Red Skin, White Masks: Rejecting the Colonial Politics of Recognition* (Minneapolis: University of Minnesota Press, 2014).

44 Anderson, Recognition of Being, 216–17.

45 Lawrence J. Barkwell, *Manitoba's Provisional Government of 1870: The Convention of Forty* (Winnipeg, MB: Louis Riel Institute, 2011).
46 *New Nation*, "Convention at Fort Garry: Very Important Debates, the Bill of Rights," 11 February 1870, 2, col. 1.
47 Farrel Racette, "Nimble Fingers and Strong Backs."
48 Émilie Pigeon and Carolyn Podruchny, "The Mobile Village: Metis Women, Bison Brigades, and Social Order on the Nineteenth-Century Plains," in *Violence, Order, and Unrest: A History of British North America, 1749–1876*, edited by Elizabeth Mancke, Jerry Bannister, Denis McKim, and Scott See (Toronto: University of Toronto Press, 2019), 236–63.
49 Leanne Betasamosake Simpson, Dancing on Our Turtle's Back: Stories of Nishnaabeg Re-creation, Resurgence and a New Emergence (Winnipeg, MB: Arbeiter Ring Publishing, 2011), 1–2.
50 Billy-Ray Belcourt, *This Wound Is a World* (Calgary, AB: Frontenac House Poetry, 2017); Waawaate Fobister, "Agoqwe," in *Two-Spirit Acts: Queer Indigenous Performances*, edited by Jean O'Hara (Toronto: Playwrights Canada, 2013), 91–133; Sarah Hunt and Cindy Holmes, "Everyday Decolonization: Living a Decolonizing Queer Politics," *Journal of Lesbian Studies* 19, no. 2 (2015): 154–72; Daniel Justice, "Notes toward a Theory of Anomaly," *GLQ: A Journal of Lesbian and Gay Studies* 16, no. 1–2 (2010): 207–42; Scott Lauria Morgensen, *Spaces between Us: Queer Settler Colonialism and Indigenous Decolonization* (Minneapolis: University of Minnesota Press, 2011).
51 If one were to return to the discussion of a legislative upper chamber, if indignant disobedience is coupled with principles of a gender-nonconforming kinship, one could argue that the upper chamber discussed above ought to become a house of gender diversity. The point is that by centring disobedience toward the structures that have sought and continue to seek the oppression of Métis women, as well as Métis women's disempowerment in a patriarchal settler state, we create the conditions for realizing hosts of new opportunities to challenge other forms of gender oppression.

14 Red Utopia

BILLY-RAY BELCOURT

We must always be future bound in our desires and designs.[1]

José Esteban Muñoz

The ordinary is a circuit that's always tuned in to some little something somewhere.[2]

Kathleen Stewart

Introduction: A Conspiracy

In this chapter, which is woven with my poetic verse,[3] I set out to show that (1) wherever Indigenous peoples are, so too is the feeling of utopia; and (2) in a world of colonial sensation, Native joy is a conspiracy. What follows is not an elaboration of a single argument, but instead an experiment in making use of the ways of un/seeing that are available to those like me who are in a world we did not want. I heed Fred Moten's call to write sentences differently, by which he means that if we are to take seriously the texts of Black feminist writers as ones who produce knowledge about the past and the world against which we conspire, then we might need to give up on the sentence that motors normative academic enquiry, which is hindered by tradition, by the strictures of form.[4] Thus, to provide an account of the cluttered affective spheres inside which Natives enact a form of geographic escape that is still unfolding, we need to write against the unwriteability of utopia. Which means that joy is somewhat of an impossible desire, but one that we cannot stop thinking about and enacting. That we experience joy, that we can identify it, if only belatedly, illuminates the dead end towards which the settler state hurls. So in this chapter I pit language against itself to evoke a register of meaning-making that is not bound by the tyranny of clarity, but one that is instead enmeshed in an affective structure that might proliferate something like freedom. If there is an object to be spotted here, perhaps it is a haptic mode of thinking and writing that engenders or mimics what it seeks to call into being. Writing is a performative practice; it has a visual component, which lays bare the imagistic quality of words. To map a queer place like a red utopia, to listen for the conspiracy of our joy, one must thus take on a form of decipherment empowered by a desire to disrupt a settler geography and its constitutive death wishes. From here I attend to the theoretics of utopia, which I cannot do without summoning those who have indelibly shaped my curiosity about the possibility of the end of this emaciated world. Next I examine a set of texts – historical and visual – that are localized to the reserve and evince a structure of feeling that is utopian.

> In the back alley of the world, joy is a utopian feeling. The back alley is a metaphor and a material condition. It is a deformity of the law: there, the codes of public life are upended and everything and nothing is criminal. A form of conduct that is both more than and before conduct proliferates. We, the ungovernables, speak a language of our own making.

We live in the ashes of an era of forced migration inaugurated by the brutal feat of race-based death policy called reservization. The Royal Proclamation of 1763, the Indian Act of 1867, and the Numbered Treaties of 1871–1921 form an aggregate of meta-principles about territoriality that suspend the Indian, who is made answerable to the Crown, in a legal limbo of sorts. In what follows, I use paradox as an optic to spot what lingers in radical excess wherever state power is marshalled. This means that reservization simultaneously demonstrates that we are at the whim of the state and utterly free from it. Sculpted with gross indifference to Native liveability, the reserve was and is a problem for emotion. It is the site of an affective opening to what Leanne Betasamosake Simpson calls "the eroding edge of pathos."[5] But "the eroding edge" is also a terrain of emotional possibility, where a culture of radical hope puts pressure on the vulgarities of settlement. Again, we are in the throes of a form of administrative power that violates via neglect. This, however, also suggests that we are the abandoned who need to escape the ditch of history to enact a new world. What interests me about reservization is thus its constitutive defect, how it spawns an ecology that erodes the mandate of the state to make us into the unseen, into something like a vaporous population, caught in the air, atomized, and swallowed up by time. The reserve, the back alley of modernity, is a liminal space that makes everywhere else in a settler state habitable. Nonetheless, it is also where we were and are left to our own devices to refashion what is thinkable in the thick of an environment that wards off the labour of regard. Anyway, we think in the register of the utopian. And so we take on a being in non-being. Then we conspire.

In "conspire," to which "conspiracy" is linked, there is a riot against something, the shape of which fluctuates according to the form of disturbance one aims to bring about. There is also the act of breathing together, which comes to us from the Latin *con-* (together with) and *spirare* (breathe). What I arrive at is fugitive breath/ing. As of late, there has been a surge of critical race theories of how it is breath that entangles us to others, for better or for worse. In *Blackpentecostal Breath: The Aesthetics of Possibility*, Ashon Crawley starts with the sparse words hurled out into the world by Eric Garner before his on-air death at the hands of police officers in Staten Island, New York. Despite efforts to sever his ability to vocalize, to make words leave his body, "I can't breathe" was the refrain that Garner managed eleven times. "I can't breathe" hung in the air like an unanswered question. At the same time, it rippled its surroundings. "I can't breathe," says Crawley, was "a rupture, a disruption, an ethical plea regarding the ethical crisis that has been the grounds for producing [Garner's] moment, our time, this modern world."[6] This modern world is interrupted by the enactment of a different sort of exhalation, one that is "a critical performative," a refusal of "the western juridical apparatus of violent control, repression, and yes, premature death."[7] Christina Sharpe likewise probes the difficulties of accessing something like "fresh air," for the wake, which is where "the past that is not past reappears," swells up from the climate of anti-Blackness in which we all ride the unstable currents of respiration; the wake is congested with "breathtaking spaces."[8] Aspiration, Sharpe notes, is how we put breath "back in the Black body in hostile weather."[9]

So "I can't breathe" repeats from those whose "daily practices of survival," to use Ann Cvetkovich's language,[10] are caught up in an atmosphere that makes a fool out of the lungs. "I can't breathe" is a theoretical claim; it draws attention to the obstruction of what, according to Crawley, "is constitutive for flight, for movement, for performance."[11] "I can't breathe" also irradiates the unfinished project of care, how some have been barred from uncomplicatedly accessing the sky. The sky, tinged with the alarm of biopower, seizes the body and makes a mockery of it. Following Crawley, "I can't breathe" potentiates; it ratchets up an excess that cannot, in the end, be wholly negated. "I can't breathe" is but one theory of how indigeneity is made to apparate in public life in Fallon Simard's "Bodies That Monetize," a master of arts thesis exhibition that took place at Blank Canvas Gallery in Toronto in the fall of 2017. Simard's "i cant breathe" (figure 14.1) is stylized with a blurred

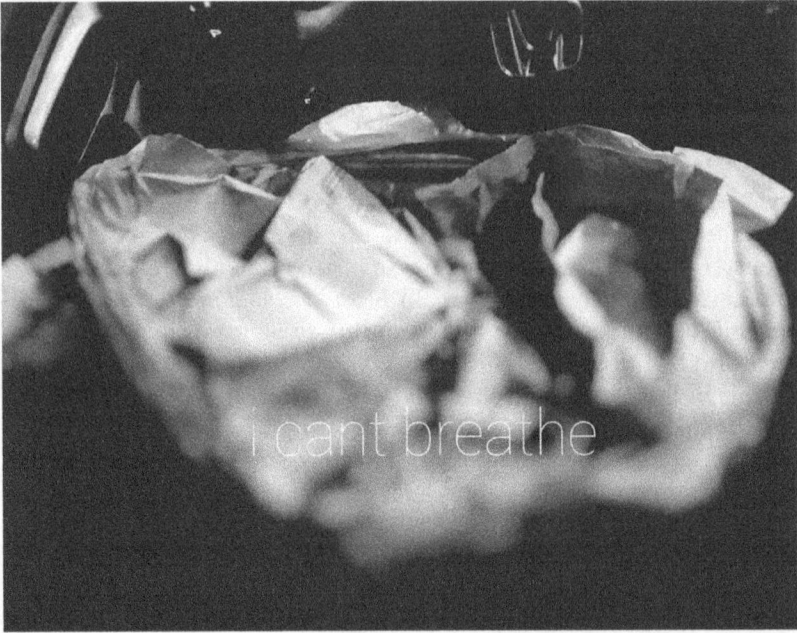

Figure 14.1. Fallon Simard, *Anxiety*, 2017. Meme printed on giclee.

photograph of crumpled brown paper bags, which are prosthetic-like household items used to assist with breathing during biosocial events such as a panic attack. Simard uses the form of the meme, which enables a mode of mobility that exceeds the gallery walls, to activate something like a poetics of putting it out there, out in the open, such that the surround of the surround, which is to say the air, is brought into focus. Out of this comes the thesis that troubled breathing is a normative facet of North American modernity. Elizabeth A. Povinelli argues that a "weak" mode of state killing proliferates sores, bad colds, and small pains in the chest in Indigenous communities, but also that uncritical deployments of care are not quick fixes for these forms of "dispersed suffering." She writes, "In neoliberalism to care for others is to refuse to preserve life if it lies outside a market value."[12] Everywhere Native suffering is embedded into the clock of modernity, so something as biologically common as the inhalation and exhalation of breath becomes a political and an aesthetic experience in and of itself.

In an archipelago of exile like ours, there are crowds everywhere. For a second or two, everyone has but one skin, which is wired to the totality of the feeling of being on the run. It is not that we are escaping life, but that we were stranded by it. An ocean flooded the basement of us.

Karyn Recollet writes, "Gestures of futurity are choreographies of possibilities and hope – not residing so much in an unattainable dreamscape, but rather they are in constant figuration and reconfiguration all around us."[13] For Recollet there is a kinesthetic component to decolonization; indeed, she beautifully posits that the moving body reveals a "map to tomorrow."[14] This refusal "of being stilled," she declares, after Crawley, is the scene of a geographic flight, what I might describe as an eschewal of ontological entrapment, which for Recollet is irreducibly gestural. Breathing is thus but one example of Recollet's "gestures of futurity." This is a time and place in which indigeneity is organized via a mode of enfleshment that is at once numbing and agonizing, one that produces again and again a social death and attendant forms of pain whose vocalizations become unhearable. To be in the world is to be fleshy and to be fleshy is to be susceptible to a form of social power that occurs at a level the naked eye cannot apprehend. Emotion strives to translate this. Part of what I am doing here is to say that yes we are subject to processes of enervation that smother, that morph the body into a sign of the failings of self-sovereignty, but there are "choreographies of possibilities and hope," to harken back to Recollet's phraseology, that abound too. Native joy is a sociological and statistical feat, but it flowers nonetheless.

The Not-Yet of Utopia

Always, inside and outside are durational concepts, and thus do not provide any sense of place. Indeed, this is a no place, so the sole orientation that one can have is that of vertigo. GPS is a relic of a bygone era. There are dead ends that open up onto dead ends. Desire makes waste out of time, but it is never a waste of time. Flags are always at half-mast, which is to say that ours is a no man's land. Tonight, we make a country out of one another.

I have to begin this section with José Esteban Muñoz; without him, something would be missing. We – queers, oddballs, weirdoes, hopeless romantics, and doomed lovers – live and think now in the space pried open in the wake of *Cruising Utopia: The Then and There of Queer Futurity*. Published a decade after his debut book *Disidentifications: Queers of Color and the Performance of Politics*,[15] Muñoz's *Cruising Utopia* is a crashing wave at which we stand open-armed, with which we become indelibly mixed. He had an eye for what was blurred by the drama of the everyday, the haze into which we all risk disappearing at the expense of a time and place that is not motored by the cannibalism of the normative. At the end of *Cruising Utopia*, Muñoz wrote, "Utopia in this book has been about an insistence on something else, something better, something dawning."[16] As he saw it, the future is queerness's turf, which means that queerness is not right now, but instead an ideality, one that is always elsewhere, gyrating to the beat of the unsung on the dance floor of the world-to-come. For Muñoz, past, present, and future collide at the site of queerness's elaboration – they torpedo into public life by way of a lisp, a wink, a beat, a tempo, a can of pop, a drug (in his case, MDMA), all of which are a part of a choreography of desire. Linearity is thus a conceptual trapdoor around which we must tiptoe. We, queers of colour, armed with the magic wand of intimacy, create a future unlike anything we know now. In Muñoz's words, "Certain performances of queer citizenship contain what I am calling an anticipatory illumination of a queer world, a sign of an actually existing queer reality, a kernel of political possibility within a stultifying heterosexual present."[17] We therefore do not sit back and anticipate the joy at the end of the ride. The here and now is a prison house, to evoke Muñoz's argument,[18] but it is also the scene of a cacophony of investments, curiosities, anxieties, presuppositions, and desires, some of which give us a sneak peek into the world of tomorrow. With the analytic of the "future in the present"[19] at the fore, there is nowhere to go but here.

Additionally, in *Secrets from the Centre of the World*, Joy Harjo, a member of the Creek Nation, makes poetry out of the photography of Stephen Strom, and in her preface she argues that "the distance he intimates make sense in terms of tribal vision. We feel how it all flows together, and time takes on an expansive, mythical sense."[20] With the caveat that I do not subscribe to a biology of race that falls short of explaining the social life of indigeneity, I do believe that there is something like "tribal vision," that there is something about the feeling of indigeneity that enables us to see via an optic unavailable to others. In my master's thesis, I called this "decolonial sight," which is an embodied mode of apprehending the riot of time, a visualizing practice that glimpses the ways in which the present already bears the world we want. Sometimes we have to tilt our heads to see the world-to-come. The otherworldly is a category of the experience of indigeneity.

From Muñoz and Harjo, I inherit a conceptual arsenal that enables me to listen to the frequencies of the modality of existence that are utopian, even if they are crowded by the miseries of coloniality. Let us consider now two case studies: (1) correspondence between Indian agents about a First Nations man who rescued his children from a residential school in northern Alberta, and (2) Adam Garnet Jones's film *Fire Song*,[21] which renders queer life where it has been made an ontological impossibility. I choose these two seemingly disparate texts that bookend a time frame that is just short of a century because they bring into focus the difficulties of discerning practices of care where care was to be quashed. I also want here to nod to the *longue durée* of hope as an emotional infrastructure and a modality of life on the reserve.

1935

The reserve is where we were and are to be done in by time, to be ousted from the shallow refuge of the body politic, made to live out a wretched existence under the watchful yet sadistic eye of the city that deals in Native misery, Ottawa. The reserve is where sociality was meant to disintegrate, where the threat of body snatching was and is always-already, where those who brutalized on behalf of the state could freely derange Native life, suspending it on the barbed-wire fence of death. This is to say that the reserve is governed by an absurd logic that Natives would not enact care against the embargo on care that is Canada. Case in point: in a letter dated 24 July 1935 from the Office of the Indian Agent at Driftpile, Alberta, H.P. L'Heureux accounts for the seizure of the "monthly ration" of the family of J.B. Gambler, "an Indian of Calling Lake" who made fugitives out of his children on the run from a residential school in Wabasca. Gambler refused to allow the state to "regain possession" of his children, to heed to the process of making-property that was state education, to accelerate the circuitry of biopower that motored state-making in the long twentieth century. Gambler refused all of this: he swore at the Indian agent and threatened to shoot him dead. In response, the Indian agent marshalled the extra-legal power of the state, tapped into its monopoly on torture and withheld food, which is of course a tactic of arresting Indigenous vitality, unleashed in the domain of the biological. I do not know what happened to Gambler or to his children, whether or not they were stolen from him again, whether or not he got revenge on that Indian agent, but I do know that what this document accounts for, against itself, against the correspondence of the grim reapers at Driftpile, Wabasca, and Calling Lake, is the unfinishability of settlement, that we protect our own, that our ancestors did resist the debilitating wrath of the settler state during some of its grisliest times. We are not sick and tired of running away. Today, everywhere thickens with the possibility of Native uprising, at the community hall, at the church addition, at the school gymnasium rumoured to have been built on a graveyard.

Can the Rez Fag Speak?

Can the Rez Fag speak?[22] The Rez Fag both is and isn't: how are we to write against the unwritability of grief? Everywhere the Rez Fag is pulverized: at the kitchen table, at the Band Office, at faculties and departments of Native and Indigenous Studies. To talk about the Rez Fag you have to talk about circuitries of unbecoming and to talk about circuitries of unbecoming you have to talk about the ghosts in the machine of relationality and to talk about the ghosts in the machine of relationality you have to give up on the allure of self-sovereignty.[23]

Garnet Jones's *Fire Song* (2015) is a film that torpedoes right into the cacophonous atmosphere of reserve life. Let's consider the film's para-text: "Andrew Martin gives a stellar performance as Shane, a gay Anishinaabe teenager in Northern Ontario, struggling to support his family after his sister's suicide. Originally Shane planned to go away to college in the fall, and he had been trying to convince his secret boyfriend to come with him. Now he is torn between responsibilities at home and the promise of freedom calling from the city. When he finally has to choose between family or future, what will Shane do?" The film is a hard one to watch, for we are made to arrive again and again at the scene of history's elaboration. Shane and David are caught up in a discourse that imbues the reserve with particularized meaning, as what cannot empower a queer world. Following Muñoz's *Disidentifications* we might wager that Shane and David disidentify with the heteronormative terrain of the reserve, and that they do this by retreating to the space of the queer bedroom, for example. They desire a reserve, but desire it with a difference.[24] They seize the crumbs of social agency to perform a reserve that "should be, that could be, and that will be."[25] Shane and David transform the cultural logic of the reserve as a queer death-world. They leave, but they leave behind kernels of radical possibility: they sneak in queer looks at the lake; they are beside themselves with desire in the bedroom. They suspend the reserve in a state of ambivalence, meaning that it is open to re-signification, to a performance of world-making that might allow us to be as queer on the reserve as our hearts desire.[26]

Conclusion

Spilled, unbound, remote, unsafe, possibility swells in the badlands of modernity. There, it troubles language. It rejigs words so as to expose that which is always in excess of what we utter, a chorus of linguistic detritus. Are we ready to give everything a name? This is not so much about the torture of classification, but a desire to beget the finality of desire, to relocate in the debris of semiotics. We speak polyphonically, against the white noise of the present, against its fable of the world. We tiptoe into the field of vision of the sky, to make ourselves judicable. At its mercy, we open unknowingly. We seek shelter in the metaphor and the material conditions of exile. Under siege in the barracks of the prairies, we concoct our own social experiment, one without end, an unmoneyed one, alive and indeterminate, but always joyous, always in the name of something like joy. In the little something somewhere, we surrender to the frenzy of the surround of the surround.

In this chapter I demonstrated something like an Indigenous theory of utopia. A poet, I also tapped into the polyphonic registers of meaning-making endemic to creative writing. I intended this to partly perform the interpretations I was swap with "undertaking." By this I mean that the image-making quality and the feeling power of the poem allow us to envision and to feel what we theorize. My objects – a piece of horrific correspondence and a film about the strains of biopower and heteronormativity on the reserve – show that political violence cannot wholly negate what it despises. This is the weak crux of settler colonialism, its inability to exhaust a peoples who have the capacity to dream up otherwise forms of embodiment, being, and temporality. With hints of a world-to-come everywhere we are, a red utopia is on the horizon.

NOTES

1 José Esteban Muñoz, *Cruising Utopia: The Then and There of Queer Futurity* (New York: New York University Press, 2009).
2 Kathleen Stewart, *Ordinary Affects* (Durham, NC: Duke University Press, 2007).
3 All poetic verses are mine. Some of them were published in my second book, *NDN Coping Mechanisms: Notes from the Field* (Toronto: House of Anansi Press, 2019).
4 Fred Moten made this remark at a conference in honour of Saidiya Hartman's ground-breaking book *Scenes of Subjection: Terror, Slavery, and Self-Making in Nineteenth-Century America.* See https://youtu.be/dJ1EDweOfB8.
5 Leanne Betasamosake Simpson, *This Accident of Being Lost* (Toronto: House of Anansi, 2017), 35.
6 Ashon Crawley, *Blackpentecostal Breath: The Aesthetics of Possibility* (New York: Fordham University Press, 2017), 1.
7 Crawley, *Blackpentecostal Breath*, 34.
8 Christina Sharpe, *In the Wake: On Blackness and Being* (Durham, NC: Duke University Press, 2016), 9, 108–9.

9 Sharpe, *In the Wake*, 113.
10 Ann Cvetkovich, *Depression: A Public Feeling* (Durham, NC: Duke University Press, 2011), 206.
11 Crawley, *Blackpentacostal Breath*, 33.
12 Elizabeth Povinelli, *Economies of Abandonment: Social Belonging and Endurance in Late Liberalism* (Durham, NC: Duke University Press, 2011), 145.
13 Karyn Recollet, "Gesturing Indigenous Futurities through the Remix," *Dance Research Journal* 48, no. 1 (2016): 91.
14 Recollet, "Gesturing Indigenous Futurities," 92.
15 José Esteban Muñoz, *Disidentifications: Queers of Color and the Performance of Politics* (Minneapolis: University of Minnesota Press, 1999)
16 Muñoz, *Cruising Utopia*, 188.
17 Muñoz, *Cruising Utopia*, 49.
18 Muñoz, *Cruising Utopia*, 1.
19 "A future in the present" is a turn of phrase that Muñoz inherits from C.L.R. James. See Muñoz, *Cruising Utopia*, 2009.
20 Joy Harjo and Steven Strom, *Secrets from the Centre of the World* (Tucson: University of Arizona Press, 1990), n.p.
21 Adam Garnet Jones, *Fire Song* (Big Soul Productions, Thunderstone Pictures, 2015).
22 This is in reference to a piece of textual art by Demian Dinéyahzí'. See their Instagram @heterogenoushomosexual.
23 An edited version of this poetic verse was published in my memoir, *A History of My Brief Body: A Memoir* (Toronto: Hamish Hamilton Canada, 2020).
24 Muñoz, *Disidentifications*, 15.
25 Muñoz, *Cruising Utopia*, 69.
26 Muñoz, *Disidentifications*, 34.

Contributors

Hōkūlani K. Aikau is a Kanaka ʻŌiwi professor in the School of Indigenous Governance at the University of Victoria. She is the author of *A Chosen People, A Promised Land: Mormonism and Race in Hawaiʻi* (University of Minnesota Press, 2012), and with Vernadette Gonzalez she has co-edited *Detours: A Decolonial Guide to Hawaiʻi* (Duke University Press, 2019). Her next ethnographic project, *Becoming Hoa with ʻĀina: Returning People and Practices to Heʻeia*, funded in part by the UH Sea Grant Program, is a collaboration with Kākoʻo ʻŌiwi, a Native Hawaiian non-profit, working to restore wetland taro farming on the windward coast of Oʻahu.

Isabel Altamirano-Jiménez is Binizá (Zapotec) from the Isthmus of Tehuantepec, Mexico. She is professor of political science and Canada Research Chair in Comparative Indigenous Feminist Studies at the University of Alberta. She has written extensively. Her current research examines the connections between body, land, dispossession, and Indigenous refusal. She has written numerous articles, book chapters, and books. She is preparing a monograph tentatively titled *Body-Land, Resource Extraction and Consent*.

Billy-Ray Belcourt is an assistant professor in the School of Creative Writing at the University of British Columbia, is from the Driftpile Cree Nation, and lives in Vancouver. He is the author of *This Wound Is a World* (Frontenac House, 2017), winner of the 2018 Griffin Poetry Prize, *NDN Coping Mechanisms: Notes from the Field* (House of Anansi, 2019), and *A History of My Brief Body* (Hamish Hamilton, 2020).

Lianne Marie Leda Charlie is Wolf Clan and Tagé Cho Hudän (Northern Tutchone speaking people of the Yukon). She has a PhD in political science from the University of Hawaiʻi at Mānoa. She is an artist and a faculty member with Dechinta Centre for Research and Learning. She lives in Whitehorse, Yukon.

Jeff Ganohalidoh Corntassel is a writer, teacher, and father from the Cherokee Nation. He is an associate professor in Indigenous studies at the University of Victoria and associate director of the Centre for Indigenous Research and Community-Led Engagement. His research and teaching interests focus on "everyday acts of resurgence" and the intersections between Indigenous resurgence, climate change, gender, and community well-being. Jeff situates his work at the grassroots with many Indigenous-led community-based programs and initiatives ranging from local food movement initiatives, land-based renewal projects, to gendered colonial violence and protection of homelands. He is completing work for his forthcoming book on sustainable self-determination, which examines Indigenous climate justice, food security, and gender-based resurgence.

Aimée Craft is an Indigenous (Anishinaabe-Métis) lawyer (called to the bar in 2005) from Treaty 1 territory in Manitoba. She is an associate professor at the Faculty of Common Law, University of Ottawa. Her expertise is in Anishinaabe and Canadian Aboriginal law and she is a leading researcher on Indigenous laws, treaties, and water. She co-leads a major research grant on decolonizing water governance and works with many Indigenous nations and communities on Indigenous relationships with and responsibilities to *nibi* (water). Her award-winning book, *Breathing Life into the Stone Fort Treaty* (Purich Publishing, 2013), focuses on understanding and interpreting treaties from an Anishinaabe *inaakonigewin* (legal) perspective. She is the former director of research at the National Inquiry into Missing and Murdered Indigenous Women and Girls and the founding director of research at the National Centre for Truth and Reconciliation. In her decade of legal practice at the Public Interest Law Centre, Craft worked with many Indigenous peoples on land, resources, human rights, and governance issues. In 2016 she was voted one of the top twenty-five most influential lawyers in Canada.

Mishuana Goeman, Tonawanda Band of Seneca, is a professor of gender studies and American Indian studies, and affiliated faculty in community engagements and critical race studies in the Law School, UCLA. She is also the inaugural special advisor to the chancellor on Native American and Indigenous affairs and associate director of the Center for the Study of Women. In 2020–1 she was a distinguished visiting scholar with the Center for Diversity Innovation at the University of Buffalo located in her home Seneca territories. Along with journal and book chapters, she is also the author of *Mark My Words: Native Women Mapping Our Nations* (University of Minnesota Press, 2013), co-editor for *Keywords in Gender and Sexuality Studies* (NYU Press, 2021), and a co-principle investigator for community-based digital projects: Mapping Indigenous L.A (2015), Carrying Our Ancestors Home (2019), and California Native Hubs.

Dallas Hunt is Cree and a member of Wapsewsipi (Swan River First Nation) in Treaty 8 territory in Northern Alberta. He has had creative and critical work published in the *Malahat Review, Arc Poetry, Canadian Literature,* and the *American Indian Culture and Research Journal.* His first children's book, *Awâsis and the World-Famous Bannock* (Highwater Press, 2018), was nominated for the Elizabeth Mrazik-Cleaver Canadian Picture Book Award. His teaching and research interests include Indigenous literatures, Indigenous theory and politics, Canadian literature, speculative fiction, settler colonial studies, and environmental justice.

Sarah Hunt/Tłaliłila'ogwa is an assistant professor in the School of Environmental Studies at the University of Victoria and Canada Research Chair of Indigenous Political Ecologies. She is Kwagu'ł (Kwakwaka'wakw Nation) and has spent most of her life as a guest in Lekwungen territories. Her publications include "Ontologies of Indigeneity: The Politics of Embodying a Concept" (*Cultural Geographies,* 2014), "Researching within Relations of Violence: Witnessing as Research Methodology" (2018), and numerous other articles, book chapters, and popular media. As an interdisciplinary scholar, her research is concerned with questions of justice, violence, gender, and self-determination, as well as Indigenous methodologies, land/water-based praxis, and the creation of decolonial and coalitional knowledges. Her research focuses on Indigenous peoples' understandings of justice across the nested scales of lands/waters, homes, and bodies via engagement of coastal peoples' embodied knowledge and land-based cultural practice.

Darcy Lindberg is mixed-rooted nêhiyaw (Plains Cree) whose relations come from the Maskwacis (Samson Cree Nation) and Battleford areas in Treaty 6 territory. He holds an LLM and PhD from the University of Victoria. Darcy's doctoral research focused on the constitutional and legal theory of the nêhiyawak (the Plains Cree peoples) in relation to the land, water, and animals, and the trans-systemic relationships with Canadian constitutional law. Darcy was called to the British Columbia and Yukon Bars in 2012 and he practised law in the Yukon Territory. He is an assistant professor with the University of Victoria's Faculty of Law.

Dian Million (Tanana Athabascan) is associate professor and chair of the Department of American Indian Studies, and affiliate faculty in Canadian studies at the University of Washington, Seattle. She is the author of *Therapeutic Nations: Healing in an Age of Indigenous Human Rights* (University of Arizona Press, 2013), "Felt Theory: An Indigenous Feminist Approach to Affect and History" (*Wicazo Sa*, 2009), "Intense Dreaming: Theories, Narratives and Our Search for Home" (*American Indian Quarterly*, 2011), as well as numerous articles, chapters, and poems. Her work centres on questions arising from the effect/affect of capitalism/settler colonialism on Indigenous family and community health in North America. Informed by two generations of Indigenous feminist scholarship, Million seeks to illuminate the ways in which Indigenous life reorganizes in the face of colonial violence and settler social welfare narratives of trauma to embrace lives that are integral to peoples, their histories, and their places.

Christine O'Bonsawin (Abenaki, Odanak Nation) is an associate professor of Indigenous studies and history at the University of Victoria. Her scholarship in Indigenous studies and sport history takes up questions regarding the appropriation and subjugation of Indigenous peoples, identities, and cultures in Olympic history. Christine's recent scholarship has mainly focused on the legal and political rights of Indigenous peoples in settler colonial Canada, particularly in hosting the Olympic Games on treaty lands as well as unceded Indigenous territories. She is a co-editor and contributor for the *Journal of Sport History Special Edition: Indigenous Resurgence, Regeneration, and Decolonization through Sport History* (2019) and *Intersections and Intersectionalities in Olympic and Paralympic Studies* (2014).

Leanne Betasamosake Simpson is a Michi Saagiig Nishnaabeg scholar, writer, and artist. She is author of several books including *Noopiming: The Cure for White Ladies* and *Rehearsals for Living* with Robyn Maynard. Leanne is a member of Alderville First Nation, in Ontario.

Corey Snelgrove is a settler and postdoctoral fellow at the University of Toronto. His research examines the politics of reconciliation and Indigenous visions of decolonization, especially Indigenous treaty visions as a critique of capitalism. His latest essay, "Treaty and the Problem of Colonial Reification," is forthcoming at *Theory & Event*.

Gina Starblanket is an associate professor in the School of Indigenous Governance at the University of Victoria. Gina is Cree, Saulteaux, French, and German, and is a member of the Star Blanket Cree Nation in Treaty

4 territory. Her research focuses on Indigenous-state relations, gender and Indigenous feminism, prairie Indigenous political life, racism and settler colonialism in the prairies, and Indigenous-Crown treaty relations in Canada. She is co-author of *Storying Violence: Unravelling Colonial Narratives in the Stanley Trial* (ARP Press, 2020) and co-editor of the fifth edition of *Visions of the Heart: Issues Involving Indigenous Peoples in Canada* (Oxford University Press, 2020).

Heidi Kiiwetinepinesiik Stark (Turtle Mountain Ojibwe) is an associate professor in the School of Indigenous Governance at the University of Victoria. She is the director of the Centre for Indigenous Research and Community-Led Engagement and the director of the Graduate Certificate in Indigenous Nationhood. She has a PhD in American studies from the University of Minnesota. Her research interests include Indigenous law and treaty practices, Aboriginal and treaty rights, and Indigenous politics in the United States and Canada. She is the co-editor of *Centering Anishinaabeg Studies: Understanding the World through Stories* with Jill Doerfler and Niigaanwewidam Sinclair (University of Manitoba Press, 2013) and is the co-author of *American Indian Politics and the American Political System* (third and fourth edition) with David E. Wilkins (Rowman & Littlefield, 2017). She has published articles in journals such as *Theory and Event, American Indian Quarterly, American Indian Culture and Research Journal,* and *Michigan State University Law Review.*

Daniel Voth is an associate professor in the Department of Political Science at the University of Calgary, and served as the director of the International Indigenous Studies Program from 2019 to 2022. He is Métis from the Métis Nation of the Red River valley. Raised in Winnipeg's inner city, Daniel earned his PhD from UBC in 2015. His research agenda focuses on the political relationships between Indigenous peoples, particularly in southern Manitoba, as well as the way settler-imposed power structures and land dispossession undermine important gender orientations to governance. His research has been published in the *Canadian Journal of Political Science,* the *University of Toronto Law Journal, Native American and Indigenous Studies, Canadian Journal of Urban Research,* and several book chapters.

Matthew Wildcat is a member of Ermineskin Cree Nation. He is an assistant professor of political science and Native studies at the University of Alberta. Matthew has published in AlterNative, *Decolonization: Indigeneity Education Society,* and the *Journal of Genocide Research.* Matthew also provides governance and strategic advice to various organizations, notably the Maskwacis Education Schools Commission.

Index

www.ingramcontent.com/pod-product-compliance
Lightning Source LLC
Chambersburg PA
CBHW030239030426
42336CB00009B/176